The Provisional Power

Studies in Critical Social Sciences Book Series

Haymarket Books is proud to be working with Brill Academic Publishers (www.brill.nl) to republish the *Studies in Critical Social Sciences* book series in paperback editions. This peer-reviewed book series offers insights into our current reality by exploring the content and consequences of power relationships under capitalism, and by considering the spaces of opposition and resistance to these changes that have been defining our new age. Our full catalog of *SCSS* volumes can be viewed at https://www.haymarketbooks.org/series_collections/4-studies-in-critical-social-sciences.

Series Editor
David Fasenfest (York University, Canada)

Editorial Board
Eduardo Bonilla-Silva (Duke University)
Chris Chase-Dunn (University of California–Riverside)
William Carroll (University of Victoria)
Raewyn Connell (University of Sydney)
Kimberlé W. Crenshaw (University of California–LA and Columbia University)
Heidi Gottfried (Wayne State University)
Alfredo Saad-Filho (Queen's University, Belfast)
Chizuko Ueno (University of Tokyo)
Sylvia Walby (Lancaster University)
Raju Das (York University)

The Provisional Power

Marx and Politics as a Critique of Society

Maurizio Ricciardi

Haymarket Books
Chicago, IL

First published in 2024 by Brill Academic Publishers, The Netherlands
© 2024 Koninklijke Brill NV, Leiden, The Netherlands

Published in paperback in 2025 by
Haymarket Books
P.O. Box 180165
Chicago, IL 60618
773-583-7884
www.haymarketbooks.org

ISBN: 979-8-88890-541-8

Distributed to the trade in the US through Consortium Book Sales and Distribution (www.cbsd.com) and internationally through Ingram Publisher Services International (www.ingramcontent.com).

This book was published with the generous support of Lannan Foundation, Wallace Action Fund, and the Marguerite Casey Foundation.

Special discounts are available for bulk purchases by organizations and institutions. Please call 773-583-7884 or email info@haymarketbooks.org for more information.

Cover design by Jamie Kerry and Ragina Johnson.

Printed in the United States.

Library of Congress Cataloging-in-Publication data is available.

Contents

Preface VII
Acknowledgements XV
Abbreviations XVI

1 The Democratic Conundrum 1
   1   Collisions 1
   2   Multitude and People 6
   3   The Discord 11
   4   Traffic 16
   5   A World History 21

2 The History of Power 27
   1   Becoming Power 27
   2   A Provisional Power 32
   3   On the Use of the State 36
   4   The Terrain of Law 40
   5   Revolution and Dictatorship 47

3 The Power of Government 55
   1   Executive and People 55
   2   Bureaucracy and Empire 62
   3   Chartism and Government 67
   4   Executive and Parliament 71
   5   Colonial Power 77

4 The Domination of Capital 83
   1   The Government of Difference 83
   2   Societal Might 87
   3   Value and Law 94
   4   The Law and the Exception 102
   5   Cooperation and Command 107

5 Despotism and Difference 114
   1   Authority and Slavery 114
   2   Western Despotism 121
   3   Domination and History 126
   4   The Subversion of Power 132

5 The Power of Difference 136

Karl Marx Works 143
Friedrich Engels Works 147
Marx and Engels Works 148
Marx et al. Works 149
References 150
Index 164

Preface

> All this combines to produce a mass writing, not a group writing (the gestures are completed, the persons do not assist each other).
> BARTHES (1982: 106)

This book does not have the ambition to propose a comprehensive reconstruction of Karl Marx's work. Instead, it limits itself to investigating it from the specific perspective of power. However, one could rightly say that, within Marx's writings, the reference to power is omnipresent; indeed, it is the main object of his critique of both politics and political economy. To my knowledge, however, Marx's semantics of power has never been the subject of a specific analysis that investigates the way in which it determines an articulate and complex concept, which is configured differently according to the different historical and analytical contexts that Marx deals with. The intention of this book is to follow the movement of that semantics in the more immediately theoretical writings, in the political interventions and, finally, in some of the articles written for the US newspaper *New York Daily Tribune*. It will thus become clear that the Indian uprisings or German, British, and Spanish constitutional history are just as important to Marx as the investigation of economic categories, even though the latter ultimately serve to identify the great novelty of modern power in relation to all its past and traditional forms. Power is the historically different configuration of relations that are necessarily located within the regime of historicity established by the capitalist mode of production. There is thus no general theory of power in Marx, but an analysis of its historical emergence in the systemic conditions in which it arises.

The novelty of the capitalist mode of production is not that its full establishment introduces a new power in addition to the existing ones. It establishes a new mode of production and legitimation that literally disrupts the way power itself can be conceived. Therefore, it goes beyond distinguishing between different powers, applying a kind of constitutional perspective in order to moderate or neutralize the excess of one power over the others. For Marx, the capital relation, rather than being one of the outcomes of modernity, is what continuously re-qualifies it by constantly redetermining its manifestations both politically and ideologically. The capital relation imposes an integration between historically different powers, managing in a quite peculiar way to make them functional to its expansion and valorization. Reacting to the existence of this unitary and global field of power, Marx also brings back within it the figures that were classically used to describe the destructive crisis of the political system, or the affirmation of exceptional and tendentially 'illegitimate' modes of command within it.

This explains Marx's recourse to certain concepts of European political discourse such as despotism, but also dictatorship or civil war, which he takes up not to describe extreme or exceptional situations, but the ordered movement of societal relations. By virtue of the redefinition of their semantic field, they no longer identify points of extreme tension in the political but rather its normality, a condition that places the action of the state and the presence of civil war in society on a plane of continuity, which does not exclude violence because there is law, just as it does not erase slavery because there is wage labour. Unlike the Schmittian political, whose genealogy can be reconstructed precisely because the exception is conceived as a function of the decision that resolves it, the Marxian political does not grant politics and its institutionalization the possibility of making a decision that is capable of neutralizing antagonism. Political power is constantly the result of the co-presence of normality and exception. This is because for Marx, against the central tradition of political modernity dating back to Thomas Hobbes, political power is the explication of a division, not the representation of the achieved unity of the people or any other universal subject.

For Marx, political power is an evanescent and provisional figure. Reconstructing this concept therefore means dealing with a complex plot that is articulated on a double register: state power, with its bureaucratic and imperial evolutions, enters into a constant tension with the configurations of power that arise historically from societal relations. This is the basis of the Marxian definition of the state itself as a specific and particular dislocation of capitalist domination. The state is the historical and institutional place in which the mediation of the clash taking place in society is constantly sought and represented. Even when it exhibits and perhaps successfully asserts a certain autonomy, the state is always an effect of society, being irretrievably marked by the differences and oppositions that run through it. The illusory character of the state's representation of political unity is not to be understood as an error in the perception of the material bearers of conflicting interests. As with the Marxian concept of commodity fetishism, this illusion is constitutive of a power that establishes all 'citizens' in the role they are called upon to play within the state. Political power is not simply the registration of the societal balance of power. It does not therefore directly express social domination in political form. Or rather, it also fulfils this task, but only by making subordination and power itself a universal necessity.

Marx's explicit rejection of political theology sets the conditions for him to conceive the class struggle, the criterion of the political, outside the almost blackmailing dialectic between order and disorder. Class struggle always presents itself as an exception that must be regulated and normalized. Similarly, the working class, the different subject, is the always unpredictable emergence from the ordered domination of capital. Its emergence, not because it is destined to establish a new order but because it challenges the sovereignty of the capital relation, redefines the contingent relation between normality and exception in each specific historically determined configuration of power. Class struggle reveals the political as a moment of interruption in the process of society's subsumption under the command of capital. It shows the current possibility of escaping from a domination based on the form of value and the corresponding capacity of money, the political object par excellence, to assign each individual a specific position within the process of the production and reproduction of society. The power of money is the real societal constraint, based on the work of an abstraction capable of making indifference to any individual existence appear as the universal independence of individuals. It is also the real foundation of the production of a domination that, despite its systemic and therefore impersonal character, is exercised over everyone but for the benefit of only a few. Without this personal component, i.e., without the opposition between capitalists and workers, it would completely lose its meaning. Even when it presents itself as a bureaucratic mode of technical governance of the production system, the capital relation always remains a power relation, for which it is not by chance that Marx uses terms such as despotism, command, autocracy.

We are thus confronted with a complex form of domination that is both abstractly systematic and concretely individual. It defines the conditions of the present globally, also because of its capacity to make productive all those relations that seem historically outdated and yet largely persist within the capitalist mode of production. This domination imposes itself thanks to its capacity to bring the past to bear on the present, to valorize anachronisms – the most important of which is undoubtedly the domination exercised by dead labour objectified in capital over living labour and its labour power. On the other hand, for Marx the state is not a "great architectonic edifice" as Hegel (1991: 321) claimed, but a gothic construction resulting from the assemblage of different instruments of power that do not allow one to think of it triumphantly as the outcome of modern rationalism. The critique of power, that is, the possibility of triggering a revolutionary process, is thus for Marx primarily a revolt against the weight that the past exerts on the present. It is a revolt against the tradition that otherwise weighs like a nightmare on the brains of the living precisely when they think they can change themselves and the world around them. The very centrality assigned by Marx to the fight against anachronisms explains his reluctance to describe the communist society of the future. The urgency to rid oneself of the past is in Marx far more powerful than the need to imagine a future, whose presence he also discerns in the processes of cooperation in which the worker as a whole imprints the mark of his "becoming power".

Marx is therefore not content with describing the constitution, distribution, internal balances, and thus the limits of power. His critique of it investigates the process of production and aims to identify the conditions under which the subordination it establishes can be suppressed. For Marx, the movement of power constantly poses the question of the subjects of power and the material conditions that produce relations of supra- and subordination. For Marx, power is not an anthropological necessity, just as it is not a zero-sum game, in the sense that the conquest of a share of power does not mechanically entail a corresponding greater powerlessness of the opponent. Precisely because it is produced within the social clash, power is not a given quantity. Rather, it depends on the quality of societal cooperation: the more the latter is removed from the immediate command of a few individuals, the more power becomes the direction that other individuals *en masse* can collectively impart to the actions they perform, becoming power.

It is therefore not simply a matter of conquering present power, with an act that should distinguish precisely between the before of the domination of capital and the after of workers' power. For Marx, the struggle for power can in no case rely on changes that recall the status of the miracle in Christian theology. The struggle of the multitude of social figures that Marx summarizes in the name of the working class, the different subject, is destined to come to terms with the provisional character of its conquests, which are constantly exposed to the return of the past, i.e., to the reassertion of modes of reproduction of society proper to capitalist domination. The class struggle cannot therefore be limited to the conquest of a position of supremacy. It must constantly come to terms with the transitory nature of its acquisitions, with their ever-precarious institutionalization. For Marx, there is no already available political form that can ensure in time the political power eventually attained by the proletariat, whose very subsistence is, moreover, already a clear sign of the continuity of the capital relation.

The radically historical character of Marx's understanding of power requires the critique of political forms considering the epochal novelty of the domination of capital. Significantly, in the *Manifesto,* the term democracy appears only once and refers to the proletariat and its struggle to become the ruling class. It thus becomes a movement that constantly registers the 'becoming power' of a materially existing subject rather than the power obtained by an abstract subject. This is the case because power does not accrue on the basis of some principle but because of the collective capacity to exercise it that it is able to accumulate. If in his writings on France and Great Britain in the 1840s and 1850s Marx analysed the failed attempt of the French proletariat and the British Chartists to become a "conquering power", the Paris Commune in its short and controversial existence points to the possibility of finally enlarging the number of subjects of power. It is the experiment that seems to be able to institutionalize a political cooperation that is not a repetition of the democratic representative form. Marx sees all the difficulties and limitations of this provisional attempt to institutionalize a non-state political form: it cannot claim to represent political unity, it cannot deny the presence of class struggles, and finally, it must be the space where the power of difference can unfold against that of social indifference guaranteed by the state.

Marx does not fear power, which for him is the collective capacity to direct cooperation, without necessarily having to take labour as the form and measure of action. Precisely for this reason, he does not see cooperation as a kind of public work, that is, literally as a collaboration, as work that everyone is more or less coercively called upon to perform for the good of all. It is only possible to bring the potential already visible in capitalist cooperation to fruition by freeing oneself from the despotism of capital, which is not merely the irresistible command exercised within the labour process by an authority that imposes itself as an autocracy. In despotism, the command of capital becomes a societal process capable of deploying a peculiar capacity to interdict individuals' access to history. Despotism is a process of constant privatization of life that prevents the empirically universal connections that are already visible within the world market. For Marx, putting an end to despotism means transforming these connections into political action, that is, into historical action that opens up to its own becoming by freeing itself from the past.

In the face of this possibility, state sovereignty is at bottom a small power for Marx. This is also why he is not interested in, or does not grasp, the transformations that are sweeping it in the second half of the nineteenth century and that will lead to the affirmation of the welfare state. For Marx, the state is always a societal production and the mediation it can carry out depends on the events of the class struggle and not on any real autonomy on its part. The state cannot therefore realistically reform society. It could even be said that the Marxian approach to the state only shows its full utility today, at the moment of the triumph of neoliberal society over the state, with the consequent reduction of the functions and benefits it provided in previous decades. The purpose of this book, however, is not the demonstration of how much and what needs to be abandoned or updated in Marx's work, let alone its rehabilitation. It does not claim to establish at what distance Marx stands in relation to our present.

In my opinion, the question should, if anything, be turned on its head, asking whether we can pose questions to his work with the same theoretical and therefore political radicality with which it posed them in its time and with which, precisely because of this, it continues to question ours.

On Marx's Semantics

All English translations of quotations from Marx's works have been revised by the author without further indication to respect the original Marxian semantics of power and society. All translations from German or Italian texts which are not available in English are mine. The German term *Gewalt* has been rendered as power, force, or violence, depending on the context. The term *Macht* has been translated as might, while the German term *Herrschaft* has been rendered as domination, dominance, lordship, or domain. For the same reason, following the Marxian semantics of society (*Gesellschaft*), the adjective *gesellschaftlich* has been mainly translated as societal using social when Marx uses *sozial* or when referring to its contemporary usage. *Vergesellschaftung* has been rendered as societalization.

Outline of the Book

The overall aim of this book is therefore to reconstruct the Marxian semantics of power and to investigate its complex articulations to identify what Marx sees as the coordinates of a political action capable of challenging the constellation of powers that legitimise and reproduce capitalist society. It is thus possible to highlight the existence of a complex semantic field in which different terms (power, domination, might, but also force, command, authority, despotism, bureaucracy, colonialism, slavery, state, law, dictatorship, monarchy, democracy) establish a conceptual constellation in which, unlike the liberal and democratic doctrines, political and social subjugation are not alternative and independent, but overlap to the point of constituting a single field of tension. The analysis of this semantic and conceptual field makes it possible to redefine the fundamental features of the Marxian critique of a society constituted by the thresholds of power that characterise it. At the same time, since power is not something that can simply be seized, it is possible to grasp how, according to Marx, the working class can constitute itself as an autonomous power capable of confronting the domination of capital.

PREFACE   XIII

    The first chapter reconstructs the Marxian confrontation with the language of power in modern politics. The analysis of the French Revolution and the comparison with Hegel serve Marx to criticise the modern subject of politics. Since the end of the eighteenth century, in fact, the people has asserted itself as the foundation of state power and for this very reason, Marx writes, democracy is the resolved conundrum of every constitution. This same people, however, cannot be regarded as an amorphous mass that must necessarily be represented by a monarch or the governing power. Against Hegel, Marx asserts those empirical differences that characterise the multitude that find their only possible representation in the legislative power. This announces the Marxian critical position of executive power that will remain a constant feature of his critique of state power. In the aftermath of 1848, however, Marxian discourse also subjects democracy to criticism, because the people as a universal subject shows its inconsistency in the face of the empirical universality of the proletariat. The reality of the world market reveals the ambiguity of any national constitution of power because the proletariat shows itself to be a political subject bearing a new universality. On its struggle for liberation, the class struggle, Marx articulates his concept of the political, which is not based on the search for political unity but assumes the productivity of struggle and differences.

    The second chapter first analyses how Marx, in his polemic with Karl Heinzen, identifies private property as a political relation capable of determining the constant reproduction of power. Property, in fact, establishes the existence of a social power far more decisive than state power. Despite its formally individual dimension, it is the basis of a collective condition of subjugation of those without it. From the Marxian writings of the 1840s, a conception of power slowly emerges that does not regard it as a zero-sum relationship, as if it could simply be distributed more fairly. It is thus not an anthropological necessity that takes on various historical forms. The discovery of capital for Marx radically changes the very history of power because it is no longer produced merely in the state but within societal relations that classical political theory considered symmetrical and egalitarian. On the basis of this recording Marx and Engels in the 'Manifesto' indicate a problematic proletarian mode of use of the state, while Marx in the years immediately following redefines the very concept of dictatorship in an original new way.

    The third chapter examines the texts Marx dedicates to the situation in France and Great Britain after 1848. In particular, the articles written by Marx as a political journalist and analyst – for the *New York Daily Tribune* – of the events that mature within the world market are highlighted. In these articles, Marx records the rise of the executive, i.e. the governmental power asserting its dominance over the parliamentary one. The defeat of the French workers is thus added to that of the Chartists, determining a new threshold in Marxian critique of the analytics of power. The inability of the European proletariat to 'become power' is for him the basis of the rise of the personal power of Napoleon III in France and Lord Palmerston in Britain. Their action imposes a centrality of the executive that, according to Marx, is the sign of new and more articulate forms of state power in its now undeniable connection with the domination of capital. In both cases the state becomes empire, in France by combining bureaucracy and the power of finance, in Britain by adding executive power to colonial supremacy.

Through the analysis of the *Grundrisse* and *Capital*, the fourth chapter reconstructs the Marxian conceptualization of society, the historical and political novelty it represents, and the unfolding within it of the power of money, which is the true source of social power. Money literally coined individuals by establishing the individual and collective position they can occupy within it. Society is both the place of genesis of the domination of capital and the place where class struggle and forms of antagonistic cooperation unfold, which for Marx establish the practical evidence of the possibility of subverting the capital relation. The formal equality of individuals clashes with the subordination that matures within the sphere of production, as well as in all forms of societal subjugation functional to the global domination of capital. The social movement of the working class, which for Marx is immediately a political movement, clashes with the legal and state forms that aim to establish the normality of social and political life, while proletarian antagonism is always reduced to an exception.

In Chapter 5, the theoretical and practical tension between the constitution of authority within capitalist society and the actual and potential forms of antagonism emerge. For Marx, capital as a social relation is made possible by determined historical processes in which the authority of capitalists is asserted through the irresistible command that they exert both in the workplace and in society as a whole. If the despotism of capital is asserted through factory command, the enslavement of wage labour, however, does not only concern the labour condition but extends throughout the entire social relationship, exploiting the existence of historically prior relations of domination such as slavery and patriarchy. The Paris Commune and the 'Critique of the Gotha Programme' provide an opportunity to investigate how Marx identifies some practical ways of deconstructing the social power of capital and the possibility of relations that are not subservient to its domination.

Acknowledgements

This book is a debt contracted with many people. I hope that in reading it, my Maestro Piero Schiera saw how important his lesson on constitutional history was. Sandro Mezzadra carefully commented on the different parts of the text. Paola Rudan discussed, solicited, and re-discussed it. The comments of Eleonora Cappuccilli, Isabella Consolati, Niccolò Cuppini, Roberta Ferrari, Maurizio Merlo, and Felice Mometti were more than helpful. Over the past few years, with laborious patience, the study group entitled *GlobalMarx* has read and discussed Marx's writings on the various parts of the world and his critique of the social sciences of his time. The outcome of this work has now been collected in *Global Marx: History and Critique of the Social Movement in the World Market* (Brill: 2023). My thanks to Luca Basso, Michele Basso, Matteo Battistini, Michele Cento, Luca Cobbe, Michele Filippini, Giorgio Grappi, Mario Piccinini, Fabio Raimondi, Veronica Redini, and Stefano Visentin for their discussions and insights. Others such as Luca Scuccimarra, Ferruccio Gambino, and Devi Sacchetto are unaware that they have contributed. A special thanks goes to Max Guareschi for how he read and accompanied the book. Finally, I want to thank Marco Meliti for his support for finalizing the manuscript, and Dave Mesing for his help in revising the English. I would like to express my deepest gratitude and admiration to Laura Montanari for the gift of the wonderful picture on the cover.

Anna and Rosa helped, stimulated, and endured me.

I dedicate this book to Mario and Maurizio for all the Marx learned, discussed, argued, rejected, and learned again.

Abbreviations

MECW *Marx Engels Collected Works*. London: Lawrence and Wishart; New York: International Publishers, 1975–2004.
MEW   *Marx Engels Werke*. Berlin: Dietz Verlag, 1956–1968.

CHAPTER 1

The Democratic Conundrum

1   Collisions

The word democracy appears only once in the *Manifesto of the Communist Party*. However, its definition expresses a real caesura within the modern history of the concept. This solitary presence is even more conspicuous when one considers that the *Neue Rheinische Zeitung*, edited by Marx from 1 June 1848 to 19 May 1849, has the subtitle 'Organ of Democracy'. The *Deutsche-Brüsseler-Zeitung*, in which Engels and Marx assiduously wrote in the months leading up to the 1848 revolution, is the organ of the *Deutscher Arbeiter Verein* and the *Association démocratique*. While clearly claiming its ongoing political relevance, the paradox of this sole occurrence of the term in the *Manifesto* significantly expresses the change in Marx's semantics of power in the aftermath of 1848. First of all, democracy has become a polemical concept, which Marx and Engels severely criticized but which they still sought to appropriate. It is 'polemical' because the concept of democracy has become a battleground for defining the general political perspectives it tries to encapsulate. Marx contrasts it to Hegel and his monarchical depiction of political unity, whereas militants and radical intellectuals pit it against the communists in order to defend the constitutive nexus between property and the individual in the face of the claim of collective property by the nascent proletariat. For all these reasons, democracy ends up contradictorily indicating the political form that confirms and organizes the universal equality of all individuals. Democracy is thus the subject of a series of confirmations and rejections, by virtue of which in the *Manifesto* it ends up consisting of the struggle "to raise the proletariat to the position of ruling class" (Marx and Engels, 1848: 504). The democratic subject is thus no longer the people and democracy is not a form of government, i.e., the only way to govern equality, but rather the achieved predominance of a part of the people on which democracy itself should be based.

Marx had already affirmed the necessary breakdown of the democratic political subject in the previous year (1847), arguing that instead of the people one should speak of the proletariat in order "to replace this broad and vague expression by a definite one" (Marx, 1847a: 222). The latter is "the real people, the proletarians, the small peasants and the plebs – this is, as Hobbes says, *puer robustus, sed malitiosus*" (Marx, 1847a: 233). For Marx, the discovery of the proletariat takes place within the search for the material subject of democracy, which begins in the showdown against Hegelian political philosophy. In this battle, Marx decisively affirms the resilience of the democratic discourse, claiming to identify the people as the empirical and not only the ideal reality of politics. He accomplishes this through a strategy that affirms the centrality of that empiricism that Hegel tries so hard to relativize in his discourse on the state. In a decidedly problematic way, to affirm the political centrality of the people one must therefore take as a starting point the actual clashes that occur both between individuals and between the different figures of state power. The people cannot be exclusively an ideal unit that must necessarily be represented to really exist. Marx thus claims to start from the people's material conditions of existence, without fearing the lines of cleavage that run through it. Hegel obviously does not ignore these conflicts and uses the term 'collisions' [*Kollisionen*] to define them. Marx constantly repeats this terminological choice and it also frequently shows up in his 1840s vocabulary before being replaced by *Gegensatz*, alternatively rendered in English as opposition, contrast, and antagonism. Understanding the conceptual status of 'collision' is thus important for establishing which 'people' Marx opposes to Hegel, i.e., whether the people is to be considered part of a structure of order or whether instead the conflicts that run through it can make it a principle of movement and thus of potential and constant transformation of society and its state.

For Hegel, collision "has its basis in a *transgression*, which cannot remain as such but must be superseded". It represents a caesura that does not yet deserve the name of action, but instead reveals and makes possible the redefinition of order according to its own criteria. Precisely because collision "sets the Ideal, inherently a unity, in dissonance and opposition", it does not show the actual insufficiency of that ideal, but only the existence of an accidental clash that takes place entirely within a given framework and reveals its substantial hold. It is exactly for this reason that upholding the legitimacy of differences based on birth can only establish the conditions for "an unsurmountable *barrier*, so that they appear as a wrong that has become natural, as it were, and they therefore give rise to collisions". On the contrary, differences between estates (such as those that existed in Prussia even after the French Revolution) and between rulers and ruled cannot generate radical conflicts, but only "essential and rational" collisions, "for they have their basis in the necessary articulation of the whole life of the state" (Hegel, 1975: 204–209).

It is therefore no coincidence that for Hegel the different determinations of law "can come into *collision* only in so far as they are all in equal measure rights". They are the expression of internal tensions within law that find their composition in it. They are *collisions* that are limited in their effects and occur within a hierarchy that constantly ensures their order since "only the right of the world spirit is absolute in an unlimited sense". (Hegel, 1991: §30). When these *"collisions of rights"* affect the right to property, it must be clear that the latter is not called into question, because it is already completely foreseen, established, and judged by the legal system, thus producing "the *recognition* of right as the universal and deciding factor" (Hegel, 1991: §85; cf. Ritter, 1982). This priority of order over collision is made even clearer when it comes to possible conflicts within the family, which is to be represented before other families by the "husband [*Mann*] as its head". The right and availability of property on the part of the head of the family "may, however, come into collision" with the claims of the other members because, despite its immediacy, Hegel sees the family as already open to "particularization and contingency" (Hegel, 1991: §171). Family conflicts thus do not challenge either the family or paternal authority, which can thereby continue to establish the basis for that substantial expectation of order that for Hegel culminates in the state.

Similarly, the possibility of a collision between "differing interests of producers and consumers" must be understood on the assumption that *"on the whole, their correct relationship re-establishes itself automatically"*, and thus collision is a kind of movement of internal adjustment within the system. This does not mean that, for Hegel, there can be an automatic rebalancing capable of re-establishing the fundamental conditions of order. In fact, he recognizes the need for "universal provision and direction", since "large branches of industry are dependent on external circumstances and remote combinations" which prevents individuals from grasping the "full implications" of those circumstances and makes them feel exposed to an invisible and impersonal power. This condition, which Marx would recognize as proper to the predominance of the world market, is instead determined for Hegel by the dominance of the selfish end and thus by a deficiency of the universal in times of crisis. Political intervention then becomes necessary "to moderate and shorten the duration of those dangerous convulsions to which its collisions give rise, and which should return to equilibrium by a process of unconscious necessity" (Hegel, 1991: §236).

In his critique of Hegelian public law, Marx is therefore committed to searching for a different legitimacy for the conflicts between the family, civil society, and the state. If, as Hegel argues, the laws of the state are an *"external necessity"* for the family and civil society, then "where a collision occurs, the 'laws' and 'interests' of family and society must give way to the 'laws' and 'interests' of the state". Marx immediately notes that, as we have seen, Hegel carries out his reasoning entirely within law and thus within a closed system that superimposes itself on reality and claims to completely represent it. Hegel "is not here speaking of empirical collisions", but only of the relationship between the spheres of private law and the state (Marx, 1843a: 5–6).[1] Only in this way can he establish the necessary *subordination* and *dependence* between them and the state itself.

It is clearly not a matter of deriving the state from the movements of the family and civil society, but rather of showing that they are a constituent part of it and not functions dependent on it. Thus, they cannot be reduced to "the dark natural ground" of the state itself, which acts by attributing "the material of the state" to them from time to time, the result of its decision and judgement. Instead, it is a question of establishing what the pathways of subjectivation within the state can be. From this perspective, Marx does not want to recognize the family and civil society as immediately political, nor does he want the only subject to be the idea that the state embodies. If the state is the condition of possibility of a material reality, then the latter must be recognised as having its own dynamic that is the only one that can truly define state reality. "The fact is that the state issues from the multitude in their existence as members of families and as members of civil society". Hegel does not ignore the existence of this empirical reality but recognizes it only when subjected to a rationality that is denied to it because it can only be found in the idea embodied in the state. "Empirical actuality is thus accepted as it is. It is also expressed as rational, but it is not rational on account of its own reason, but because the empirical fact in its empirical existence has a different significance from it itself" (Marx, 1843a: 7–9).

In order to dominate factual reality, Hegel therefore ignores an "ordinary empirical fact", opposing it with the primacy of a universality that is the norm to which it must necessarily conform. Conflicts within the family and civil society are only relevant when they are provided for by legal codification. "Family and civil society are the premises of the state; they the genuinely active elements, but in speculative philosophy things are inverted" (Marx, 1843a: 8). They find their sole and possible subjectivation in the state and its law, becoming the objects of their defining activity. Marx is not claiming the particular importance of the family as a natural society or civil society as a space for the freedom of individuals here; he does not therefore intend to assert the dignity of the law of private individuals over that of the public. His criticism concerns the way in which Hegel codifies the universal, questioning whether it is possible to conceive it only from the idea rather than from the material conditions of its

---

[1] According to Arndt (2014), "Marx is not a clear alternative to Hegel, but remains within the sphere delineated by the concept of freedom in the *Elements of the Philosophy of Right*". This may be true with regard to Marx's *Critique of Hegel's Philosophy of Law*, but is not consonant with *Capital*.

production. The assertion that the state is a "superior *might* [*höhere Macht*]" is unfounded if the problem of the constitution of that state is not resolved by clearly referring the basis of its power back to the individuals who guarantee its obedience. This redefines the question of the subject, because "the *actual distinct aspects* or *various facets of the political constitution* are the premise, the subject" (Marx, 1843a: 12). This is the empirical foundation that Marx contrasts with Hegel, thereby not only carrying out a philosophical critique of the logical form of his discourse, but also affirming the priority of democratic practice over democracy understood solely as the form of the state.

Marx thus aims to break the dialectic between content and form, which for Hegel and the tradition from Hobbes to Kant is the very foundation of politics, by adding the dialectic between form and matter, understanding the latter as the set of individual and collective empirical relations to which he nevertheless assigns priority.[2] In this way, the problem is no longer one of putting a content into form that otherwise constantly presents itself as formless. Instead, it is a matter of understanding that material conditions are not systematically intended to be the content of a form, but themselves establish the conditions of possibility of the form itself. Each individual cannot only be considered as private or for his immediate natural qualities. What matters is "its *social quality*, and that state functions, etc., are nothing but modes of being and modes of action of the social qualities of men" (Marx, 1843a: 21–22). If social qualities are the stuff of which individuals are made, they do not yet establish the political centrality of society that progressively ousts the anthropological reference within Marxian discourse. In order to support the priority of the democratic movement over the state form, Marx opposes Hegelian idealism with the "generically human", which is supposed to establish the foundation of a problematic equality that, unlike that asserted by Hegel, is real. It is true that for Marx the multitude also immediately becomes the people with a conceptual leap of no small significance. Nevertheless, there remains the search for a political dynamic that cannot stop because it cannot ignore the empirical conditions in which it unfolds in the name of universalism.

This understanding of the democratic subject necessitates the rejection of the constitutive role Hegel assigns to the monarchy in the belief that the formless multitude still needs to be represented. For Hegel, the monarch is the necessary and visible presence of an individual will. This is a concrete necessity, because there is a need for an individual and not for any formal

---

2 Touboul (2004: 275–289) emphasizes Marx's Aristotelian debt in this rehabilitation of the 'material'. On the persistent presence of Aristotle in Marx, DeGolyer (1992) remains a fundamental text.

demand representing unity. In this way, however, for Marx the very possibility of democracy and therefore the republic is undermined, which become contingent political expressions, because the only inalienable principle of any political form is that the unity of the people is represented by an individual. This leads to the paradox whereby democratic politics is only possible if monarchical representation guarantees it an otherwise non-existent form (Cesaroni, 2006: 82). On the contrary, for Marx "democracy is the truth of monarchy". It is the original movement of all politics, since it is the only one that is based on the manifestation of the will of the people. "Democracy is the genus Constitution", with respect to which there can then be different species. Since any political form can only derive from the people, democracy is the necessary basis of any political form. "Democracy is the solved *riddle* of all constitutions" (Marx, 1843a: 29).

2 Multitude and People

This historical and political judgement matured in Marx through the study of the French Revolution, which became the momentous event of the manifestation of the people as a universal political subject (Balibar and Roulet, 2001). Marx's critique of the logic of Hegelian discourse echoes that already formulated by Trendelenburg on the relationship between empiricism and dialectics, just as it abundantly echoes Feuerbach's critique of the constant inversion of subject and predicate (Finelli and Trincia, 1983: 282–283; Rossi, 1974: 60). The question of Marx's empiricism, which has certainly provoked much interest (Farr, 1983; Hudelson, 1982, 1983),[3] concerns us here insofar as he refers to it with increasing intensity in order to challenge the centrality of the abstract individual as the highest expression of the universal. This is evidently a very problematic reference to an empiricist that only gradually finds its clear determination, given that it is only in 1844, in the *Introduction* to the *Critique of Hegel's Philosophy of Law,* that the reference to the proletariat appears for the first time in his writings (Balibar, 2011a; Tommasello, 2012). The vagueness of the reference to the empirical, however, prevents the democratic conundrum within the critique of Hegel from being truly resolved. The people as subject should actually be both matter and form, with a splitting that does not find a solid justification. After the French Revolution affirming that it is no longer

---

3   For Renault (2001: 50): "Marxian epistemology is realist, rationalist, constructivist and pluralist. ... Rationalist rather than empiricist because Marx defends the theoretical value of hypotheses even if they lack an empirical foundation".

possible to argue for the equivalence of different forms of government means affirming the priority of the legislative over the executive. It means affirming the priority of the people as a political subject and consequently its existence before any representation. The prince cannot therefore make the people exist, which for Hegel is an "independent state" only outwardly, i.e., at the moment when it opposes other peoples.

> He is sovereign inasmuch as he represents the unity of the people [*die Volks Einheit*], then he himself is only the representative, the symbol, of people's sovereignty [*Volkssouverainetät*]. People's sovereignty does not exist by virtue of him, but he on the contrary exists by virtue of it.
> MARX, 1843a: 28

The prince is thus reduced to an official of the people, and his representation is not recognized as having the capacity to establish an otherwise non-existent unity. The people cannot be thought of as a "formless mass", as Hegel claims. If the foundation of the state is in the people, "each is in actual fact only an element of the whole demos". It is thus not possible to say that the life of the people must necessarily revolve around a fixed and determined point such as the monarch. Monarchy is not "the genus Constitution. Monarchy is one species, and a poor one at that. Democracy is content and form". If democracy is a movement that can find different configurations, monarchy on the other hand is a form that continually falsifies its eventual democratic content. Indeed, democracy seems to function for Marx as the antithesis to the representative institutionalization of state power, to the point of being able to state that the "The French have recently interpreted this as meaning that in true democracy the *political state is annihilated*" (Marx, 1843a: 29–30).[4] With its entire *demos*, which however can hardly also be the empirical *demos*, democracy nevertheless demonstrates the possibility of a political dynamic that does not have its predetermined outcome in the state. On the other hand, this was also the idea of democracy that Marx had found in Spinoza, namely the seamless continuity between people and government. Democracy is the "political regime in which the health, not of the sovereign, but of the whole people is the supreme law", so in this regime obedience does not mean servitude, because it entails the utility "of the agent himself" rather than only the utility "of the ruler". In short, rather than a representative, it is the holder of power who should be the interpreter

---

4 Abensour (1997) has particularly stressed this Marxian position, showing, beyond the questionable category of 'total people', a line of thought that continues in Marx's later writings. See also Leopold (2007: 254–262) who focuses on the Marxian problem of the end of politics.

of a reason that is recognized in everyone to the same potential degree (Marx, 1841: 241; see also Chauí, 2017; Morfino, 2013).

This investment in the democratic political dynamic also motivates the centrality accorded to the legislative, in which Hegel sees the bearer of potential disorder within the state with the consequent necessity to contrast it with the power of government, when it is not the articulated expression of society due to the estates (Duso, 2013: 226–227). For Marx, the legislative does not seem to be part of that mechanism which in Hegel is entrusted the putting into stable and definitive form of the continuity of the political state. The Marxian legislature is a figure of movement that knows no stabilization and for this very reason is elected as the democratic institution par excellence. There seems to be no representative gap between the legislative and the people and, precisely for this reason, it appears intrinsically revolutionary to Marx. The legislative is the irruption of the multiple into the order of the state. In other words, it should allow for the explication of that dynamic that the empirical people constantly produce. As a product of the revolution, the legislative is also intended to make its time and movement permanent. It should be the demonstration that change has not happened once and for all, but that it continually recurs as a political necessity that is now undeniable.

The legislative expresses the time of the revolution, a time that cannot be confined to an original event, but rather to its lasting unfolding and its ability to impose itself on state institutions. In other words, the legislative is the constitution in motion, because it is the revolution that continues over time, whereas the gradual time of the executive, with its slow and judicious changes, entails the renunciation of the possibilities opened up by the French revolution. "The category of *gradual* transition is, in the first place, historically false; and in the second place, it explains nothing". It is the practice of an executive that rebels against the very idea of a constitution. On the contrary, "the collision between the constitution and the legislature is nothing but *a conflict of the constitution with itself*", that is, the constitution is exposed to change, because the same individuals who are materially part of the constitution also attend the legislature. This explain why the constitution is "a compromise between the political and the unpolitical state". It establishes a dynamic space of communication between civil society and the state. For Marx, the legislature articulates the constitution in a way that the governing power cannot, to the point that he writes that "the legislature does not make the law; it only discovers and formulates it" (Marx, 1843a: 57–58).

Marx is not interested in resolving the collision between constituent power and constituted powers, as "in recent French history this proved to be a hard nut to crack" (Marx, 1843a: 55). He does not oppose an institutionalization of politics contrary to Hegel's own. He does not simply assert the priority of the legislative over the power of government; rather, he claims to save the dynamics of the universal within the state without its representation ending up preventing any possible articulation.

> The legislature made the French Revolution; in general, wherever it has emerged in its particularity as the dominant element, it has made the great, organic, general revolutions. … The executive, on the other hand, has produced the small revolutions, the retrograde revolutions, the reactions.
> MARX, 1843a: 57; cf. KOUVÉLAKIS, 2003: 367–371

For Marx, governmental power is a limit that operates within a constitution understood as a dynamic expression of the empirical life of the people. As Rousseau and the Jacobins had argued,[5] democracy is a particularity that *pars pro toto* claims to represent the constitution as a whole and, for this very reason, rebels against the very idea of a constitution.

The conflict that Marx detects between the two powers is not a question of constitutional balances, but rather the way that the tension between empirical reality and the universal arises, because the necessity of the independence of governmental power and its bureaucracy is based on the Hegelian conviction of political limits of what he calls the "*empirical universality* of the views and thoughts of the *many*", clarifying that the expression the *many* "denotes empirical universality more accurately than the usual term '*all*'" (Hegel, 1991: §301). For Hegel, it is evident that "*universality* is something entirely different from a large multitude [*Menge*]", precisely because the latter "affords us perceptions of changes *following upon one another*, or of objects *lying side-by-side*, but no connection involving necessity" (Hegel, 2010a: §39). This absence of connection brings the multitude to the threshold of *vanishing fury*, being capable only of negation, rather than autonomously formulating a proposal, a judgement, and consequently also producing an action that does not only apply to the majority of cases, to a plurality of individuals. Empirical universality thus ends up referring either to those elements that simply last the longest in time, or to "a universality resulting from comparison with other concrete wholes, in which case it does not get beyond commonality" (Hegel, 2010b: 710).[6]

---

5 Bongiovanni (1981: 70–73) emphasizes Marx's distance from Rousseau and the politics of the French Revolution, while Screpanti (2013) highlights some significant proximities.

6 "If it is *allness* that universality brings to mind, a universality that ought to be exhausted in singulars as singulars, then there has been a relapse into that bad infinity; or else it is mere

Distrust in the multitude leads Hegel to outline a double mediation that organizes and governs it: the articulation of society into estates and the governing power with its bureaucracy. The estates are the evidence of the necessary existence of a hierarchy within civil society. Thanks to them, political opinions and sentiments are presented according to an order, without being the immediate expression of the multitude of individual wills. The estates literally pre-order a society that would otherwise present itself under the sign of the multitude and its singularities. In Hegelian discourse, as Marx himself acknowledges, they are not simply the residue of a now defunct conception of civil society, but instead perform an ideological function. They do not determine an overall ideology of society, but rather articulate the partial ideologies linked to the system of needs and labour. Precisely because the ethics of society are always exposed to the action of the multitude of figures that animate it, there is a need to produce a mediation that connects society to government on a stable and not occasional basis. "It is significant", Marx notes, "that Hegel, who has such a great respect for the state spirit, for the ethical spirit, for state consciousness, positively despises it when it confronts him in an actual, empirical form". Just as bureaucracy (to which we will return at length later) has the function of making the public consciousness "empirical", so do the estates in their connection with the government produce that mystique of the state that Marx criticizes in Hegel and otherwise. Estates and bureaucracy make the universal an affair of the government, so that it exists "without *actually* being matters of *general* concern", its empirical dimension, i.e., the material conditions of its production, being denied, so that "the actual business of the people has come into being without action by the people" (Marx, 1843a: 60–62).

If for Hegel "the *multitude of members* [*Menge der Glieder*] remains the best reason that can be advanced against the direct participation of all", for Marx the problem is instead that the discriminating factor in excluding and governing individuality cannot be number. On the other hand, for Marx private property is primarily a mechanism of power precisely because of its ability to establish a hierarchy between individuals, so that equality is constantly neutralized by the specific ownership qualification of the individual. The equality of individuals is inalienable precisely because the multitude is made up of different individuals. One cannot, in other words, make the individual act against the universal by establishing a politically constitutive difference in the behavior of individuals when they present themselves as a mass. "*One* individuality,

---

plurality which is taken for allness. But plurality, however great it might be, remains inescapably only particularity: it is not allness" (Hegel, 2010b: 572–573).

many individualities, *all* individualities. One, many or all – none of these descriptions alters the *essence* of the subject, individuality". For the possibility of expression of these singularities, "*numbers* here are not without significance", as Marx adds. The paradox of singularity is not its uniqueness, but its multiplicity. The fact that individuals present themselves *en masse* establishes the fundamental difference between the estate-based representation of society and the politics of the legislature, since the latter is "a *social* function, ... a function of *sociality*" (Marx, 1843a: 116–119).

From the enthusiastic and not always consequential exaltation of democracy that Marx opposes to Hegel, certain elements emerge that remain problems even in later years. First, there is the material determination of what the empirical conditions of existence of the multitude of individuals consist in. Then, there is the matter of which specific collisions constitute this multitude and, again, how they can be empirically determined. Finally, there is the question of how democratic individuality can be conceived, knowing that through it the presence of all individuals is legitimized regardless of their social location.

3 The Discord

In any case, it is clear to Marx that democracy is a polemical field on which different configurations of political power can be articulated, but in itself it is not the ultimate solution to the problem of power. Even when it is only imaginary, its presence explains the predictable failure of the reforms hinted at by the Prussian monarchy in the early 1940s. It is no longer possible to distinguish monarchy from tyranny and despotism because, contrary to Montesquieu's claim, they all respond to the same principle. "Where the monarchical principle has a majority behind it, human beings constitute the minority; where the monarchical principle arouses no doubts, there human beings do not exist at all". Democracy, on the contrary, represents a kind of evolutionary leap from the animal world to the "human world" that constantly shows the anachronism of any political choice that thinks it can go in another direction (Marx, 1843b: 138–139). From this point of view, therefore, democracy is a given even when it is not institutionally present. Yet at the very moment when it now appears to be a politically inevitable condition, it also shows the limits of its assumptions.

In the age of potential social democracy, men are not truly emancipated. They live a split existence: the man of bourgeois society and the man of political life. Here it is not only Hegelian ethics that shows its limits in the face of the empirical universality of society, but it is the theological-political core of democratic discourse that is unable to react to the potential expansion of equality. In democracy, an individual that has no real counterpart in reality is sovereign.

> Political democracy is Christian since in it man, not merely one man but every man, ranks as *sovereign*, as the highest being, but it is man in his uncivilised, unsocial form, man in his fortuitous existence, man just as he is, man as he has been corrupted by the whole organization of our society, who has lost himself, been alienated, and handed over to the dominance of inhuman conditions and elements – in short, man who is not yet a *real* species-being.
> MARX, 1844a: 159

Christianity is the foundation of legitimacy for a universality that is not only abstract with respect to the empirical conditions of contemporary society, but is placed in a pre-social past, i.e., completely alien to the real conditions of bourgeois society. It constantly introduces the past into the present, preventing the latter from developing and addressing its own contradictions. Christianity performs the entirely political function of constantly legitimizing the presence of an anachronism that is perfectly functional to the present conditions of power. This is the constitutive pattern of political theology for Marx. He makes this clear in a note from these years, written while reading and annotating Ranke's essay on the Restoration in France. As often happens, Marx finds the material to formulate his political judgements in historians. Given a historian's account, the inversion of subject and predicate shows the materiality that the logical operation would erase. If the king makes the law in absolute monarchy, whereas in Louis Philippe in France it is the constitution that makes the king, then Hegel's position must be considered in a new light, because it is enough to overthrow subject and predicate, law and power, to account for the real and radical change that is taking place. Hegel makes the different moments of the ethical idea the subject, while he makes the old forms of state existence, such as the articulation of society into estates and the continuing dominance of the monarch, the predicate. For Marx, this seems to be Hegel's mistake, because in historical reality the idea of the state depends on the material (albeit antiquated) configuration of the state: "he only expresses the general character of the time, its *political theology*". In this way "all forms of non-reason become forms of reason" and this is the result of making religion the fundamental grammar of the state. "This metaphysics is the metaphysical expression of reaction, of the old world as the truth of the new worldview" (Marx 1843c: 181).[7] Marx does not criticize Hegel because he restores an inverted order to the world, but because he offers a philosophy of its continuity in which theology functions as a principle of order.

Just as Marx does not simply intend to overturn Hegelian philosophy, neither does he consider Christendom "as an 'inverted world'" that must be put back on its feet by recovering the fullness of the broken community. For Marx, the problem is not to affirm the proletariat as a "messianic community" (Taubes, 2009: 165, 192), but rather to break the historical hierarchies that political theology legitimizes far beyond the Middle Ages (Taubes, 1996: 257–267). It is therefore a matter of breaking out of the conceptual scheme that the nexus between theology and politics ends up imposing on the historical and juridical level (Scattola, 2007). Ultimately, Marx accuses Hegelian political theology of not only identifying "the basic, radically systematic structure" (Schmitt, 2006: 45) of an epoch, but also of making it normative, continually transposing historical contents of the past into the present. Similar to what Hans Blumenberg reproaches Carl Schmitt with, Marx imputes to Hegel the stubborn denial that the legitimacy of an epoch or political action can be based on its novelty rather than on "duration, antiquity, historical extraction and tradition" (Blumenberg, 1985: 99). This conviction is fundamental to understanding Marx's concept of the political. It identifies the past as the fundamental problem and, precisely for this reason, cannot accede to an uncritical celebration of the present, nor can it confidently point to the future as the time when contradictions will find their necessary solution. What Marx is concerned with is questioning the mortgaging of the past to the present, the effect of which is the radical de-historicization of relations between men, who are interpreted not for what they are, but for what they are presumed to always have been and consequently always will remain, thereby legitimizing the necessary and unquestionable transcendence of power.

It is precisely for this reason that Marx states that a representation devoid of reality of man "becomes in democracy tangible reality, present existence, and secular principle" (Marx, 1844a: 159).[8] The diachronic tension between past

---

7 On Hegel's political theology, see Theunissen (1970).
8 This is a critique of the theological foundation of democracy at least in part different from the vaguely Volterrian one proposed by Engels, for whom "Democracy is, as I take all forms of government to be, a contradiction in itself, an untruth, nothing but hypocrisy (theology, as we Germans call it), at the bottom". (Engels 1843: 393). This does not detract from the fact that Engels's studies of Carlyle and the situation of the working class in England are fundamental to understanding the Marxian critique of democracy. On Engels's overall work, see Sgro' (2017); Liedman (1986).

and present that affects democratic individuals is further intensified by that which places them all in the same society, but in different positions. There is thus a problem of democracy with the society of which it is supposed to be the expression, a problem that was already being considered in those years to be solved by directly connecting democracy with the social. Whether one speaks of social democracy, as opposed to merely political democracy, or whether one uses social democracy directly, the real democratic conundrum is how to respond to the obvious difference in power that individuals have in society. In this respect, the democratic conundrum thus proves never to be solved. It is on this terrain that Marx's discovery of political economy introduces elements of substantial innovation in the semantics of power. As early as 1844, in fact, he writes:

> Capital is thus the *governing power* over labour and its products. The capitalist possesses this power not because, not on account of his personal or human qualities, but inasmuch as he is an *owner* of capital. His power is the *purchasing* power of his capital, which nothing can withstand.
> MARX, 1844b: 247

The *governing power* which, according to Hegel, "'*subsumes*' the individual and the particular under the general" (Marx, 1843a: 48), now describes the ability, through the possession of certain goods, to command the labour of others. This is the purchasing power that Adam Smith had referred to, who for his part had already introduced a decisive innovation in the definition of the concept of power itself, shifting its center of gravity from politics to social traffic. Indeed, in *The Wealth of Nations*, we read the famous statement:

> It was not by gold or by silver, but by labour, that all the wealth of the world was originally purchased; and its value, to those who possess it and who want to exchange it for some new productions, is precisely equal to the quantity of labour which it can enable them to purchase or command. Wealth, as Mr. Hobbes says, is power.
> SMITH, 1981: 48

The fact that Smith is taking up the Hobbesian concept of power is already evident at the beginning of the chapter, where he states that "Every man is rich or poor according to the degree in which he can afford to enjoy the necessaries, conveniences, and amusements of human life" (Smith, 1981: 47). What Hobbes generically refers to in his definition of power as means,[9] Smith makes depend on wealth, which thus reveals itself to be much more than a set of accumulated goods – it is a social technology capable of establishing a criterion of distinction between individuals.[10] It is no coincidence that, while for Hobbes wealth is a power insofar as it is "honorable", i.e., because it enables an individual to assert himself socially (to obtain services, yes, but also to arouse the envy of others), for Smith wealth constitutes individuals. It is a type of power distinct from political and military power – a power through which the latter can eventually be purchased, thus being somehow "degraded" to secondary goods that can be acquired on the market of power. The *power of purchasing*, Marx's "purchasing power", is, however, exercised primarily over the *productive powers of* labour.

It is thus "a certain command over all the labour, or over all the produce of labour which is then in the market". Wealth is the real foundation not only of the power of individuals, but also of "the power of every country" (Smith, 1981: 48, 372) and establishes the co-ordinates of a semantic field which in Smith exclusively comprises the "purchasing power" and the overall power of the state, whereas in Marx it is immediately enriched by that power of government which in Smith is not there, but which we have already seen in the critique of Hegel. On the other hand, the difference between the Smithian doctrine of value founded on commanded labour and the Marxian theory of value, founded on the domination of the social reproduction of labour power, is also explained by a different understanding of production and the accumulation of power. Indeed, a new type of collision emerges in the field of labour, different from the previous ones: "*Wages* are determined through the hostile [*feindlich*] struggle between capitalist and worker" (Marx, 1844b: 235). This "hostile struggle", the forerunner of the class struggle, works the Marx's concept of society by breaking its naturalness and the anthropological necessity that still characterises it, even though there is already a concern not to postulate "'society' again as an abstraction *vis-à-vis* the individual. The individual *is the social being*" (Marx, 1844b: 299). However, he is so by virtue of a constitutive split that Hegel failed to grasp, because he "sees only the positive, not the negative side of labour" (Marx, 1844b: 333). Democracy itself can be founded on a universal subject precisely because it must necessarily ignore this hostile struggle.

---

9   "The power *of a man*, (to take it universally,) is his present means, to obtain some future apparent good. And is either *original* or *instrumental*" (Hobbes, 1998: 58).

10 For Small (1972: 77), wealth is the outcome of an economic policy understood as "the technology of a practical art which was strictly responsible to a moral philosophy that correlated all human activities".

This is not only a philosophical-political consideration, because the negative side of labour immediately produces a struggle with absolutely practical effects in Germany as well. Indeed, the 1844 Silesian workers' revolt showed both liberal public opinion and the nascent workers' movement that the proletariat also existed in Germany (Wolff, 1952) and that consequently the problem of pauperism was taking on an entirely new form (Ricciardi, 1995). It is no longer a question of dealing exclusively with a mass of individuals who are in fact regarded as outside society, but rather of responding to the demands of individuals who actively come forward *en masse* to change their living conditions. In this context, it makes no sense for Marx to demand, as Arnold Ruge does, that the state, and more specifically the monarch, take on the task of enlarging the universal so that more individuals can be included within it (Ruge, 1844). Social reform cannot be seen as a strategy to reconstitute the common essence [*Gemeinwesen*] that capitalist development is erasing. Social reform is a state policy, and this has a double consequence. First, the problem of the universal cannot be considered abstractly, perhaps by comparing real democracy with eighteenth-century pure democracy; second, and at the same time, the judgement on the state is no longer only about its constitution, but in addition its practical activity.

The year before, Marx had written to Ruge that "the political state expresses, within the limits of its form *sub specie rei publicae*, all social struggles, needs and truths" (Marx, 1843b: 143). However, this overall definition – which combines the movements of society, the motivations of individuals and the ideological dimension of their actions – does not lead to an investigation of the potential of state action. Instead, its limitations are constantly emphasised, in the conviction that the state cannot significantly alter the present condition of society. "From the *political* point of view, the *state* and the *order* [*Ordnung*] *of society* are not *two* different things. The state is the order of society" (Marx, 1844c: 197). To save the order of society, social issues are always blamed on a defect in its administration and thus on the need for its reform to adapt its functioning to changed conditions. For Marx, the buzzword of social reform, which for the entire second half of the nineteenth century would run through Europe determining the social policy of almost all states, is simply an empty phrase.

4   Traffic

Marx perfectly grasps the role of administration as "the *organising* activity of the state" (Marx, 1844c: 198), but does not seem to recognise that, precisely from the 1840s onwards, administrative action assumes society as its privileged object, showing that the state is able of intervening in its order by taking it on as a fundamental political problem. Taking his cue from the social movement and the disruptive reality of communism and socialism produced by it, another left-wing Hegelian, Lorenz von Stein, theorises not only the need for administrative measures to intervene in the distribution of property, but above all the need to recognise a constitutional dimension to administration, i.e., the ability to continuously redetermine the relationship between state and society. The Stein hypothesis, which proved successful until the 1970s, does not limit administration to the organization of the state, but makes it an organizational mode of society itself (Ricciardi, 2010: 89–115). Stein has no particular interest in introducing elements of democracy into political decision-making processes and is certainly convinced that by democratising access to property, it can be avoided. Marx, on the contrary, thinks that the state is possibly a poor instrument for democratising society and that, consequently, the work of the administration has a structural limit. It must limit itself to "a *formal* and *negative* activity, for where civil [*bürgerlich*] life and its labour begins, there the might [*Macht*] of the administration ends". Consequently, "*impotence* [*Ohnmacht*] is the *law of nature* of administration" (Marx, 1844c: 198). It is so because of the insatiable nature of bourgeois society, because of the collisions that run through it, and because of the history of the state itself. For Marx, the latter is the history of an anachronism, which the historical vicissitude of Germany shows in the most obvious way (Ricciardi, 2023). The state is a survival of the *ancien regime* within social relations that constantly show its inadequacy. Marx is not blind to the transformations of state administration, but he does not consider them up to the overall evolution of society. If the latter is a kind of evolutionary universal that contains within it both the reality of exploitation and subjugation and the possibility of liberation, then the state as an instrument of domination cannot evolve in a direction other than that which its origin imparts to it.

For Marx, the relationship between state and society must not be secured over time according to the Stein hypothesis but must instead be broken. He rejects the idea that the class antagonism is a kind of historical invariant, which can only repeat itself in different forms and must therefore be governed. Marx's enigmatic statement that "it is only in an order of things in which there are no more classes and class antagonisms that *social evolutions* will cease to be *political revolutions*" (Marx, 1847b: 212) poses a stark alternative between the evolution of society and its political constitution, two different times and two different modes of movement. It is clearly a matter of seeing how these polarities act on each other and how Marx's position changes over time, although the idea remains constant that the state at its fundamental core cannot be changed, i.e., it cannot take a different form and thus literally cannot be reformed. For Marx, the state is in any case the expression of something static, which comes into constant collision with society, with its dynamics based on the economy of its traffic. Marx credits Stein with understanding that the history of the state is intimately connected to the history of capitalism. However, he does not consider this specific "state moment" capable of producing a reform of society. This does not mean that for Marx the state as an anachronism is destined to disappear with the evolution of capitalist society. On the contrary, their intertwining is one of the fundamental aspects of the history of society itself.

In a letter to Annenkov, Marx explains how, according to him, with the rise of the productive forces the "traditional social forms" are exposed to change and that for the modalities of this change he uses the term traffic [*Verkehr*]. The latter is a dynamic that does not end in the political form, nor does it necessarily culminate in the democratic movement that Marx had affirmed before Hegel. Rather, traffic establishes conditions that men cannot freely choose, but which produces its effects on their individual existence.

> A history of mankind, which is all the more a history of mankind as man's productive forces, and hence his societal [*gesellschaftlich*] relations, have expanded. From this it can only be concluded that the social history [*sociale Geschichte*] of man is never anything else than the history of his individual development, whether he is conscious of this or not.
>
> K. MARX to P.V. ANNENKOV, 28 December 1846, MECW, vol. XXXVIII: 96.

Traffic produces an extension and intensification of social relations, not only by establishing constantly new positions for individuals, but also by introducing ever new individuals into it. With its laws removed from the free concertation of individuals, traffic establishes the conditions for a configuration of power that politics, with the primacy it accords to the will, cannot fully grasp. Traffic cannot be governed through a more or less consensual relationship between individuals, or between the people and their representative, with which classical political philosophy had sought to define modern power. Traffic establishes the coordinates of a social might that accompanies and overrides political power. For Marx, it is thus once again a matter of establishing the empirical location of individuals within this economy of traffic. "Empirical observation must in each separate instance bring out empirically, and without any mystification and speculation, the connection of the social and political articulation [*Gliederung*] with production" (Marx and Engels, 1845–1846b: 41).[11] In this program, the centrality that Marx nonetheless recognises in empiricism as a tool for the critique of the universal is reaffirmed. This now appears even more important because it is not just a matter of opposing empirics to abstraction but, precisely from the empirical condition of individuals, of determining the possibilities of the critique and subversion of a reality that is beyond their control.

The basis of the traffic economy is the division of labour with its correlate of private property. Thanks to them, the community interest that binds individuals together "does not exist merely in the imagination, as the 'general interest', but first of all in reality, as the mutual interdependence of the individuals among whom the labour is divided" (Marx and Engels, 1845–1846a: 46). Yet, it is precisely the gap between one's own private interest and the inscrutable collective interest – the fact that the division of labour appears as something natural – that makes "man's own deed [become] an alien might opposed to him, which enslaves him instead of being controlled by him" (Marx and Engels, 1845–1846a: 47). There is thus no external dominator able to compel certain behaviour, but it is human activity itself that is thus consolidated "into a material power [*sachliche Gewalt*]" that escapes all control and expectation. It is a power that arises directly from social relations and is thus a social might [*soziale Macht*]: it is consolidated within those relations by the intensification and enlargement of traffic; it is a might that establishes an obligation based on what Marx calls the "reproduction of life" of individuals.

> The social might, i.e., the multiplied productive force, which arises through the co-operation of different individuals as it is caused by the division of labour, appears to these individuals, since their co-operation is not voluntary but has come about naturally, not as their own united might [*vereinte Macht*], but as an alien force [*fremde Gewalt*] existing outside them, of the origin and goal of which they are ignorant, which they thus are no longer able to control, which on the contrary passes through a peculiar series of phases and stages independent of the will and the action of man, nay even being the prime governor of these.
> MARX and ENGELS, 1845–1846a: 48

---

11 The quotations and adherence to the Marxian lexicon of power were all compared with Marx et al. (2004) and with Marx and Engels (1845–1846b). However, it is now known that the *German Ideology* was never written in the form of its first publication in 1932. See Carver T (2010).

The term *Gewalt*, understood as power legitimised by force that ends up determining social relations from outside, occupies a particular position in Marx's work. It emerges with particular significance after 1848, and not by chance, when in Germany the nexus between force and law will show itself in all its violence, when it comes to reconciling revolutionary claims with the persistence of a largely pre-revolutionary state. In this context, instead, the unified might of the many is pitted against a power that is individualised precisely because it determines the possibilities of action of individuals without reprieve, whose action seems only to be able to aim at regaining a communitarian dimension not mortgaged by this social might that has become power. On the other hand, the very term communism derives from the communitarian semantics dominant in the first half of the nineteenth century (Granjonc, 1989) and with difficulty manages to free itself from it. The spectral presence of the community makes social might a systematic violence exercised to drive and maintain individuals in their individual powerlessness while, at the same time, alluding to the possibility of a "real community" in which that power would be inoperative. The tension between the individual and the communitarian is thus in the foreground, with the consequence that alienation is the perception of this absence of community. The political form – be it democratic, aristocratic, or monarchical – exists as an impossible communitarian supplement, which claims to represent the absent community as universal. There is a compulsion towards the universal to the extent that each class must present its own domain as such, and to do so it must conquer the political power that is the instrument that enables that representation. Concerning the need to conquer political power, which Marx nevertheless continues to recognise, we will return at length later. Here, however, political power fails to mask the dissonance between the actions of individuals who constantly aim at their own interest and the collective interest that appears to them as something foreign and independent. Precisely in democracy, which in the critique of Hegel had been indicated as the only possible nexus between individuals and the universal, men "must remain within this discord [*Zwiespalt*]", because in the face of material dependence on the conditions of production in society even the democratic state necessarily presents itself as the representation of an "illusory 'general' [*allgemein*] interest" (Marx and Engels, 1845–1846a: 47). The criticism is here once again clearly directed at Hegelian philosophy, for which the universal is only present in the state, and individuals who do not recognize its necessity can only participate in it in a limited and partial manner. What is even more important to emphasise, however, is that if the universal has the task of stabilising the community by establishing its boundaries (Balibar, 2020: 38), the Marx-Engelsian discourse produces a deviation from this very idea of community when it assumes the world market [*Weltmarkt*] as the historical and current presupposition of the rearticulation of the universal.

5   A World History

The power of the world market is not an abstraction. It is represented and embedded in a specific object, whose political centrality Marx begins to emphasise in this period. Money is the operational instrument of the world market, although a clear conceptual difference between money as money and money as capital is not yet delineated. Money is at first the social object that determines a new way of constituting individuals; it establishes the social form of power, but not yet the specifically capitalist form of domination. It rearranges individuals, imposing forms of action and submission, but does not constitute society as a whole. However, the vocabulary necessarily begins to refine in the face of the contradictions that the discourse brings to the fore. If the starting point becomes the "antagonistic struggle" that determines wages, it is very difficult to consider the social and the human as synonymous, and society as the overall horizon of meaning of collective action. To claim that "*society* is the complete unity of man with nature – the true resurrection of nature – the accomplished naturalism of man and the accomplished humanism of nature" (Marx, 1844b: 298) must come to terms with the fact that, by becoming the social object par excellence, money makes man a "dehumanised" being. Here, to say *society* is to affirm a universal condition in which money, "a *real God*, for the mediator is the *real power* over what it mediates to me" (Marx, 1844d: 212), establishes such modes of relationship and communication that the understanding of sociality as an expression of human nature is problematic. Marx is aware of this and in fact is not concerned with the loss of an authentic and integral common essence, but with the current constitution of a "common essence" completely dominated by money. The problem is, if anything, the failure to distinguish the differential effects that money produces on individuals. If its dominance is indeed universal, not all individuals are equal before money. And yet, this reflection on the effect of money on individuals is fundamental to the redefinition of the relationship between power and domination that Marx makes in the run-up to 1848.

By virtue of its position, money reconfigures individuals, imposing a criterion of estimation based on quantity alone. It allows an objective judgement, because it is indifferent to individual qualities, but based only on the prediction that a certain individual possesses or may possess money in the future. Just as Adam Smith recognized wealth as the new technology of power of nations, so does access to money require each individual to master specific techniques in order not to be devalued overall in front of society. One ought to consider how vile it is that "to *estimate* the value of a man in *money*, as happens in the credit relationship" (Marx, 1844d: 215) establishes the basis for a judgement on the morality of the debtor. Economy becomes the measure of individual morality. Being poor, being denied credit, knowing that one cannot guarantee one's solvency are all conditions that sanction alienation from the *"true community [Gemeinwesen]* of men", isolating them from each other. Private property itself is the sanction of a distance between individuals whose only bond becomes the objects alienable through money. "The *social* connection or *social* relationship between the two property owners is therefore that of *reciprocity* in *alienation"* (Marx, 1844d: 217–218). The common human essence becomes a universal dependence on objects, a triumph of their might that prevents the individual from becoming the embodiment of freedom as affirmed by the long Lockean moment that had found its final emergence in the Atlantic revolutions. The private character of societal appropriation, however, is not primarily captured in its capacity to differentiate individuals; on the contrary, their reciprocal opposition is resolved into a universal dependence, which establishes the distance that modern freedom necessarily produces. The modern individual is not only characterised by a constitutive split between his private being and his public existence, but also enters into relations with others on the basis of the expectation that they are a constant potential threat to his freedom. Indeed, if the extent of one's freedom is the insurmountable limit of that of others, then the space of freedom is necessarily established by the boundaries that constitute it.

This confined freedom "is based not on the association of man with man, but on the separation of man from man" and this is the foundation of a society that "makes every man see in other men not the *realization* of his own freedom, but the *barrier* to it". For this reason, security becomes the "highest social concept of civil society, the concept of *police",* ensuring that each man can freely enjoy his own self-interest, to the point that "species-life *[Gattungsleben]* itself, society, appears as a framework external to the individuals, as a restriction of their original independence" (Marx, 1844a: 163–164). Precisely because private self-interest is the fundamental social bond, society presents itself as a foreign might, as a social power that opposes individuals, leaving them in their mutual isolation without them being able to oppose a different configuration of their forces (Basso, 2012).

> Only when man has recognised and organised his *'forces propres'* as *social* forces, and consequently no longer separates social power from himself

in the shape of *political* power, only then will human emancipation have been accomplished.

    MARX, 19844a: 168; see also DARDOT, 2014

The criticism of Rousseau is clear in this passage. He argues that men can only add to the forces they possess, but not produce new ones. For Marx, on the contrary, cooperation is a multiplication of forces that not only allows for a different management of available resources, but also makes it possible to conceive and practically pose the question of emancipation by going beyond the narrow limits of individual action. If individuals want to achieve their emancipation, they cannot therefore stick to an economy of their forces; if they want to force the boundary that is continually established between the social and the political, they must overcome their own isolation, knowing that "the greater and the more developed the social might appears to be within the private property relationship, the more *egoistic*, asocial and estranged from his own nature does man become" (Marx, 1844d: 220). The law of social might is in fact the disavowal of the collective power of individuals, being "the expression of my *loss of self* and of my *powerlessness* that is objective, sensuously perceptible, obvious and therefore put beyond all doubt" (Marx, 1844d: 228).

The reflection on the position of the individual in the money society that Marx undertakes from 1843 onwards is essential for the subsequent attempt to determine the conditions under which social might becomes "unendurable", i.e., a "a might against which men make a revolution". In other words, he aims to determine the threshold beyond which those individuals can escape their isolation by redefining their own individuality. This cannot only be done by resolving the aporias of universalism as discourse, but by establishing as practical those assumptions that allow the world market to deploy its social might on isolated individuals. First of all, the opposition between the mass of non-owners and those who live off wealth and culture must be suppressed. This would make an enormous development of the productive forces possible, "which at the same time implies the actual empirical existence of men in their *world-historical*, instead of local, being". This establishes the semantic field that makes the very definition of the universal mobile. It is no longer rendered solely with the term '*allgemein*', but rather with '*universell*', precisely due to the practical mediation of '*weltgeschichtlich*'. In this way, the former is in fact reserved for the universal as an abstraction, whereas the latter refers to a universal that is empirically given in the concrete existence of individuals – that is, on the level of the global history of society. The universality of individuals is thus realised in a process, in which "with this universal development [*universelle Entwicklung*] of the productive forces a *universal* traffic [*universeller*

Verkehr] between men established", which produces *"world-historical,* empirically universal individuals [*weltgeschichtliche, empirisch universelle Individuen*] in place of local ones". As the world market – which makes the connections between people material – is established, the empirical universality that Marx had opposed to Hegel, accusing him of disregarding the concrete movements of ethicality, now takes on a real possibility – both individual and collective. These empirically universal individuals can finally oppose the *"forces* of traffic" by asserting their completely world-historical dimension. The very definition of the proletariat is only possible from the actual presence of this mass of empirically universal individuals. For it "can thus only exist *world-historically* [*weltgeschichtlich*], just as communism, its activity, can only have a 'world-historical' existence. World-historical existence of individuals, i.e., existence of individuals which is directly linked up with world history" (Marx and Engels, 1845–1846a: 48–49; see also Krätke, 1991).

With their specific universalism, these empirical individuals are an alternative to community closure based on a hypothetical common anthropology. Even Marx and Engels' famous assertions on ideology in this context about dominant ideas being the ideas of the ruling class, rather than a kind of general theory of ideology or basis for a sociology of culture, must be understood within the antithesis between abstract and empirical universalism. Both have obvious historical reasons for their existence, and for this reason it is not simply a matter of the clash between a false and a true universalism, nor even only that between reality and mere appearance. Rather, the issue is how the universalism that emerged from the French Revolution can, through the ideas of liberty and equality, claim absolute and irrefutable validity, thus establishing the basis of the "ruling *material* force [*Macht*] of society". Those ideas, intentionally without any reference to the material reality that produces them and in which they act, become an "eternal law" without history just waiting to be applied (Marx and Engels, 1845–1846a: 59). If, as Carl Schmitt wrote, "elites are those whose sociology no one dares to write about" (Schmitt, 1995: 147), universal ideas have precisely the function of making that sociology impossible. This is the function that ideology plays for Marx in the very constitution of power relations, and it can only fully develop if it appears as a general necessity based on universal ideas (Ricciardi, 2015). Ideology thus operates not through "'reflexes,' 'reflections,' and 'disguises' of economic relations" (Schmitt, 2006: 43), but as a constitutive part of the relations of power and domination that they historically establish.

Ideas such as freedom, equality, or democracy lead to a caesura and a prohibition at the same time: while they liberate themselves from any possible material conditioning, they forbid the investigation of the actual sociology of the power they legitimise, on pain of renouncing their universality. Precisely because it intends to remove the ruling classes from their position as elites, Marx's position claims to solve the mystery of their power by tracing it back to the materiality of the class confrontation, going so far as to argue the insufficiency of the bourgeoisie as the ruling class for the full unfolding of the domination of capital. It will thus be seen that the material action of universal ideas is possible due to the homology of functioning with the division between intellectual and manual labour, which for Marx establishes the very presupposition of class domination. To question this domination, to question the social might of money, is to prevent the reproduction of both those divisions. "Whenever a practical collision occurs in which the class itself is endangered", ideas again show their material character, their connection with the production of society. The domination of the ruling class does not come about thanks to ideas, but thanks to the fact that they "increasingly take on the form of universality". Those ideas, in fact, end up expressing the interest of a single class as a community interest, and that class can consequently present itself as "the representative of the whole of society". The appearance is not so much that of the ideas themselves, but that of a domain that claims to be universal and universally necessary. Thanks to this appearance, it can present itself as a "societal order" and present "a particular interest as general interest or 'the general interest' as ruling" (Marx and Engels, 1845–1846a: 60–61).

It is clearly not a question of contrasting the universal of ideas with "empirically universal individuals". The problem is rather to find a connection between individuals that, starting from their material location within the world market, produces a bond that is not objective because it is superior and indifferent to their movements, but derives directly from the empirical collisions they produce. As Marx and Engels write: "All collisions in history have their origin, according to our view, in the contradiction between the productive forces and the form of traffic" (Marx and Engels, 1845–1846: 74). Here "form of traffic" occupies the semantic and conceptual space of what Marx would later refer to as "relations of production". This is perhaps a more indeterminate formulation, with a less precise reference to the centrality of capital as a social relation, but which precisely because of that refers to a set of movements, exchanges, relations, and political clashes that should not be ignored even when encountering the later formulation, and which is explicitly foregrounded here. As we have already mentioned, traffic encompasses a broader dynamic than the political-institutional one that, in his critique of Hegel, Marx had summarised under the concept of democracy. Traffic refers to a complex of empirical dynamics that demonstrate the impossibility of a universal subject such as man or people, rather highlighting the fracture lines that traffic itself produces. With reference to the example of the bourgeoisie, Marx retorts to Bruno Bauer that classes do not pre-exist individuals, but it is the latter who can eventually constitute themselves as a class. The bourgeoisie does this in its struggle against the territorial nobility. "The separate individuals form a class only insofar as they have to carry on a common battle against another class; in other respects, they are on hostile terms with each other as competitors" (Marx and Engels, 1845–1846: 77).

Class is not an automatic effect of society's existence, although a given social location establishes, to use Pierre Bourdieu's term, a habitus that individuals do not freely choose, because they "find their conditions of life predetermined". The class that is constituted in struggle functions through a double register: it is both an individual habitus and a process of modification of that habitus in view of a common struggle, which in the case of the proletariat is not simply the struggle against another class, but against the relations that produce and reproduce its conditions of existence. "The transformation, through the division of labour, of personal powers (relations) into material powers" makes individuals simultaneously freer, because they have no ascribed status to which they must correspond, and less free "because they are to a greater extent governed by material forces [*sachliche Gewalt*]" (Marx and Engels, 1845–1846a: 77–78). The contingency of the bourgeois individual with respect to his class, determined by the success or failure of his economic performance, is for proletarians a contingency with respect to their overall living conditions, over which they can have no control and "over which no *social* organization can give them control" (Marx and Engels, 1845–1846a: 79).[12]

---

12   The insistence on the division of labour is the conceptual opposite of its celebration within neoliberalism, for which the category of risk functions as the legitimation of precisely that contingency; see Ricciardi (2017).

CHAPTER 2

The History of Power

1 Becoming Power

Marx's entire discourse has a radical individualism at its foundation that refuses to consider the members of a community as "average individuals" [*Durchschnittsindividuen*], i.e., as individuals who must necessarily replicate certain general qualities that, due to their indifference, are the condition of possibility of community life.[1] Individuals can "participate as individuals" only within the "real community" (Marx and Engels, 1845–1846: 80), because in it proletarians should be able to control the conditions of the reproduction of their lives. While it establishes a distance that is difficult to measure between the imaginary community represented in the state and the real community, the change in adjective also shows that this community is something other than a reference to a generic common essence. The empirical character of this individualism establishes the conceptual opposite of both the abstractly universal individual, in his function as the political *a priori* of society, and the sociological individual, understood as the median configuration of the member of a class. The democratic man in particular is the outcome of this median configuration of individuality, which makes him the member of a social homogeneity that traffic, competition, and struggle continually take it upon themselves to deny. The average individual, who is always supposed to be able to adapt to his democratic universe, is also constantly exposed to the weight of a tradition whose critique prevents the "real community" from being considered as the restoration of a condition of past perfection. Social evolution is not a linear process, but follows profoundly different paths that, by determining the empirical position of individuals, also differentiate and complicate the configuration of the powers to which they are subject and to which they may possibly rebel.

> It follows from this that even within a nation the individuals, even apart from their pecuniary circumstances, have quite diverse developments, and that an earlier interest, the peculiar form of intercourse of which

---

1 See Forbes (1990). Beyond other obvious interpretative limitations, also Elster (1985) emphasizes Marx's specific individualism. Gilbert (1990: 198) argues that Marx "actualizes rather than dissolves democratic individuality" and, again emphasizing the link with Aristotle, shows its effects in particular with regard to Marxian internationalism.

> has already been ousted by that belonging to a later interest, remains for a long time afterwards in possession of a traditional might in the illusory community (state, law), which has won an existence independent of the individuals; a might which in the last resort can only be broken by a revolution.
>
> MARX and ENGELS, 1845–1846: 83

This is also why the Marxian idea of revolution privileges its processual character above all, refusing ever more firmly to reduce it to the event. The social might that is produced in traffic – the might of tradition, political power – establishes too dense a network, too complex a configuration to think it can be erased in a single move. This is also why the collective power that the proletariat or the working class can use in opposition is constantly a provisional power that cannot be thought of as a zero-sum game, in which a share of power taken away from one part immediately becomes power available to the other. Since power is constantly being produced and amplified in trafficking, it is not possible to simply imagine countervailing power as equal and opposite power.

Yet, as we have seen, only a revolution can dissolve the network of powers. The time of revolution must retrace the time of powers in order to defuse them, to produce the material conditions that prevent their reproduction. It is thus shown that for Marx the real problem of power in all its various manifestations is not so much its foundation as the constancy of its exercise. Modern politics has focused on the foundation of power, be it a hypothetical social pact or a constituent moment. As will happen later in the social sciences, for Marx the functioning, internal dynamics, and stratification are far more important than the moment of the constitution of power. It is on this ground that the break between communism and democracy takes place, between the proletariat that is becoming a party and the party of democrats. Here, party does not primarily mean a political-institutional organization that stands in opposition to others, but the active presence of a social party that acts politically as such, thus without the prospect of having to or being able to represent the political totality. This idea of the party presenting itself as a social part, and hence not as a faction but neither as a particular articulation of the overall political system, will be one of the innovations of the political semantics used in the *Manifesto* that is anticipated, sometimes literally, in the previous year's vehement polemic with Karl Heinzen. The latter is an exponent of the radical democratic movement in Germany and will continue to be so after his emigration to the United States. For Marx and Engels, this polemic represents a reckoning with political radicalism and its republican and democratic positions, because of the centrality they assign to political power over power based on traffic and money.

Heinzen reacts to the accusation of starting a "war against communists" and explains his reasons against what he sees as the fundamental errors of communist doctrine. The first concerns the social function of private property which, according to an argument dating back to Locke, also defines the individual personality for Heinzen. With the separation "of all private property from the individual person, communism also abolishes individual existence". To abolish proprietary singularity means to erase all public and private space between one individual and another, to impose barrack-room socialism as in the phalansteries, to destroy all individual and independent expression. It still means sacrificing the individual to the "ghost of community or society", which should instead only be the means to his or her affirmation. The fundamental difference with communists such as Engels and Marx consists in their refusal to regard the individual as something prior to society itself, because otherwise – in a Lockean manner – property would also be abhorrently placed prior to and outside the social relationship, for that reason being if not a natural right, then at least a natural expression of personality. Since in this manner it is not a relation, property would not establish a position of power, and therefore could not be the source of any injustice. Only power concentrated in the state, and even more so in a single person, would consequently be responsible for both the violence of power and the scandal of injustice. Since, even if communism were the answer to this condition, it would still not be possible in the short term, for Heinzen everyone would have to recognize that a combination of political and social aspirations must be achieved to combat power [*Gewalt*] and its injustice [*Unrecht*]. Thus, "in place of the state of power and violence [*Gewaltstaat*], a real state of law [*Rechtsstaat*] must be founded, a purely democratic state, a republic that recognises the equal right of all its citizens. Only within this state will it be possible to undertake those social reforms that everyone recognises as necessary in theory and practice" ([Heinzen], 1847a). As is evident, denying an immediate political value to private property implies not only a separate constitution of the political itself, but also a specific definition of the social as a space that individual owners can freely determine if they are not subject to the control and coercion of political power. It is precisely for this reason that the social is, so to speak, a secondary sphere, whose eventual problems can only be addressed after the fundamental problem of political power has been solved, because the right solution to this problem already contains the solution to the social question as well.

This first article by Heinzen, published with a decisive distance from the editorial staff of the *Deutsche-Brüsseler-Zeitung*, immediately triggered the reaction of Engels, who strongly affirmed that communism was not a doctrine but a movement, and Stephan Born, who questioned the political form outlined in it (Engels, 1847; [Born], 1847). In his rejoinder, Heinzen reiterates his position, stating that "communists are too *blind* to see that power also dominates *property* and that injustice in property relations is only maintained by power. I call *foolish and cowardly* those who attack a bourgeois for his acquisition of money and leave a king alone with his *acquisition of power*. [...] Power also dominates property!". Beyond the tones that the polemic takes on both sides, it becomes clear that Heinzen here denies what, as we have already seen, is becoming a central category of Marx's discourse, namely relation. If property is not a relation, then it also cannot be the locus of manifestation of some personal might, but instead only the ultimate outcome of a personal commitment from which others can also benefit. This calls for a further definition of the social figures of property in their relation to political power, and Heinzen does not shy away from this necessity:

> I cannot help it, if I am less indignant in the face of a 'subject' who has casually become a 'bourgeois', who without the compulsion of violence [*Gewaltzwang*] makes a dozen other subjects work for a wage, than in the face of a despot who by means of organised violence [*Gewalt*], established and sanctified as a system and dogma, not only economically but also ethically erases every choice of thousands, even millions of bourgeois and proletarians.
>
> HEINZEN, 1847b[2]

Certainly, this judgement is also motivated by the judgment of the German situation in comparison to that of other states which, like the United States, have a democratic and republican political constitution. The first and fundamental choice for Heinzen is in fact between republic and monarchy, between democracy and despotism. In the democratic republic, the positions of possible supremacy would be contingent and therefore unrelated to the overall political organization. As we have already seen, however, the communist discourse also turns against this contingency of social location, not because it claims to plan all positions precisely, but because social contingency seems to it to be governed by different rules depending on the social class in which individuals are placed. In other words, contingency is not an uncontrolled effect of societal traffic, but a systematic production of its order. Societal contingency differentiates individuals according to society's material forms of production. It thus ends up assigning different possibilities of success to self-ownership in

---

2 On the continuity of the Lockean paradigm up to the nineteenth century see Brocker (1992).

such a way as to make it difficult if not impossible to consider all individuals as an undifferentiated mass of powerless owners.

It is precisely for this reason that, where Heinzen sees only one despotic power that must be attacked and eliminated, and then occasional positions of supremacy, Marx sees two and criticizes their relationship. "We are therefore faced with two kinds of power [*Gewalt*], on the one hand the power of property, in other words, of the property-owners, on the other hand political power [*politische Gewalt*], the might of the state [*Staatsmacht*]". The discourse in Marx's response is characterized by a series of semantic shifts that end up depriving *Gewalt*, power/violence, of the centrality and meaning Heinzen attributes to it. Political power is in fact referred to its state organization and not to its individual and collective representative and thus immediately becomes the power of the state, that is, the might that the state deploys within the relations that its citizen subjects entertain with each other. This is certainly not to deny the nexus between violence and the state, but to affirm the even more important one between the state and the relationship of society: for Marx, the state is a power that must be grasped in the social process of its production. It is these links that define the Marxian concept of power and the semantic constellation that defines it at its root. Heinzen's definition of power is meaningless because in "countries where the bourgeoisie has already conquered political power and political domination [*politische Herrschaft*] is none other than the rule, not of the individual bourgeois over his workers, but of the bourgeois class over the whole of society" (Marx, 1847c: 318).

Domination is a fundamental term in the semantic constellation that defines the Marxian concept of power. Indeed, it becomes most relevant when the centrality of the capital relation is affirmed. Against its etymology and history,[3] domination in this context does not refer to personal power exercised directly over the body of each individual subject, but to the ability to collectively determine the activity, and thus the existence, of a multitude of individuals. The power relationship no longer takes individual submission as its model but must necessarily be thought of as a collective condition. It does not simply refer to an asymmetry or even an act of will. Power is a relation and a condition. This is precisely why Marx does not accept that property is presented as the effect of individual performance. "*Bourgeois* property relations" are such

---

3   We will obviously return to the Marxian concept of *Herrschaft* of which – to my knowledge – there is no specific analysis. It should be noted that the concept returns significantly in Max Weber within an unresolved tension between the abstraction of power and its being necessarily exercised over men. See Piccinini and Rametta (1987); Nobili Schiera (2015); Basso M (2012).

because they correspond to a specific organization of society, guaranteed by state might. "The proletariat must therefore overthrow the political power where it is already in the hands of the bourgeoisie. It must itself become a power [*Gewalt*], in the first place a revolutionary power [*revolutionäre Gewalt*]" (Marx, 1847c: 319).

2　A Provisional Power

Marx does not share Heinzen's horror towards power, just as he does not think that state power is the fundamental instrument of the subjugation of individuals. The means to achieve certain ends, to use the Hobbesian definition, are produced elsewhere, i.e., within society and, precisely for this reason, "the political domination of the bourgeois class arises from these modern relations of production". As long as the proletariat is unable to overthrow these relations and merely fights the "the political domination of the bourgeoisie, its victory will only be temporary" (Marx, 1847c: 319). For Marx, this is what happened in France in 1794, when the proletariat fought in the service of the bourgeois revolution. The latter is thus not a more or less necessary stage in a universal classification of revolutions culminating in the proletarian revolution, but rather the revolution in which the proletariat's inability to change the conditions of its own production emerges. Nor is it a question of political immaturity, because for Marx, the social domination of the bourgeoisie cannot be overthrown simply by political revolution. The proletariat's coming to power is a process that deconstructs the society that produces it, redefining the network of powers that determines it.

Where republicanism and democratic thought see distinct and hierarchically differentiated processes of power, Marx instead sees a unified process running through the whole of society. "*Money* and *power*, *property* and *rule*, the *acquisition of money* and the *acquisition of power*" are connected by relations that go as far as "they merge". Society is not the sphere in which a kind of antithesis of power is produced, but rather the place of production of certain materially produced 'thresholds of power' capable of dividing men, establishing the rules of their subjugation. Therefore, it is not enough to say that "the *political* relationships of men are of course also *social, societal* relationships", making all relations between men into social questions, because this does not account for the "conflicts of modern times" that occur within society. Solving the social question in the sense of a republic or monarchy "did not mean that even a single 'social question' has been solved in the interests of the proletariat" (Marx, 1847c: 320–322).

The question of property is thus no longer linked to individual self-assertion, but increasingly to overcoming "the collisions which have arisen from large-scale industry, the development of the world market and free competition". Precisely for this reason, the question of property can no longer be thought of as an instrument of individual sociality. It is a "question of world-historical significance" (Marx, 1847c: 322, 323), because it depends on those "collisions" that now occur with increasing frequency in the United States, which is simply not the finally realized democratic republic, because of the credit system and speculation more than the specific constitutional form of the state. For Marx, the limitation of Heinzen's discourse – but this is a reproach he regularly addresses to many of his compatriots – is that they regard the Prussian monarchy as a state form that is both backward and degenerate, thus attributing to the coveted democracy the ability to resolve the question of power comprehensively and definitively. They not only ignore the fact that democracy is not a neutralization of power, but above all that in democratic society, power does not circulate indefinitely, instead moving through determinate channels that lead it to thresholds where it can increase or decrease depending on the subjects it affects.

Within the complex constituted by state and society, specific thresholds of power differentiate the possibilities of action of different classes of individuals, even and precisely when the norms claim to have a universal character. This is concretely demonstrated by taxation, which, as much as market logics, pushes the level of workers' income towards the minimum necessary for their reproduction. "Taxes form a part of this minimum, for the political calling [*politischer Beruf*] of the workers consists precisely in paying taxes". From the workers' point of view, there is no difference between the centralizing absolute monarchy or the "federal republic with social institutions" that Heinzen takes from Rousseau's projects for Poland and Mably's for Corsica. For Marx, the dream of the republic is shattered by the relationship that it concretely has with its different citizens, because it is "perfectly 'possible' that what individual persons do is not 'always' determined by the class to which they belong", which for the class struggle decides nothing because the conditions of the latter do not depend on the will of individuals and, in the last instance, not even on the political form (Marx, 1847c: 329, 330).

Marx's polemic with Heinzen brings us back to where we started, namely the solitary presence of the term democracy in the *Manifesto*, which declares that "the first step in the revolution by the working class is to raise the proletariat to the position of ruling class, to win the battle [*Erkämpfung*] for democracy" (Marx and Engels, 1848: 504). This identification would not be understandable without referring to Engels's analysis of Chartism, which will be so important for Marx in later years. Engels recognizes the Chartist movement's ability to approximate that nexus between social struggle and political power that was to prove increasingly crucial. Despite the limitations arising from its composite character, and although it nominally sought above all to eliminate competition between workers, it affected, albeit "to a limited degree", the "very corner-stone of modern society", and thus proved "to be so dangerous to the existing social order" (Engels, 1958: 248).

For Engels, Chartism redefines the very meaning of democracy, enriching it with a social content that would otherwise be foreign to it. The genealogy of Chartism reveals the global dynamic of the democratic movement of which it is a part (Battistini, 2017). What is interesting to emphasize is that Engels – as is also the case for Marx – rejects the language of pure democracy, albeit for different reasons than its rejection in both the Federalist Papers and Kant. The problem posed by Chartism is not more democracy nor even a pure, i.e., direct form of democracy.

> An English Chartist is a republican, though he seldom, if ever, uses the term. He prefers to describe himself as a democrat, although he gives his sympathy to republican parties all over the world. Indeed, he is more than a republican, because the democracy that he supports is not only political.
> ENGELS, 1958: 259).

The "characteristic *social* aspect of the working-class side of the Chartist movement" is expressed in the constant striving to improve the social conditions of the workers. However, this is not merely the presentation of a catalogue of demands different from previous ones, but a specific difference between "Chartist democracy and all former brands of bourgeois political democracy" (Engels, 1958: 261). The materiality of the democratic subject, i.e., its composition and the social claims it expresses, redefine what can be understood as politics. The fact that, as Engels writes, "not one of the Chartists today is content to agitate solely for the political objectives" (Engels, 1958: 267), verifies for him the conviction that politics does not end in itself and thus does not establish a separate and stand-alone activity. On the contrary, this is Engels's criticism of socialists who do not recognize "historical development. They want to realise the Communist ideal immediately and do not grasp the fact that the transition to this state of society can be achieved only by the pursuit of a definite policy culminating in the dissolution of the existing social order" (Engels, 1958: 269). For Engels as well as Marx, the critique of politics means a practice that completely dissolves its object by showing its radical historicity. This critique can only be practical (Hindrichs, 2006). It cannot consequently resolve itself into an exclusively intellectual operation, just as it cannot refer to an abstractly universal subject programmatically and exclusively directed towards the future. The ahistorical nature of the English socialists' claim is motivated by their failure to "account of the extent to which modern man has been moulded by the past. In fact the whole world and, indeed, all individuals in it are the product of historical circumstances" (Engels, 1958: 269). This radically historical character of workers' democracy, the burden that the past continually ignites on the behavior of social subjects, prevents it from being considered an exclusively political form. Precisely for this reason, Engels can tersely argue that:

> *Democracy nowadays is communism.* Any other democracy can only still exist in the heads of theoretical visionaries who are not concerned with real events, in whose view it is not the men and the circumstances that develop the principles but the principles develop of themselves. Democracy has become the proletarian principle, the principle of the masses.
>
> ENGELS, 1845: 5; see also, CARVER, 1996

As it is easy to see in the *Manifesto*, the identification of democracy and communism is in reality not so peaceful, given that its authors not only understandably avoid calling themselves democrats, but in the conclusions end up recognizing a distance that must be bridged, entrusting communists with the task of working "everywhere for the union and agreement of the democratic parties of all countries" (Marx and Engels, 1848: 519). There is thus the recognition of democracy as a political movement of the proletariat, but there are also parties that evidently do not recognize its centrality, with which it is possible and indeed necessary to forge alliances. In any case, it is clear that in the *Manifesto*, the proletariat cannot be assimilated to the people that Marx spoke of in his critique of Hegel, just as democracy is not understood as a form of government, nor is it fundamentally understood as the constitution that shapes the state.

As a whole, the rhetoric of the text (Martin, 2015) is characterized by a continuous series of semantic oscillations that include some indisputable innovations and an equally indisputable deflagration of the vocabulary of power with an almost uncontrolled multiplication of terms. This is at least partly explained by the fact that the text is the outcome of an authentic struggle for the political naming of the social clash to be affirmed against both the vocabulary of the nascent social sciences and that of socialist currents. The *Manifesto* opens by affirming the class struggle as the criterion of the political (Balibar, 2013) and, immediately afterwards, declares that "Communism is already acknowledged by all European Powers to be itself a Might" (Marx and Engels, 1848: 508). It is precisely this position of might among the powers that makes it necessary to make manifest, and thus public, a specific political program. It is not simply a matter of transforming the might of communism into the power of the proletariat, because in this way power would be re-proposed without changing its presuppositions in the slightest, whereas the communist problem seems to be precisely that of establishing the conditions of possibility for an evolution that does not endlessly reproduce the need for political power. Quite paradoxically, might must establish the basis of power in order to revoke its centrality and necessity. This theoretically and politically central point corresponds to the way the *Manifesto* describes the subject of its program. The proletariat, in fact, is not a universal subject. However much its rise is recounted with the tones of a universal story, the proletariat is an empirical subject that cannot be the universal foundation of a political order because it cannot univocally represent the society that oppresses it (Althusser, 1993). The proletariat cannot be the definitive subject of power, but necessarily has a discontinuous and always revocable relationship with it.

3 On the Use of the State

"Now and then the workers are victorious, but only for a time [*nur vorübergehend*]" (Marx and Engels, 1848: 493). The *Manifesto*'s political problem is to secure workers' power over time, not just temporarily, i.e., to maintain the effects of any victories won, the institutional changes introduced. However, this power is a provisional power which cannot take its duration for granted.[4] For Engels and Marx, the real result of each of these successes is above all the

---

4 Rosa Luxemburg fully grasped the provisional character of power not only for Marx, but for the working class. Meanwhile, Luxemburg argues that the "fate of democracy is bound up with the fate of the labour movement", thus avoiding making democracy an abstraction that must in any case be held as a presupposition if politics is to be done and thought. That is, in a Marxian guise, she links democracy to workers' power and not to the people in the abstract. In this way she redefines the nexus between reform and revolution, making it clear that the latter is necessarily the foundation of the former and its legal order, since "in the history of classes, revolution is the act of political creation". Thus, reform and revolution have a fundamental difference that cannot be reduced to a problem of time and speed. This approach produces the discourse on political power and its conquest. "Since the proletariat is not in the position to seize political power in any other way than 'prematurely'; since the proletariat is absolutely obliged to seize power 'too early' once or several times before it can enduringly maintain itself in power, the objection to the '*premature*' seizure of power is nothing

further subjective constitution of those who took up the struggle, the "ever-expanding union of the workers". Their victory deconstructs the existing order but, as it is not a founding event, it does not open a new time. Instead, it coexists with that order, having to come to terms with its persistence and thus with the limits of its own action: "this organization of the proletarians into a class, and consequently into a political party, is continually being upset again by the competition between the workers themselves" (Marx and Engels, 1848: 493). The *Manifesto* affirms the politically central presence of class struggle, but immediately recalls the counter-trend that always threatens to render it ineffectual. The theoretical problem of the *Manifesto* is the attempt to dissolve the political through its specific institutionalized form, namely the state. Solving the problem of the transience of workers' achievements imposes a tension on the discourse with respect to the state and the very location of the political with respect to the social. The criterion of the political is not so much an existential division, but the material struggle of the "proletariat, the class of modern wage-labourers" against the "the sway of the bourgeois class" (Marx and Engels, 1848: 496). While the identification of the enemy is now clear, the relationship the proletarians establish with the bourgeoisie is not a matter settled once and for all, but must be continually addressed. It is no coincidence that the division "into two great hostile camps" is described as an ongoing process, not an acquired fact. The division between the bourgeoisie and the proletariat is the story of the apparently triumphant march of the bourgeoisie that is recounted not without emphasis in the first part of the *Manifesto* and, at the same time, "the more or less veiled civil war raging within existing society" (Marx and Engels, 1848: 495). This reference to civil war as an everyday and continuous experience, rather than as a moment of dramatic rupture in social and political life, is one of the examples of how Marx redefines certain classical political concepts, such as civil war but also dictatorship, removing them from their extreme and exceptional position, to make them moments of a continuity that demands to be interrupted. To use Hans Blumenberg's terms (1976), Marx carries out a "reoccupation" of certain concepts, highlighting their historical contents that would otherwise be neglected and usually left in the background. This reoccupation ends up showing the historical epoch of modern capitalism as a precarious structure because it is exposed to change that potentially interrupts its continuity. The Marxian civil war is not a struggle for the dominance of the existing and thus it prevents one from thinking of the epoch

---

other than a *general opposition to the aspiration of the proletariat to take state power*" (1971: 113, 115, 123).

as a structure of order capable of reproducing itself through its own conflicts. As the truth of the class struggle, it makes it a "political struggle" (Marx and Engels, 1848: 493), which does not aim to redefine citizenship and membership of the body politic, but the relations of supra- and subordination that define society. Thus the "overthrow of the bourgeois domination, conquest of political power by the proletariat" does not end the civil war, but only redefines its overall framework (Marx and Engels, 1848: 498).

Precisely for this reason, Marx's notion of the political is always suspended, because it does not provide for some political decision to reconcile the antithesis that produces the same concept. Unlike the Schmittian political, in which the exception is conceived as a function of the decision that resolves it (Schmitt, 2003; Galli, 2015),[5] the Marxian political does not grant politics and its institutionalization either a founding moment, such as sovereignty, that proves its necessity, or a resolving event, such as a purely political revolution, that can put an end to its antitheses. It does not exist in view of the unity produced by the decision, but because of the presence of the struggle of a class against the societal organization that constantly reproduces the conditions of its existence. In this sense, for Engels and Marx, history is indeed the history of a class's struggle against the bourgeoisie as holders of shares in wealth, but also against the domination of capital: the subordination of proletarians cannot be equated with a master-servant relationship. "To be a capitalist is to have not only a purely personal, but a social *status* in production". The tension between domination and power that runs throughout the *Manifesto* is motivated by the acquisition, increasingly clear and important in Marx's later work, that "capital is, therefore, not a personal [but] a societal might [*gesellschaftliche Macht*]" (Marx and Engels, 1848: 499).

However, in the *Manifesto*, the political struggle against the domination of capital, which is now a world power, is linked to the conquest of "political supremacy" on a national scale. Not only that: with the empirically universal individuals, the proletariat must "rise to be the leading class of the nation, must constitute itself *the* nation". This would be a necessary and transitional phase, motivated by the modern identity of political power and state might, *politische Gewalt* and *Staatsmacht*. In order to access the possibilities offered by the latter, it is necessary to conquer the former, which allows the state to be used as an instrument. However, this also explicitly declares a difference between the

---

5 Iorio (2003: 310 ff) argues that, except their 'ideological' differences, there is a continuity between the Schmittian concept of the political and Marx's concept of the political, because both would be oriented towards the identification of the unity of a group, thanks to the opposition to an enemy. In Marx the outcome would be a specific socialist democracy.

national form of the proletariat's struggle and its content, which should ignore national boundaries. By virtue of this distinction, moreover, the communists, who should not constitute a "separate party opposed to other working-class parties" (Marx and Engels, 1848: 497) – but should value the content against the form of the struggles, upholding their transnational and overall dimension – end up constantly intensifying the tension of the conception of power that the *Manifesto* expresses. In any case, "political supremacy" should be used to take capital away from the bourgeoisie through the introduction of certain "despotic inroads on the rights of property, and on the conditions of bourgeois production; by means of measures, therefore, which appear economically insufficient and untenable" (Marx and Engels, 1848: 504). Meanwhile, it is worth noting the appearance of the reference to despotism that plays a central role in the Marxian vocabulary of power. Those measures are despotic because they do not stand on the 'terrain of law'. They contest property without producing those 'legal collisions' that, as Hegel argued, always find their solution within the systematic order of law.

The "despotic inroads" aim to suspend the reproduction of bourgeois society by changing its internal order, which presents itself as tradition. They do not establish a different order, since their inadequacy from an economic point of view is clearly recognized, but they claim to alter the course of societal evolution by establishing conditions that are incompatible with the existence of classes and the law that reproduces them. These are largely administrative measures that have the state as their center of disposition and control. This brings us back to the problem of Marx and Engels's relationship with administrative action.[6] Here the despotic character of the measures should obviate the impotence that is otherwise, as we have seen, the law of administration for Marx. Despotic in this context thus means the ability to impose certain measures against the force of inertia and opposition that the social power of capital can still deploy. The seizure of power of which the *Manifesto* speaks is thus not a single event, but a new phase in the class struggle and thus also in the use of the state (Luporini, 1979). This struggle around administration is moreover the defining feature of French '48, when Lorenz von Stein writes that two republics – the social republic and the bourgeois republic – are fighting for domination over administration because it allows them to control the redistribution of the social product. The Marxian problem is clearly the bureaucratic

---

6 Demirović (2006: 463, 477) acknowledges that for Marx, "politics itself is heteronomous and participates in societal illiberality" and that "democratic politics has within it a tendency to become authoritarian, for it wants to make individuals equal by political means, when they are socially unequal".

form that administration has taken, and it is against this specific connection between political power and bureaucratic power that he continues his criticism until the Paris Commune. For Marx, bureaucracy is a political instrument for the preservation of the social relations of capital.

When, in the course of development, class distinctions have disappeared, and all production has been concentrated in the hands of the associated individuals, the public power [*öffentliche Gewalt*] will lose its political character. Political power, properly so called, is merely the organised power of one class for oppressing another (Marx and Engels, 1848: 505).

The association of individuals does not eliminate power as such, which is indeed something they can finally share, precisely because it is no longer the sign of struggle and oppression. If it is now public without being political, it is because the latter is the indelible sign that social relations exhibit when they have to govern the potential insubordination of a class. On the other hand, this remains a characteristic feature of proletarian rule as well, because the necessity of the state is the sign that class antagonism is still present. The state can in no case be the representation of the universal, but always and only the outcome of a split that it helps to reproduce. It is the evidence that one part of society manages to transform its social domination into political power.

The proletarian use of the state clearly entails the risk of perpetuating the political while claiming to suppress it. On the other hand, the *Manifesto* is not Marx's last word on the use and function of the state. At the same time, the identification of democracy with the rise of the social domination of the proletariat shows that the democratic conundrum is not always solved, because democracy cannot be regarded as the truth of every constitution. The conundrum has changed form and concerns precisely the possibility that the proletariat can actually assert itself as power, not as an undifferentiated mass, but as a multitude presenting itself as a mass. Engels and Marx, like much of the European revolutionary movement, expected 1848 to show the solution to the conundrum empirically. But it did not.

4 The Terrain of Law

The revolutions of 1848 were defeated. "With the exception of only a few chapters, every more important part of the annals of the revolution from 1848 to 1849 carries the heading: *Defeat of the Revolution!*" (Marx, 1850a: 47). This defeat is in part salutary, because it sheds light on what the revolution actually is, removing it from the hitherto dominant dimension of a historical-universal event and allowing a specific part of the social movement to appropriate its overall meaning. The unravelling of the revolutions of 1848 is the loss of the illusion of the universally progressive character of history that in the *Manifesto* was expressed in the linearity with which economic exploitation immediately produced the revolutionary occasion. At the same time, it signals that the proletarian revolution did not live up to its political task. Although it presented itself as a novelty, it failed to introduce the innovations for which it fought, thus remaining an episode within the more general social evolution. The social revolution lost because it did not live up to the set of pressing and tumultuous changes that set the tone for the nineteenth century. That is, it failed to make the evolution of the proletariat the decisive novelty in the midst of the scientific, technological and productive revolutions taking place. This is precisely why it becomes the unsolved enigma not only of democracy, but of society as a whole. It is no coincidence that, on 14 April 1856, speaking in London at the annual party of the Chartist newspaper *The People's Paper*, Marx was able to state that "the so-called revolutions of 1848 were but poor incidents – small fractures and fissures in the dry crust of European society" (Marx, 1856a: 655). The elaboration of the defeat therefore takes place on both grounds on which it had matured: by further deepening the analysis of the concept of society in order to affirm its definitive centrality, on the one hand, and by analysing the response of the state on a European scale on the other, because its government ultimately proves to be something more complex than the "committee for managing the common affairs of the whole bourgeoisie" to which the *Manifesto* had reduced it (Marx and Engels, 1848: 486; see also Fernbach, 1973). At the same time, the class opposition is treated in a more articulate manner, as it becomes clear that economic position does not immediately produce readiness for political struggle. Rather, Marx records that there is *"no necessary correspondence* between the 'economic' and the 'political' constitution of classes", capturing the movement that establishes what Stuart Hall has called the "specificity of the political" (Hall, 1977a: 26, 40).

The first attempt at analysis takes place practically in real time, i.e., during 1848 itself, when the *Neue Rheinische Zeitung* intervenes in European affairs and with particular and inevitable continuity in German affairs. One problem is certainly the position of the communists in relation to the factions and parties with which the *Manifesto* had given the indication to establish alliances. The reality of the democratic movement is not only given by the wavering behaviour of its exponents in the *Paulskirche* assembly (Marx, 1848a), but also by the proposal of an old militant of the workers' movement such as Wilhelm Weitling, who claims to establish a "dictatorship of the wisest" (Mayer, 1951; see also, Stedman Jones, 2016: 212 ff) in order to limit the disruptiveness of a revolutionary movement that together with the old estate-based governments also overwhelms the compound world of the socialist sects. Marx publicly opposes this dictatorship of the few, while the journal he directs aims to bring out both the antagonism between the social movement and the bourgeoisie, and the tension with the positions and behaviour of those who refer directly to democracy.[7] The new journal's presentation of itself as an organ of democracy is motivated precisely by the attempt to combine social movement and democratic movement. This understanding of democracy as a movement and not as an institutional form remains a constant in Marx's work, although in 1848, with the progressive defeat of the revolutionary movement in Germany, it inevitably ends up being less important than the constitutional clash between the various German governments, and in particular the Prussian government, and the Frankfurt and Berlin assemblies. The radical and democratic positions appear inconclusive. While recognizing the need for a central power [*Zentralgewalt*] formed within the national assembly itself, these end up proposing an improbable Germanic federation of republics, principalities, and constitutional monarchies. Marx is a political realist who, as far as circumstances allow, tries to find the conditions for the social movement to have a political voice within a Germany for which, given the situation, a republican form cannot immediately be demanded. "Both German unity and the German Constitution can result only from a movement in which the internal conflicts and the war with the East will play an equally decisive role" (Marx, 1848b: 51). The clash with the democratic parties is thus motivated by their propensity to imagine republics that in no way correspond to the actual truth in the German situation. This Machiavellian tension of the political Marx becomes even more clear after the Paris massacre of June 1848 when, despite the fact that he emphatically announces that the workers "have been *defeated* but their enemies are *vanquished*", he ends up proposing a tumultuous form of state that allows social traffic to express itself in all its components (Marx, 1848c: 144).

> Collisions proceeding from the very conditions of bourgeois society must be fought out to the end, they cannot be conjured out of existence. The best form of state is that in which the societal contradictions [*gesellschaftliche Gegensätze*] are not blurred, not arbitrarily – that is merely artificially, and therefore only seemingly – kept down. The best form of state

---

7 As Engels writes (1848: 74): "to recognise the revolution under these circumstances meant recognising the democratic aspects of the revolution, which the big bourgeoisie wanted to appropriate to itself. Recognising the revolution at this moment meant recognising the *incompleteness* of the revolution, and consequently recognising the democratic movement, which was directed against some of the results of the revolution".

is that in which these contradictions reach a stage of open struggle in the course of which they are resolved.

MARX, 1848c: 149; see also SCHIEDER, 1991: 43 ff

This is a proposal that is as realistic as it is defensive, dictated by the perception that, given the importance of the French revolution of 1848, the June defeat in Paris is a sign of a closure of the spaces of political viability for the revolutionary movement as a whole in Europe. For Marx, democratic movement does not primarily address the political form, but rather questions the order of society. From November 1848, however, this movement has to deal with the conflict between the Prussian government and the national assembly in Frankfurt, against which Marx forges the categories he then uses to interpret the conflict over the working day. The conflict matures from the Frankfurt assembly's claim to control the army and is exacerbated by the Prussian king's refusal to allow it to move to Berlin on 5 November. The assembly failed to produce a credible response until a state of siege was declared in Berlin and a bloodless and unopposed coup d'état put an end to the March revolution. On 5 December, the assembly is dissolved, and the King of Prussia grants his constitution (Nipperdey, 1984: 648 ff; Winkler, 2000: 114 ff). At this juncture Marx sought to reaffirm, as he had already done against Hegel, the superiority of the legislative over the executive and its monarch. On 9 November, a fateful day in German history, Marx had already asserted the presence of two sovereigns both claiming to establish the constitutional ground of a clash that can only end with the defeat of one of them. The different historical foundations of the different claims to legitimacy show with increasing clarity that "*Right* is on the side of *force* [*Macht*]" (Marx, 1848d: 4). For Marx, the critique of the German situation is both a constant reflection on the relationship between power and law, and on the way in which the latter transposes what matures on the level of social relations.

What Lenin would call dualism of powers seventy years later is here the clash between two governmental claims, both of which aim to determine administrative action concerning both taxation and the possibility of forming autonomous militias. In this context, the polysemy of the term *Gewalt* stands out to the highest degree, because the government claim can only be supported by its material strength, since the Prussian king does not recognize the assembly's right to defense. "Where counter-revolutionary authorities seek forcibly to frustrate the formation and official activity of these committees of public safety, *force must be opposed by every kind of force. Passive* resistance must have *active resistance* as its basis" (Marx, 1848e: 38; see also, Derrida, 1993). However, it was precisely on the question of resistance to the

Prussian government that the break between the Frankfurt assembly and the Prussian assembly in Berlin took place. The latter, in fact, faced with the monarch's counter-revolutionary turn, declared tax resistance to be contrary to law and therefore illegitimate. Having already established that paying taxes is the "political calling" (Marx, 1847c: 329) of the workers, Marx cannot help but side with the Berliners, signing a call for a tax strike and supporting the municipalities' obligation to comply with the decision of the Prussian national assembly (Marx, Schapper and Schneider II, 1848: 41). For him, the fact that the Frankfurt assembly declared the tax resistance illegal demonstrates the obvious futility of the assembly itself. Precisely in response to the tax resistance, the Prussian monarch declares a state of siege, revealing the paradoxical truth that "states of siege everywhere, such are the achievements of the March revolution" (Marx, 1848f: 53), since they multiply in all those Prussian cities that claim to establish their own militias. The state of siege sets the co-ordinates of what is emerging as the terrain of law [*Rechtsboden*], on which the compromise between the Prussian bourgeoisie and the government matures. The terrain of law is the opposite of the revolutionary process. It incorporates some of its instances, establishes an order between the subjects that participated in it, carries out a synthesis between the old configuration of power and the new one, and establishes the subject that can claim the rights that emerged from the revolution, but also their limits.

> "Terrain of law" simply meant that the revolution had gained no ground and the old society had not lost its ground; that the March revolution was only an "occurrence" that gave the "impulse" for an "agreement" between the throne and the bourgeoisie, preparations for which had long been made within the old Prussian state, and the need for which the Crown itself had already announced in earlier royal decrees, but had not, prior to March, considered as "*urgent*". ... The "terrain of law" meant that the legal title of the people, *revolution*, did not exist in the *contrat social* between the Government and the bourgeoisie.
>
> MARX, 1848g: 166

When Marx rejects the terrain of law (1848g: 154) he does not simply claim the illegal character of revolutionary action but poses a broader historical and political question. The terrain of law is in fact the outcome of that political theology that allows the constant reconciliation of the past with the present. Only through it, in fact, can the anachronism of the ancient estate-based society penetrate into bourgeois civil reality. Only on the terrain of law does political theology reveal its practical usefulness, showing that "metaphysics is the most intensive and the clearest expression of an epoch" (Schmitt, 2006: 46) by establishing the fundamental conditions of the uninterrupted legitimacy of order. For political theology, there is always an order to be saved and, in case of necessity, it is perfectly consequential that the search for this salvation produces states of siege. The state of siege is not a suspension of law, but the cogent and irresistible indication of the legal modalities through which thresholds of power are confirmed and established.

The emergence of the force of law makes it a "paradigm of government" (Agamben, 2005). As one of the most eminent fruits of politics after 1848, it reaffirms the unity of the people by force, establishing an ordered people to replace the disordered and revolutionary one, while making the "miracle" of sovereignty (Piccinini, 1989) an ordinary and repeatable event. Marx accuses the bourgeoisie of being counter-revolutionary because it puts an end to the overall movement of the revolution by accessing the terrain of law, i.e., by choosing to represent "renewed interests within an obsolete society" (Marx, 1848g: 162). The state of siege highlights the intimate union of force and right, showing that "he who has force [*Gewalt*], has right" (Marx, 1848h: 50). In order to once again become the centre of gravity of the political system, the government must make that connection evident, because only in this way does it show the ineffectuality of the claim to create new law, breaking the ambitions of the national assemblies in Frankfurt and Berlin. The government successfully asserts the claim to be the only figure capable of determining the coordinates of the terrain of law and derives its legitimacy from this.

"The March revolution, as seen by the Crown, was a savage fact", which forced it to interrupt the continuity of law, becoming revolutionary itself. The revolution obliges other revolutions, producing in fact a legal vacuum that prevents criminal or civil law from applying to those defeated in the revolution. After a victorious revolution, "one can hang one's opponents, but one cannot convict them" (Marx, 1849a: 324; see also, Guastini, 1974: 349–356; Lascoumes and Zander, 1984), because law cannot judge the revolution, which can only be subjected to historical judgement. Indeed, the entire press, regardless of its political leanings, recognizes that "this was a struggle between two powers [*Gewalten*], and only force [*Gewalt*] can decide between two powers" (Marx, 1849a: 325). In *Capital*, the same sentence is rephrased as two equal rights between which only force can decide, showing how law always remains within the logic of the society of capital. Defending himself in court against the charge of treason, Marx does not even claim the legality of his actions under the laws established by the national assembly, which would have absolved him. The issue is in fact not obedience or disobedience to laws, but the recognition of the social character of legal production. Despite the autonomy of his discourse, law in the society of capital can only be positive law. Marx clearly opposes a historical foundation of law, whereby estate-based society finds its own presupposition by assigning to each the position it must necessarily occupy. Positive law, like money in other respects, expresses the material order of bourgeois society. Revolution is the work of constantly deconstructing the law of society. In the German '48 it turned as much against absolute monarchy as against estate-based representation, not only showing that its laws are now in contradiction to the world of traffic and industry, but also questioning that the law of the ancient estate-based society is the fundamental normative expression of society.

> Society is not founded upon the law; that is a legal fiction. On the contrary, the law must be founded upon society, it must express the common interests and needs of society – as distinct from the caprice of the individuals – which arise from the material mode of production prevailing at the given time.
>
> MARX, 1849a: 327; BURKETT, 2000

In the rhetorical flourish of his defence, Marx asserts that he holds that the *Code Napoléon* does not claim to create bourgeois society, but only to express its mode of functioning, clearly taking the individual as its foundation and renouncing the terrain of law that legitimizes estates and corporations.

Marx's position clearly takes up the terms of the polemic against the historical school of law, brutally defined as the "*sole frivolous* product" (Marx, 1842: 203) of the eighteenth century, not least because of its worship of sources that immediately turns into absolute respect for authority. Even more remarkable, however, is the inability it shows to grasp the profound diversity of the processes of social "dissolution", that only in certain cases, as in the activity of the French National Assembly, "appears as the *liberation of the new spirit* from *old forms*, which were no longer of any value or *capable* of containing it" (Marx, 1842: 205–206).[8] The *Code Civil*, on the other hand, is the outcome of this liberation, which does not, however, result in the passage from one normative order to another, from natural and historical law to the predominance of positive law. The real shift consists in the priority that society takes over legal production, in the fact that law literally becomes the law of society. Similarly, the powers that confront each other are powers in society, which represents the new

---

8 On Marx's understanding of law in his early writings, see Basso M (2023); Kelley (1978); Levine (1987); Mascat (2018).

political space for the production of the rules of law. The clash taking place can only be decided by "material might [*materielle Macht*]", because what appears to be a clash between two irreconcilable claims to sovereignty – since "two sovereign powers cannot function simultaneously, side by side, *in one state*" (Marx, 1849a: 331) – is actually a clash between two societies. What had just concluded was thus not the "a political conflict between two parties within the framework of *one* society, but a *conflict between two societies*, a social conflict, which had assumed a political form" (Marx, 1849a: 335). This is even more evident in Marx's stance regarding the vote on the constitution granted by the monarch. Marx does not appeal to the democratic values of the bourgeoisie in order to oppose them to those of the "political constitution representing the 'social' interests of the feudal aristocracy, the bureaucracy and the monarchy by the grace of God". He does not seek a political compromise so that different sides can jointly oppose the constitution. Instead, he delineates two models of society, with the explicit intention of showing even the Prussian bourgeoisie that the estates-based articulation of society is not the result of the division of labor, but an attempt to control the movements of a society destined to move outside of governmental protections anyway. Marx therefore demands a vote for this society from the bourgeoisie, because the constitution granted by the Prussian monarch does not simply outline a politico-legal architecture, but imposes a specific authoritarian and bureaucratic solution to the "social question" (Marx, 1849b: 263). This clash of societies, which Marx takes from the French historians (Bongiovanni, 1989), is initially used in a rather scholastic manner to describe the incompatibility between the ancient estate-based society and the modern, industrial society. In a far more significant manner, and precisely rejecting the outcomes of the post-revolutionary historiography of Guizot and Thierry (Consolati, 2023), Marx however rereads that clash as a social civil war and not simply as a conflict between two populations of the same society. When social positions are not secured in advance by law, society itself becomes a space in which cooperation produces collisions that cannot be avoided or cancelled except by changing the conditions of production and reproduction of society itself.

5   Revolution and Dictatorship

The imposition of the terrain of law reduces the revolution in Germany to a contingent event. In France, it paradoxically appears to become one due to its continuance. If in Germany law institutionalizes the anachronism of the ancient estate-based society within bourgeois civil society, then in France the ghost of the grand old revolution is brought out to legitimize the burden that the past imposes on the present. The double life of the revolution, first as tragedy and then as farce, reveals that it becomes part of that repertoire of past elements that serve to prevent the radical change of the present.[9] The hallmark of the period from 1848 to 1851 is thus the spectral character of the revolution, represented by forms and figures that are constantly evoked when the risk of new changes becomes concrete. The great revolution of 1789 functions as a compulsion to repeat and not as a real and effective opening; thanks to it, "an entire people, which had imagined that by means of a revolution it had imparted to itself an accelerated power of motion, suddenly finds itself set back into a defunct epoch" (Marx, 1852a: 105). The connection between the event and the revolutionary process as a whole was shown to be weak, revealing the unexpected retrograde function of the revolution, which thus shows that it does not respond to any philosophy of history, be it idealistic or materialistic, that refers to a metaphysics of the revolution itself (Marx, 2007: 209). For Marx, however, it is a fact that in 1848 the revolution "moves in a descending line. It finds itself in this state of retrogressive motion before the last February barricade has been cleared away and the first revolutionary authority constituted" (Marx, 1852a: 124). The proletarian revolution must therefore show that it knows how to resist the return of the past, aware that the "tradition of all the dead generations weighs like a nightmare on the brain of the living" (Marx, 1852a: 103) just when they think they can revolutionize their present. In order not to be relegated to the ranks of the merely political, the social revolution "cannot begin with itself before it has stripped off all superstition about the past" (Marx, 1852a: 106). This is an important passage because it shows how for Marx, history is not completely available to the action of men, who can only act "under circumstances directly encountered, given and transmitted from the past" (Marx, 1852a: 103).

The weight of tradition makes the revolution a process in which different actions and expectations, both collective and individual, are condensed. Tradition prevents the emerging cult of progress, which also seems to surface in some pages of the *Manifesto*. Marx had already recorded that "in spite of the pretensions of *'Progress'*, continual *retrogressions* and *circular movements* occur" (Marx and Engels, 1845: 83). We have already seen that in any case he does not attribute any specific and particular significance to history. 1848 shows that it has no end either. There is no linear progression of time along which the proletarian revolution follows the bourgeois revolution once the latter has

---

9   Carver (2002) speaks of an imaginative anachronism enabling the birth of the new.

completed its task. For Marx, revolution is a struggle against anachronisms and therefore it cannot only be directed towards the future. 1848 shows that revolution does not move on the wings of an enthusiasm that reveals its universal character, because that enthusiasm spreads as quickly as it suddenly dissolves (Ricciardi, 2001: 143–152). The time of proletarian revolutions is the time of the movements of their subjects – it is not a universal time. It is the time of those who must constantly return to their action to modify themselves and not just their environment. Proletarian revolutions "criticise themselves constantly, interrupt themselves continually in their own course, come back to the apparently accomplished in order to begin it afresh" (Marx, 1852a: 107): they can only draw on the future if they avoid succumbing to the domination of anachronisms, against which a great historical planning aimed at the future is not enough, because the past burdens the very existence of individuals and the relationship they have with the classes they belong to. This is the temporality that Engels and Marx assigned to what they, like many others at the time, called *revolution in permanence*. Compared to the buzzword popular in democratic circles and later taken up by Blanqui (Draper, 1978: 201 ff; see also, van Ree, 2013), Marx and Engels do not mean an endless revolution, but a practical policy based on the realization that the proletariat's dominance in society is still largely in question. Revolution in permanence does not refer to a hypothetical infinite character of revolution. It does not identify the moral character that in fact can never be achieved, because that would return revolution to being a figure in the philosophy of history. Instead, it has a precise historical determination and is rather the political revolution that recognizes its own insufficiency; it is the sign of the unresolved tension between political power and class domination. Its specific temporality determines the contents of the dictatorship of the proletariat, which it prepares for and overlaps with. In any case, they cannot be thought of separately. In the moment of their superimposition – as for example in the April 1850 declaration of the *Weltgesellschaft der revolutionären Kommunisten* (MEW 7: 553) – those despotic interventions on property, which were already indicated in the *Manifesto*, return. It is, however, a sign of conscious weakness, of the impossibility of governing alone and the need to deepen and amplify the social measures proposed by the democrats. A plan of continuous and uninterrupted conflict is thus indicated to shift the focus of electoral, fiscal, economic, and organizational measures so as to improve the condition of the proletariat and to foster their independent organization. Using the terms of the *Manifesto*, to make the revolution permanent means to produce the continuous conditions for the contestation of the dominion of the ruling classes and not just the power of the state (Marx and Engels, 1850).

The nexus between permanent revolution and dictatorship of the proletariat establishes the temporal and organizational framework that makes it possible to deconstruct the social dimension of class domination through the management of power and its articulation. The dictatorship of the proletariat is not the declaration that the revolution is over, but rather corresponds to the possibility of further accelerating it, but paradoxically also of slowing it down and still directing its effects. By recording that the purpose of the state is "to perpetuate the rule of capital, the slavery of labour" (Marx, 1850a: 69), it should question the state character of politics. This means that it not only raises the question of the subject of power, but immediately also how it is exercised and for what purpose. For Marx, the necessity of the dictatorship of the proletariat seems to derive from the simple observation that without a radical redefinition of power, the proletariat cannot in any way alter its condition.

In a famous letter to Joseph Weydemeyer, Marx convincingly declares that "class struggle necessarily leads to the *dictatorship of the proletariat*" and that "this dictatorship itself constitutes no more than a transition to the *abolition of all classes* and to a *classless society*" (Marx to Weydemeyer, 5/3/1852: 62–65). Although it is exercised through the state, the dictatorship of the proletariat is a different social and political configuration than historically state power. In other words, it should not be understood as the specific politics of the post-revolutionary state, just as the "seizure of power" is not central to it, but its holding (Balibar, 1977: 65). It is Marx's embryonic, and never fully delineated, attempt to conceive a non-state political power, the momentary realization of which he finds in the Paris Commune. The dictatorship of the proletariat aims to destroy the continuity in time of the social effects of capitalism: it is not designed to abolish this or that capitalist institution by degree, but rather is the transitory political form of the proletariat's domination in awareness of the limits of its power. It does not aim to produce another right to oppose bourgeois right but should directly invest what Marx would call the natural laws of capitalist production, knowing that the norms of the former are also the expression of the latter. The dictatorship of the proletariat is at the same time the deconstruction of the representation of the universal. It depends, however, on the understanding that the revolution cannot be the immediate dissolution of all capitalist connections. Instead, it is a dictatorship that is not the opposite of democracy, but its inversion as vague in the *Manifesto*: "to raise the proletariat to the position of ruling class" (Marx and Engels, 1848: 504) must coincide with the dissolution of the social power of money and the forms of domination it establishes. The dictatorship of the proletariat immediately after the 1848 revolution says nothing about how power should function, but turns against its existing forms.

It is probably not coincidental that, although there is a clear derivation from Filippo Buonarroti's *Dictatorship of the People*, Marx's concept originated as a polemical concept directed against other dictatorships that he saw coming during the revolutions of 1848: "the transfer of *Cavaignac's military dictatorship* from Algiers to Paris" (Marx, 1848i: 128), which in reality "was not the dictatorship of the sabre over bourgeois society; he was the dictatorship of the bourgeoisie by the sabre" (Marx, 1850a: 76), made possible, moreover, by the initially journalistic and then political activity of Armand "Marrast the dictator in civilian clothes" (Marx, 1848i: 128).[10] The "dictatorship of the bourgeoisie" is initially a "legislative dictatorship" (Marx, 1850a: 107) and becomes effective after the abolition of universal suffrage. The French peasant is also caught up in this game of dictatorships because, if "the *constitutional republic* is the dictatorship of his united exploiters; *the social-democratic,* the *Red* republic, is the dictatorship of his allies" (Marx, 1850a: 122). Marx's opinion of social democracy actually changes significantly in the months that follow; what is worth emphasizing, however, is that for him dictatorships are not just a kind of involution of state power in the face of the revolutions of 1848, but are the sign of a general tendency that will lead him to call Lord Palmerston a dictator as well. The 'reoccupation' of the concept of dictatorship, which for Marx is the collective exercise of a force for an indefinite period of time not with a view to the constitution of a new power, but for the destructuring of the existing domination, thus takes place within the clash between revolution and other dictatorships. Already in the aftermath of the German events, Marx had clearly stated the connection between revolution and dictatorship: "Every provisional political set-up following a revolution requires a dictatorship, and an energetic dictatorship at that". The chief sin of Prussian Prime Minister Camphausen was precisely that of not being dictatorial enough, thus allowing the old powers of the bureaucracy and the army to reorganize themselves. The constituent assembly in Frankfurt, as we have seen, thus ended up with the same power that the king retained. This produced a juxtaposition of powers that no constitution could tolerate: "it was this very division of powers in a provisional situation that was bound to lead to conflicts" (Marx, 1848j: 431).

However, the dictatorship of the proletariat does not take place in a *Provisorium,* just as it does not aim to avoid the collisions caused by the presence

---

10   Schmitt (2013: 179) also recalls the presence of different linguistic and political meanings of dictatorship in the France of 1848, only to hasten to questionably enclose the dictatorship of the proletariat within its concept of sovereign dictatorship. If, as Schmitt shows, there is a dictatorial origin of the political form, the dictatorship of the proletariat in its Marxian sense does not aim to constitute any political form.

of divided powers. It does not aim to produce a decision to prevent these collisions, it does not aim to re-establish the contested order, and it is not the constituent process in view of another political order. In the time of revolution in permanence, the dictatorship of the proletariat is a process that invests social domination through the empowerment of a multitude of subjects who are not simply deprived of it, but who literally are not, because they are strangers to its social construction. In this sense, in the midst of the clash within the *League of Communists*, Marx addressed his opponents saying: "Whereas we say to the workers: You have 15, 20, 50 years of civil war to go through in order to alter the situation and to train yourselves for the exercise of power, it is said: We must take power *at once*, or else we may as well take to our beds" (Marx, 1850b: 626). To come to power, as Marx had argued against Heinzen, is not simply to conquer existing power but, without holding back from it, to change the very conditions of its production. This is, moreover, the limit of the French proletarians' revolutionary action that establishes the most obvious sign of their defeat. They first supported the democratic republic thinking that its social content would modify their condition. In June 1848, they rose up against a republic that decided to ignore those contents, and finally they adapted to bourgeois rule by not opposing the electoral reform that effectively excluded them "from any participation in political power" (Marx, 1852a: 146). They renounced any active role, leaving the scene and allowing themselves to be represented only by the democratic party.

> By letting themselves be led by the democrats in face of such an event and forgetting the revolutionary interests of their class for momentary ease and comfort, they renounced the honour of being a conquering power, surrendered to their fate, proved that the defeat of June 1848 had put them out of the fight for years and that the historical process would for the present again have to go on *over* their heads.
> MARX, 1852a: 146

It thus becomes clear that precisely because it only exists politically in the struggle against another class, the working class is not in itself a revolutionary subject. Society constantly produces collisions, but in order not to suffer them the workers must either pose as a conquering power or accept that they are conquered. The renunciation of the struggle against their exclusion from suffrage throws the workers into the "position of a political pariah" (Marx, 1850a: 105) they had before the revolution: they submit to the rules of what Marx calls despotism, whose first characteristic is precisely that it excludes its subjects from the possibility of historical action. Here again we show that in

Marx there is no historical teleology culminating in revolution. The political condition of the proletariat can regress not only through repression, but also through the choices it makes when faced with the alternatives that present themselves. On the other hand, universal suffrage is for Marx one of the intersections between political power and social domination. If, by renouncing to defend it, proletarians have abdicated the possibility of becoming power, of being a conquering power, it is because they have not fully exploited the contradiction produced by the constitution. Universal suffrage, in fact, grants the oppressed classes, "proletariat, peasantry, petty bourgeoisie", a "political power ... And from the class whose old social power it sanctions, the bourgeoisie, it withdraws the political guarantees of this power" (Marx, 1850a: 79). In other words, universal suffrage functioned as an instrument to neutralize the social power of the bourgeoisie, while it established the condition of possibility of the transition from the political emancipation of the proletariat to social emancipation. It fixed the space for a struggle that could make the proletariat a political class. Precisely because the latter does not seize the opportunity, universal suffrage establishes the basis of legitimacy of an executive power representing a mass of individuals without autonomous connections. This is the basis of Napoleon III's legitimacy and his privileged relationship with the peasants and not only them.

For Marx, the proletariat can only give itself politically as a subject of power and not as an abstract and universal subject. The dictatorship of the proletariat is in this respect the transition from democracy as a universal form of production and management of power, to its practice linked to the material condition of its subject. The record that "just as the word *'people'* has been given an aura of sanctity by the democrats, so you have done the same for the word *'proletariat'*" (Marx, 1853a: 403) is a clear sign of the defeat of the communists in the revolution. They thus end up succumbing not only to the repression of the political power, but also to a discourse that does not recognize the necessity of the revolution in permanence as a "necessary transit point" for the abolition of class relations in general and for "the revolutionising of all the ideas that result from these social relations" (Marx, 1850a: 127). Revolution in permanence remains only on paper because those ideas continue to present themselves as tradition, as a normative constraint that constantly challenges revolution. If it must claim its practical extraneousness to the terrain of law, it is also because the weight of the collective past emerges not only in the institutionalization of power relations, but also in the forms of social action of individuals.

> Upon the different forms of property, upon the social conditions of existence, rises an entire superstructure of different and distinctly formed

> sentiments, illusions, modes of thought and views of life. The entire class creates and forms them out of its material foundations and out of the corresponding social relations. The single individual, to whom they are transmitted through tradition and upbringing, may imagine that they form the real motives and the starting-point of his activity.
>
> MARX, 1852a: 128[11]

Revolution is not only directed against the present institutions, but against all those disciplinary rules that continuously establish the class habitus and thus also the forms of action and relations of individuals. This explains why Marx stubbornly refuses to assign the future a preponderant role in revolutionary temporality. Since revolution must first and foremost rid itself of the past, it cannot consist in "a passive glorification of the future" (Marx, 1852b: 107).

---

11 As Spivak (1999: 260) writes: "Marx's irreducible emphasis on the work of the negative, on the necessity for defetishizing the concrete, is persistently wrested from him by the strongest adversary, 'the historical tradition' in the air".

CHAPTER 3

The Power of Government

1   Executive and People

The concept of the dictatorship of the proletariat also suggests that the relationship between history and revolution, between process and event, needs to be reformulated, in contrast to the always episodic character that Marx sees in the continuous revolutions of the French, whose method is "beginning and accomplishing a revolution in three days". The case of Spain, on the other hand, is different: in this context revolutionary cycles have been taking place since 1808 that are the sign of a vehement and lasting clash between certain segments of society and the traditional aristocratic and monarchical power structures (Marx, 1854: 391). There is not that bourgeois, and therefore tactical, use of revolution which is actually increasingly aimed at establishing a compromise with the traditional powers, so as to reset the class struggle to zero. In Britain where that compromise has constitutional significance, the bourgeoisie does not occupy the space of revolution, yet demonstrates that it is able to alter state institutions in a consequential manner and thus holds a now established social power. The specific difference of Britain is literally the extension of its society beyond the borders of the metropolis. Colonial power is a central element in the overall configuration of power to the point of establishing its timing within the ever-shifting space of a world empire. Britain is also traversed by the movements of society but seems able to respond to them in a less frenetic and confused manner. The British "[b]ourgeois are not excitable Frenchmen. When they intend to carry a Parliamentary reform they will not make a Revolution of February" (Marx, 1852b: 334).

Unlike Germany, however, in France the process of decomposing the ancient estate-based society is now complete, just as, unlike in England, there is no need to reconcile different forms of social power on a daily basis. In France, the social conflict initially takes the form of the democratic republic, giving at least apparent voice to the hostility running through society. Soon, however, the tension to reform society gives way to the dominance of the executive, which reaffirms the necessary unity of the state. It is no coincidence that when he assumes the power of government, Napoleon III declares that he wants to "end the era of revolutions, satisfying the legitimate needs of the people and protecting them against subversive passions". Ending the revolution means "creating institutions that will outlive the people and finally be a foundation on which to build something lasting" (Napoleon III, 1853a: 192). Government thus assumes the primary task of guaranteeing the durability that Marx would like to see permanently unfolded by the revolution instead: the centrality of the executive is the political opposite of the revolution. The promise to permanently stabilise society is constantly repeated by Napoleon III, who in this way affirms the legitimacy of his personal claim to rule, harking back to the revolution of 1789 and his more famous ancestor, but at the same time promises to finally reorganise a society that had lost the certainties of its feudal articulation. In the *Preamble* to the 1852 Constitution, these elements are clearly stated:

> Our present society (it is essential to note this) is nothing other than France regenerated by the revolution of '89 and organised by the Emperor. Nothing remains of the ancient regime except great memories and great benefits. But everything that was organised then was destroyed by the revolution and everything that was organised after the revolution was organised by Napoleon.
>
> NAPOLEON III, 1853b: 204

Only organization can confirm and close the revolution, establishing the conditions for the constant and lasting reproduction of society. Napoleon III has been called a 'Saint-Simon on horseback' (Anceau, 2008) or a 'Saint-Simonian Caesar' (Girard, 1952). This is true if, in addition to the organizational obsession with which he approaches what he elects as his political task, the personal element that he considers essential for there to be a government is also assessed (De Boni, 2003; Scuccimarra, 2006). If formally plebiscitary legitimation is presented as opposed to parliamentary legitimation, the affirmation of the organizational autonomy of the state that it entails nevertheless takes place on the same basis as popular sovereignty. For Marx, the Saint-Simonian trace is not so much organizational as it is linked to the instruments and financial intermediaries with which 'Bonapartist socialism' (Marx, 1856c: 15) effectively governs French society. Under the cloak of equality to be safeguarded, the profile of the order of society clearly emerges, which cannot only be restored, but literally must be reconstituted. The plebiscitary response is thus not a degeneration of parliamentary legitimacy but is based on the common recognition of the formless character of the people and the consequent need to organise it. This tension within the configuration of power is grasped by Marx, who refuses however to see Napoleon III as an important historical figure in himself, because he considers him the outcome of a historical process that he cannot really determine. For Marx, Bonaparte is at the same time the product of the bureaucratic continuity of the French state and the effect of the crisis of the constitutional regime, who through his personal representation establishes a direct relationship with the society he claims to want to save. One must add from itself, that is, from the plurality and conflicts that run through it. "The *play of the constitutional powers*, as Guizot termed the parliamentary squabble between the legislative and executive power", is the sign of the crisis of a specific political representation of societal interests. It is a clash that pits the representatives of the people against each other. These should instead collectively possess absolute power – since the National Assembly is "uncontrollable, indissoluble, indivisible" – but they can only act individually, thus showing themselves to be a fraction of the power of the people or rather of society (Marx, 1852a: 116). Universal suffrage shows how difficult it is to represent the unity of the French people. The republicans thought that the people really did consist of "*citoyens* with the same interests, the same understandings", but instead "of their *imaginary* people, the elections brought the *real* people to the light of day, that is, representatives of the different classes into which it falls" (Marx, 1850a: 65). The youthful democratic enthusiasm with which Marx had celebrated the revolutions of the legislature is thus shattered. The legislative assembly is not the people, but a collection of individuals in conflict with each other on the basis of the different interests they represent. The evanescence of the very premise of the democratic republic is thus shown, for this is how the French republic defines itself in Article 2 of the *Preamble* to the Constitution of 28 December 1848. The institutional form does not unify the political subject, but shows all its instability, if not its impossibility, because the assembly reveals its inability to act by not being able to transform the movements of society into an effective power dynamic: the Assembly "ought rather to have allowed the class struggle a little elbow-room, so as to keep the executive power dependent on itself. But it did not feel equal to the task of playing with fire" (Marx, 1852a: 162).

Instead, the connection between democracy and communism shows all its precariousness. When filled with social content, i.e., as social democracy, it in fact aims to use republican institutions "as a means, not of superseding two extremes, capital and wage labour, but of weakening their antagonism and transforming it into harmony" (Marx, 1852a: 130). Democratic practice is still tied to its constitutive presupposition, namely the unity of the people, presenting itself as an unworkable form of mediation in a context in which it is impossible to assert a general and shared interest within society. Far from being the normal political form of bourgeois civil society, democracy is instead a form of mediation that cannot really be an alternative to imperialism. It corresponds to the culture and political action of "a *transition class*, in which the interests of two classes are simultaneously mutually blunted" and for this very reason the democrat "imagines himself elevated above class antagonism generally".

Whereas by reintroducing universal suffrage, Napoleon III effectively creates the people to legitimise it, democrats start from the conviction that the people are necessarily united and that when their divisions manifest themselves materially they depend on a corrupt political will. "Now, if in practice their interests prove to be uninteresting and their potency impotence", then the fault mainly lies with "pernicious sophists, who split the *indivisible people* into different hostile camps" (Marx, 1852a: 133).

Marx thus records a succession of institutional forms that sanction the descending line of the revolution: first the republic overcomes democracy, then the empire overcomes the republic. The republic ignores the dialectic between the proletarian and democratic social movements, and consequently presents itself as the political articulation of the present society, while the proletariat imagines it to be the realization of its projects as a "republic with social institutions" (Marx, 1850a: 66). The failure of these hopes coincides with the defeat of 22 June, after which the semantics of power used in the *Manifesto* undergoes a decisive change. The question of political power is certainly not obliterated, nor is it reduced to a mere functional articulation of society, but the very fact that it is an immanent production of society complicates the forms of subordination, causing domination to take on increasing relevance at the expense of what was previously termed alienation. In the writings on the French revolutions, the term capital begins to be employed with a political meaning. It is the manifestation of a domination that goes beyond the social power of the bourgeois ranks because it is relatively autonomous even with respect to their immediate interests. It should be added that while the proletariat only registers the relevance of social domination with its defeat, the bourgeoisie immediately recognises that the direct management of political power and the forms that had hitherto legitimized it could even be counterproductive. "It understood that all the so-called civil freedoms and organs of progress attacked and menaced its *class rule* at its social foundation and its political summit simultaneously". It thus quickly renounces the dogma of public discussion, which it identifies as the primary cause of the propagation of socialist ideas. Above all, the bourgeoisie grasps that "in order to preserve its societal might [*gesellschaftliche Macht*] intact, its political power must be broken" (Marx, 1852a: 142–143). From this point of view, Napoleon III's victory surprises France less than Marx himself had previously stated; it is the outcome of the bourgeoisie's choice to be politically absent but socially dominant. The civil war dissolves the possibility of any viable mediation. For the bourgeoisie, the republic was the condition for exercising its dominion without having to go through mediation with monarchical power, which in any case also included the social power of the aristocracy. The republican form of its rule, however, imposed on it a direct confrontation with the new social strata, with their growing social power and the influence they could then exert on political power. This was a completely new, constant, and horizontal conflict, which produced a fear for the resilience of society and nostalgia for the monarchy, which prevented direct contact between the classes. "It was a feeling of weakness that caused them to recoil from the pure conditions of their own class rule and to yearn for the former more incomplete, more undeveloped and precisely on that account less dangerous forms of this dominion" (Marx, 1852a: 129).

For all these reasons, the uprising of 22 June 1848 following the abolition of the *Ateliers nationaux* represents much more than a riot suppressed in blood (Sewell Jr, 1980: 265 ff). In it, the Parisian proletariat does not make a claim on political power, but directly expresses its quest for social dominance. Alexis de Tocqueville, for whom "the insurrection of June" was "the most extensive and the most singular that has occurred in our history, and perhaps in any other", also confirms this from an opposite perspective to Marx's. Tocqueville is struck by two different but converging aspects: the first is that the insurgents acted in an absolutely organised manner without having a visible hierarchy and leaders to command them; the second aspect is that "it was not, strictly speaking, a political struggle ... but a struggle of class against class, a sort of Servile War". Nor was it the enterprise "of a certain number of conspirators, but the revolt of one whole section of the population against another" (Tocqueville, 1948: 150–151; see also, Tommasello 2018). In Tocqueville, too, the echo of post-revolutionary historiography with its war between peoples is evidently very deep, but for him what needs to be recorded is a clash that eludes political definition, a dull clash without reparations that directly affects society. In other words, for Tocqueville, the fact that the insurgents had ceased to seek any mediation, for example by moderating their demands, was also a sign of the non-political character of the struggle. For Marx, on the other hand, the "terrible material defeat of June" (Marx, 1850a: 98) was a political clash and marked the transition from the struggle for the "overthrow of the form of government" to that for the "overthrow of bourgeois society" (Marx, 1850a: 71). Faced with this eventuality comes the choice of relying on the strength of the executive, i.e., a government that has far less need for mediation, but for this very reason can take on the task of organizing society. For Marx, Napoleon III's executive is the final episode in that enormous process of bureaucratic centralization that had found its decisive junction in the French Revolution.

The Marxian rejection of bureaucratic domination had already emerged clearly in the critique of Hegel, who had considered it necessary to ensure the "*separation* of the 'state' and 'civil' society, [of] 'particular interests' and the 'intrinsically and explicitly general'". For Marx, bureaucracy presents itself as domination because it does not respond from the simple necessity to administer but is the combined compounding of traditional state power with the claim to control social movements that arises in society itself. Bureaucracy is the illusion of the state, that is, the illusion that the state really thinks the universal, thanks to the specific knowledge of society that it is able to accumulate. "The bureaucracy is a circle from which no one can escape. Its hierarchy is a *hierarchy of knowledge*". For Marx, however, bureaucratic knowledge is not simply directed towards knowledge of social relations, but towards the legitimization and continuity of the state. "The bureaucracy is the imaginary state alongside the real state" and, to guarantee this double life of the state, it demands the secrecy of its acts in order to establish its authority. Consequently, it does not produce a universal and universally accessible knowledge, but a particular and specialized knowledge instrumental for the construction of the social authority of the state. "*Authority* is the basis of its knowledge, and the deification of authority is its *conviction*" (Marx, 1843a: 45–47; see also, Liebich, 1982). By the end of the 1840s, Marx had also read and annotated Alexandre de Laborde's book, *De l'esprit de l'Association dans tous les intérêts de la communauté,* which, in 1818, described administrative development in terms that later return in the Marxian critique of bureaucracy. For Laborde, the administration is the "new providence, modern guardian angel, which does not leave him [*sc.* man] a moment to preserve him from the dangers of free will in civil affairs". Even more important is the relationship it establishes with the representative regime, relativizing its real weight within the overall field of political decision-making: "national representation is an isolated body at the centre of an administrative network that surrounds it, circumscribes it on all sides" (MEGA III, 1: 223).[1] Bureaucratic knowledge, authority, and centralization are thus the characters that allow the executive to show itself as a form of government autonomous from society, but capable of organising it. Napoleon III is only the point of arrival of this gigantic historical process, which had already begun before the revolution of 1789.

> This executive power with its enormous bureaucratic and military organization, with its extensive and artificial state machinery, with a host of officials numbering half a million, besides an army of another half million, this appalling parasitic body, which enmeshes the body of French society like a net and chokes all its pores, sprang up in the days of the

---

1 Marx also transcribes the following statement by Laborde, which anticipates the Tocquevillian analysis and which he evidently shares: "it's a strange thing that a popular revolution should have ended up mainly extending and perfecting taxation".

absolute monarchy, with the decay of the feudal system, which it helped to hasten.

MARX, 1852a: 185

For Marx, the empire of Napoleon III is the culmination of the progressive assertion of the executive over the legislative, just as that of the first Bonaparte had completed the process of state centralization. The consequent limitation of the autonomy of society takes place through the transfiguration of every *common interest* into the *general interest*, as Marx writes so poignantly, continually using the metaphor of the bureaucratic *boa constrictor* that suffocates every autonomous movement of society in its coils. The bureaucratic synthesis is not oppression in the classical sense, but a resemantization of the common and the collective. The general interest replaces relations between individuals and between classes with their hypostatization, transforming every social relationship into an activity that, if not directly managed by the state, must nevertheless receive governmental authorization: "whether it was a bridge, a schoolhouse and the communal property of a village community, or the railways, the national wealth and the national university of France". The parliamentary republic did not hesitate to use centralization to combat the revolutionary ferments that agitated society. This is precisely why Marx can conclude by writing that "All revolutions perfected this machine instead of breaking it" (Marx, 1852a: 186). Universal bureaucratization and the dominance of the executive have their necessary counterpart in the fragmentation of society, thanks to which an abstract interest can be asserted that is general because it presents itself as different from all particular interests.

The executive therefore "represents" the general interest, i.e., for Marx the interest of the capitalist as a whole, and only mediately that of the bourgeoisie as a class. It needs the support of a mass unable to represent its interests directly. It is the ultimate expression of the atomization that characterizes bourgeois society and, for this very reason, can emancipate itself from the immediate needs and interests of the bourgeois themselves. Marx does not approve of the term Caesarism, which began to circulate as early as the 1850s, because he does not believe much in the effectiveness of the action of the solitary leader. He is rather interested in the societal structure on which his power is based. The combination of centralism and universal bureaucratization is a process far more far-reaching than Napoleon III's personal rule might suggest. As stated in a note of 1852, Marx is convinced that "the demolition of the state machine will not endanger centralization. Bureaucracy is only the low and brutal form of a centralization that is still afflicted with its opposite, with feudalism" (Marx, 1852a: 193). Bureaucratization is thus not the fatal and irresistible completion of the rationalization process, but the active presence of a political anachronism, which makes subordination an irrefutable technical necessity. The bureaucratization of society is the progression of the entrenched feudal core of state power. Its foundation lies in a historically non-contractual type of relationship – which, according to liberal critics, is its original defect – but it derives its dominance from the general organization of society. The power manifested in it not only denies the sovereignty of the individual but imposes a structure of the collective that coercively composes individual elements into a commanded and organically connected unity. The empire founded on the centrality of the executive and universal bureaucratization is the accomplished political expression of what Marx later calls the despotism of capital.

2 Bureaucracy and Empire

As previously stated, this possibility is dependent on a specific constitution of society, wherein the minimal number of autonomous connections must exist, as the state can only appear to be the universal representative of the universal if it loses all of its immediate social connections. Marx claims that this happens most clearly during the Second Empire when the societal function of the state becomes so autonomous that it "seems to have made itself independent of society and subjugated it. The independence of the executive power emerges into the open when its chief no longer requires genius, its army no longer requires glory, and its bureaucracy no longer requires moral authority in order to justify itself" (Marx, 1852a: 186). This appearance is such because, while it seems to register the full political autonomy of the state, it also reveals the total freedom of society, which no longer recognises any 'political' ties between its members. The irreconcilable proliferation of societal norms is summed up by Marx in the figure of the lumpenproletariat, which is not simply a decomposed set of social figures characterized by their material and moral misery, but the result of that specific 'democratization' of society which, by indifferently placing one figure next to the other, allows its imperial rule. It is therefore not a residue of the past,[2] of the stigmatization of social marginality that so embarrasses Marx's contemporary readers (Stallybrass, 1990; see also Draper, 1972; Cowling, 2002; Barrow 2020), but the identification of a set of social figures functionally

---

[2] The lumpenproletariat, "that passively rotting mass thrown off by the lowest layers of old society may, here and there, be swept into the movement by a proletarian revolution; its conditions of life, however, prepare it far more for the part of a bribed tool of reactionary intrigue" (Marx and Engels, 1848: 494).

subordinate to the constitution of imperial political command. Since there is no constitutive split of the social from the political in Marx, every sociological description must be immediately connected to the political form that social behaviour legitimizes or denies. The Marxian problem is not the heterogeneity of the social and its pluralistic representation, but the legitimization that empire obtains through the presence of behaviours that confirms societal disintegration and the consequent need for a visible and undisputed executive power. The lumpenproletariat is thus not the sociological expression of a mass anomie, but the empirical presence of a normative atomization instrumental for the imperial evolution of the political system, which establishes a hidden symmetry between the behaviour of the lumpenproletariat and the peasantry.

The critique of the lumpenproletariat is not reducible to the moral condemnation of some specific social behaviour, which is clearly present in Marx's text. The perspective Marx describes it with is that of the working class, here still of the industrial proletariat, or in Machiavellian terms that of a multitude that is able to give itself its own 'laws' and obey them and not that of a 'loose multitude'. The working class also does not indicate a particular social stratification or a specific labour position. The working class is the all-political ability to establish a position of collective power against the domination of capital. In this sense, the overall worker is not a unitary transfiguration of the multiplicity of production figures, but the multitude of social and labour figures that follow a common political norm in the struggle against the impersonal domination of capital. Significantly, Marx establishes a symmetry between the lumpenproletariat and the financial aristocracy, which would be nothing more than the reproduction of the former "at the top of bourgeois society" (Marx, 1850a: 51). In fact, it too is indifferent to the social relationship in which it is embedded, in order to assert its own interest disengaged from any societal logic. The rest of the bourgeoisie accuses this tendency of being at the root of the corruption of society. For Marx, on the other hand, corruption is not the result of moral decadence present in certain forms of economic action, in those of bureaucratic officials or the political class, but the inevitable effect of sharing in the direct domination of capital. The financial aristocracy, like the lumpenproletariat, also counts as an expression of the maximum individualization of society, towards which it has the same negative attitude about cooperation (as well as towards the possibility of constituting collective forms of action) that Hegel attributes to the plebs and liberals with respect to the state.

The peasants' position is different but generally symmetrical. Peasants constitute a dispersed mass due to their physical distance and their difficulties in communicating, but their adherence to the symbols of the nation as well as their attachment to the achievements of the revolution functions for them as compensation for a condition that is far from prosperous. They are an individualized mass, connected by material and symbolic values, but without any capacity to collectively assert their social position. The acceptance of a substantial political impotence makes their representation by an executive possible, which can only exist if no part of society constitutes itself as a class, thus escaping individual fragmentation and consequently acting autonomously within society itself. Rather than the sociological condemnation of the peasantry as a social stratum, Marx seems here to be describing the condition of the citizen with only the right to vote. Smallholder peasants are unable to go beyond their local ties, unable to establish those connections that could make them "hostile" to another class.

> They are consequently incapable of enforcing their class interests in their own name, whether through a parliament or through a convention. They cannot represent themselves, they must be represented. Their representative must at the same time appear as their master, as an authority over them, as an unlimited governmental power that protects them against the other classes and sends them rain and sunshine from above. The political influence of the small-holding peasants, therefore, finds its final expression in the executive power subordinating society to itself.
> MARX, 1852: 187–188

Again, however, Marx does not seem to delineate an opposition between the sociological and the political. Rather, the latter emerges by traversing and overcoming the sociological condition at the moment it does not merely establish an identity. Indeed, it is not even some specificity of their position within capitalist production that determines the particular isolation of the peasantry. "It can be seen that their exploitation differs only in *form* from the exploitation of the industrial proletariat. The exploiter is the same: *capital*" (Marx, 1850a: 122). Thus, the fate of the peasantry appears to Marx to be different not for sociological reasons, but because of the different way in which they stand vis-à-vis the government. Far from being confined to the experience of the small peasants in France, their attitude is paradigmatic for Marx of any situation in which the executive takes over to represent the material constitution of capitalist society. In this situation, the mutual recognition of belonging to the same social circle, the partial and confined identity, is the prerequisite for the absence of an autonomous class political initiative and the condition of possibility for the dominance of the executive over society as a whole. This is precisely why the empire shows "the opposition between the state power and society" in "pure form" (Marx, 1852a: 193). It is not so much a question of establishing a more or less relative autonomy of the state *a priori*, but rather of recognising that the function of the state is not mechanically deducible from the immediate interests of certain strata of society, which also have a greater specific weight in determining state power (Wetherly, 2002). What appears as a relative autonomy can thus be seen as a closer integration of the state with the forms of domination of capital. This registration keeps Marx at a distance from an abstract re-legitimation of the state in the face of the bureaucratic ability to make the state machine operate within and despite the clashes of society. The same estate of functionaries is for him not the universal estate that Hegel imagined, but the ultimate repository of the state as an anachronism. It shows the present history of the state as a legacy of the *ancien regime* (Bourdieu, 1998). The bureaucratization of society, however, does not only reveal the indelible past of the state, but opens up the institutional space for the specific domination of capital, which can only come about through its integration with the state itself.

This becomes clear in the series of articles Marx dedicates in 1856 to the events of the *Crédit Mobilier*, "one of the most economical phenomena of our epoch", which he sets out to investigate, because without it, it is not possible to "either to compute the chances of the French Empire or to understand the symptoms of the general convulsion of society manifesting themselves throughout Europe" (Marx, 1856b: 10). The activity of the financial brokerage institute shows the trend towards integration between state power and French industry. The centralization of financial activity that it pursues is the other face of the bureaucratization of society that becomes possible because money, besides being the mediator of exchanges, is now the real organizer of society. Bureaucratic dominance becomes possible and necessary for financial dominance to expand over society as a whole. The mission that Bonaparte had promised to fulfil had, moreover, a double status: on the one hand "to save the *bourgeoisie* and 'material order' from the Red anarchy ... and on the other hand, to save the working people from the middle-class despotism concentrated in the National assembly" (Marx, 1865c: 14).

The *Crédit Mobilier* is wanted by the Bonapartist government to emancipate itself from the large private banks and the Orleanist aristocracy. It is the centre of a vast work of capital centralization that corresponds to the affirmation of joint-stock companies, whose managers are "a sort of industrial kings ... whose might stands in inverse ratio to their responsibility" (Marx, 1856d: 21), since they can govern the entire wealth of society by owning only part of the shares. However, Marx is not interested in the moral critique of this capitalist mutation; rather, he is interested in how speculative capital establishes a new power structure and what lines of crisis can be glimpsed within it (Bologna, 1974; Krätke, 2008a; Krätke, 2008b). The constitution of large capital corporations comprises an "oligarchic Board of Directors" that relies on a bureaucratic body to practically manage business. Beneath both is the "mass of mere wage labourers – whose dependence and helplessness increase with the dimensions of the capital that employs them" (Marx, 1856d: 21). This subordination not only establishes the homology between the state and capitalist enterprise, but also highlights the constitutive mediation that money as capital now operates within society as a whole, establishing the criteria of integration between private savings and financial and industrial enterprises. This means that, at the moment of crisis, Napoleon III, "the imperial Socialist" (Marx, 1856d: 24), i.e., the representative of the state as lender of last resort, will have to take over the *Crédit*'s bad debts, turning them into state bonds, part of the public debt. Crisis does not only mean the breaking of the link between financial capital and the exploitation of labour by industrial capital, but also the immediate involvement of the state at a time when "the mania of getting rich without the pains of producing" (Marx, 1856e: 115) generates a socially unsustainable situation.

For Marx, this is after all the most striking result of the 1848 revolution. It imposed a restructuring of society that depended not so much on the more or less small and more or less organised groups of revolutionaries who pursued it, but on the tumult of social subjects whose uprising materially threatened the order of society. Now those who emerged victorious from that clash realise that they were in fact the "the instruments of a revolution in property greater than any contemplated by the revolutionists of 1848" (Marx, 1856e: 114). It imposes a new and different role on the state, because the crisis is not simply a more or less catastrophic pathological event, but the effect of the complex and contradictory coexistence of immediate surplus-value extraction and financial profits. Even the capitalist crisis can no longer be considered merely as the event to be awaited in order to seize it as an opportunity, but as an eventuality always potentially present in the new configuration of the capital relation. Far from being a merely economic fact, it calls into question the material configuration of power. This is precisely why the role of the state cannot be reduced to exceptional intervention but must be a constant presence within the economic cycle. "On the other hand, the money must be found; the suspension of the works would not only be bankruptcy but revolution" (Marx, 1856f: 132; see also, Ricciardi J, 2015). The overall integration of economy, finance, and state is the hallmark of what Marx calls Empire in France and government in Britain, and of which he will point out the opposite in the Commune.

3   Chartism and Government

The empire emerging in France is not fully comprehensible without what unfolded in Britain. Already on 31 December 1848, taking stock without too many illusions of the revolution in Europe, Marx recalls the elements of great novelty that it had nevertheless introduced, but he cannot avoid emphasizing its global limitations. The European peoples who had dared to rise up in the name of their national liberation had now been defeated, the proletariat in France was unable to put itself forward as a conquering power, while the French bourgeoisie had also failed in its role as the European vanguard in political and civil demands. Already at the end of 1848 all these events appear somewhat dated, because the real clash does not take place on the continent: England "seems to be the rock against which the revolutionary waves break". Britain is the dominatrix of the world market, which presents itself as traffic regulated by the rules it produces, but it is also a hierarchical set of relations between nations, an international power relationship. However, Marx is not interested in the game of sovereignty. If Britain "turns whole nations into its proletarians", the problem for him is to see how the class struggle determines this process that is no longer conceivable on a national scale, since any social reform in the rest of Europe is doomed to failure if Britain's world domination is not shaken. The international context determines the national ones, because if every war against Britain, regardless of where it is fought, is a world war, every national uprising is also a challenge to its international power. It is from these considerations that Marx identifies the Chartists as the only force capable of bringing down British hegemony, undermining it from within. "Only when the Chartists head the English Government will the social revolution pass from the sphere of Utopia to that of reality" (Marx, 1849c: 214–215). The change of perspective is radical. What is not relevant here is the plausibility of the Marxian prognosis, which turns out to be little more than wishful thinking based on the hope that the conjunction of the individual wars of national liberation and the social revolution could prevent 1848 from closing in defeat. Instead, what is key is that the shift in perspective towards Britain does not only occur because of the advanced degree of development of its capitalism, but because of the strength that the Chartists' struggle is demonstrating. Marx is not interested in the objective reasons for the economic dynamic, but in the way the class struggle produces an organized perspective of power, which in the case of the Chartists seems to be even a power of government.

Great Britain also has its 1848. Far from indifferent to what is happening on the continent, thousands of workers mobilize in the first months of the year. On 10 April 1848 the Chartists marched *en masse* to parliament to present their third motion, in which "the claim for the vote implied also further claims: a new way of reaching out by the working people for social control over their conditions of life and labour" (Thompson, 1966: 828; see also, Briggs, 1962; Thompson, 1971). The Chartists thus attempted to assert for the umpteenth time some rights of political citizenship and some elements of social citizenship. Although the signatories of the petition and participants in the demonstration are not actually as numerous as the Chartists claim, to control them the British government mobilizes exorbitant numbers of police, reserve soldiers, and volunteers (Chase, 2007: 301–302). The fear of the revolution reaching London, endangering the established edifice of British constitutionalism, is enormous. Nevertheless, the Chartist act of force fails even though this last great mass event with its well-established political language represents the deepest intention of the Chartist political project. For Marx, "not only was the revolutionary might of the Chartists *broken in London on April 10*, but the *revolutionary propaganda impact of the February victory* was also for the first time *broken*". The "victory of 'order'" in London does not so much signal the end of the revolution, but rather the confirmation of the European scale of the revolutionary process. The contrast between process and revolutionary event thus proves to be anything but a scholastic distinction. Process does not so much indicate the gradualness or waiting for the times to mature, but rather the ability to organise the revolution within the concrete conditions of the class clash. While the *Manifesto* sought to reconcile the indication of a necessary national phase of the revolution with the internationalist position of the communists, in Britain the problem is posed in a decidedly different form. A strong national workers' movement is in fact faced with a power that legitimizes itself not least through its colonial, imperial, and global projection. It will be England that "will dictate the revolution to the Continent" (Marx, 1848k: 101, 102) because, even though the umpteenth Chartist petition finds no audience with the British government, the confrontation between Chartism and the specific British configuration of power forces Marx to rethink the timing and manner of the revolutionary process.

The demand for the Charter had allowed the outcomes of eighteenth and nineteenth century radicalism to become the class language of a formidable mass movement thanks to "its identification of political power as the source of social oppression, and thus in its ability to concentrate the discontent of the unrepresented working classes upon one common aim" (Stedman Jones, 1983: 161). The conception of political power as a perverse effect of an otherwise potentially harmonious social constitution had revealed all its limitations at the moment when that same political power had shown itself capable of acting not only for its own preservation, but also to affect the structural conditions of societal production. The stalemate of the Chartist position therefore goes beyond the failure of a mass event. It highlights the gap between the organizational mode, the composition of the movement and its political objective. For Julian Harney, one of the movement's historical leaders, overcoming this stalemate therefore means abandoning the classic watchword *The Charter and No Surrender*, which had accompanied the movement in the previous decades, because the problem is no longer the residual and corrupt political power of the old ranks, but the presence of a "new aristocracy" that "monopolising the soil, and commanding the sources of toil ... would possess a power over the lives of both agricultural and manufacturing workers unexampled in the world's history". In the changed situation, to demand *The Charter, and Something More* is thus to recognise that the terrains of oppression, and thus of struggle, intersect in an evidently new way (Harney, 1850: 351). That 'something more' now being claimed expresses an awareness that the sources of power are not only located in political institutions, but that the clash for social domination has opened up.

In Britain Marx sees the process of social emancipation of the industrial proletariat underway (Berta, 1979). There is a massively present working class which, despite the defeat of the Chartists, contributes decisively to the substantial instability of the political system to such an extent that, with the elections of July 1852, the difficulty of forming a stable and lasting government becomes apparent (Hawkings, 1998: 50–56). Marx follows the vicissitudes of the British parties punctually, showing how their movements are the result of a social constitution that is changing profoundly. Not surprisingly, the real turning point in recent British constitutional history for him is the repeal of the Corn Laws on 16 May 1846. From that moment on, the Tories lost their hegemony over society and were no longer able to defend the ancient constitution of which they could present themselves as the political linchpin. What was changed was a social constitution that for Marx had its most important foundations in protectionism and the land rent. "Rent of land is conservative, profit is progressive; rent of land is national, profit is cosmopolitical; rent of land believes in the State Church, profit is a dissenter by birth" (Marx, 1852c: 328). This progressivism of capital is the sign of a transformation that Marx had welcomed in 1848, stating that free trade "breaks up old nationalities and carries antagonism of proletariat and bourgeoisie to the uttermost point. In a word, the Free Trade system hastens the Social Revolution" (Marx, 1848l: 465). A few years later, rather than the intensified possibilities of the class struggle, Marx must record that it overwhelmed the Tories' "social foundation of political power" and they reacted with a "*Counter-Revolution*, that is to say, by a reaction of the State against Society". They mobilized all the interests in some way connected to land rent – "the Colonial Interest, the Shipping Interest, the State Church Party" – who did not want manufacturing to assume hegemony because it promised a "social revolution". Similar to his writings on India, with this phrase, here Marx seems to mean, however, a 'revolution of society', its hierarchical restructuring, rather than its radical overthrow. Free trade, in other words, imposes a reconfiguration of society that involves both the Conservatives and their traditional Whig adversaries, who had been an oppositional force, but respectful of all the traditional hierarchies of British society. The British Whig "in the natural history of politics, forms a species which, like all those of the amphibious class, exists very easily, but is difficult to describe". He represents the middle class, though not in its autonomy, but rather in its necessary relationship with the landed aristocracy. His party is thus destined to share the fate of the Tories, for the moment when "the landed aristocracy is no longer able to maintain its position as an independent power, to fight, as an independent party, for the government position" (Marx, 1852c: 328–329, 331), those who had built their political fortunes by opposing that power lose much of their significance.

The irruption of capital relations thus imposes a new dynamic on the political system. The free-traders present themselves within it as the "*official representatives of modern English society*, the representatives of that England which rules the market of the world". They are a party of the bourgeoisie that in order to represent its interests, aims to "make available its social power as a political power". It is precisely for this reason that they want the organization of the state to respond to a principle of economics, that is, they want there to be only "that *minimum* […] of government which is indispensable for the administration" (Marx, 1852b: 333, 334).[3] For Marx, this would be the structure of the bourgeois republic everywhere, that is, a state command that leaves the maximum room for action to the movements of society. His model of reference, as is already evident in his writings on France, is US democracy. In Britain, however, the term democracy is carefully avoided because it is the overall name for Chartist claims (Gurney, 2014). Instead, the silent democratization of the free-traders consists in their tendency to annihilate the old British constitution, although they want to do this in a non-traumatic way, showing all their willingness to compromise, knowing that it is better to make concessions to tradition than to the Chartist enemy growing in society. While Marx points out to the Communist International the need to connect political power and social domination so that they are mutually reinforcing, the British bourgeoisie would

---

3   On Marx's overall relationship with Chartism, see Collins and Abramsky (1965).

instead have the clear understanding that when *"exclusive political dominion …* and *economical supremacy* will be united in the same hands, when, therefore, the struggle against capital will no longer be distinct from the struggle against the existing Government – from that very moment will date the *social revolution of England"* (Marx, 1852b: 335).[4]

Once again in relation to the *Manifesto*, Marx is forced to acknowledge the tension, if not the distance, between the political and the economic. If, as we have seen, in reconsidering the class struggles in France, Marx no longer mechanically identifies economic location and class behaviour, so the economic dominance of certain fractions of the bourgeoisie does not mean that they want to achieve political power at all costs. The structural limitation of the democratic political form is precisely its promise to change the economic condition through generalized access to political power. Although clearly wary of this power of the form, Marx nevertheless defends the Chartists because they are the "the politically active portion of the British *working class*". In their Charter, the demand for universal suffrage is an instrument which, given the numerical size of their social majority, should be "the equivalent for political power for the working class of England". Their fight for suffrage is not the affirmation of an abstract principle as it was in France. On the contrary, it is the moment of a process by which "in a long, though underground civil war, [the English proletariat] has gained a clear consciousness". Universal suffrage is therefore not the prerequisite for the acquisition of fuller citizenship, but the "inevitable result" of *"the political supremacy of the working class"* (Marx, 1852b: 335, 336).

4   Executive and Parliament

Following the political, social, and parliamentary chronicle of Britain in the 1850s for the *New York Daily Tribune*, Marx comes to terms with a configuration of power that reacts in an articulate and complex manner to variations in the economic cycle. He thus discovers that, while crises can perhaps be a revolutionary occasion, moments of growth allow for an equally radical redefinition of the political system's resilience. Although Marx may argue for several reasons that the issue of pauperism has not improved in the slightest with the success of free trade, and may trust that the current growth will be followed by a trade crisis (Marx, 1852d), he is also forced to note that the prosperity which begins

---

4   In the fragment of the German draft of the same article, Marx uses '*Herrschaft*' for 'supremacy'.

to spread in the second half of 1852 once again benefits the Tories. Having now renounced the reintroduction of the Corn Laws, they can "consolidate their political power", using it to increase the social power of their classes (Marx, 1852e: 364). As the horizon of crisis recedes, and with it the immediate possibility of a new revolution, governing the tension between social and political power becomes the fundamental concern of each successive executive. And it is in registering that tension that Marx delineates with increasing clarity the figure of Lord Palmerston, who becomes the English expression of the centrality already recognized in France to the executive. In the mid-1950s the coalition government that had managed to remain in office for the previous three years went into crisis because of the way it had handled the Crimean War. Within this conjuncture, Palmerston resigns as Minister of the Interior, managing to show his personal autonomy by separating his responsibilities from those of the executive. "His act becomes a great national event. He is transformed at once into the representative of the people against the Government from which he secedes. He not only saves his own popularity, but he gives the last finish to the unpopularity of his colleagues" (Marx, 1853b: 544).

In Palmerston's political parable, Marx sees a movement symmetrical to the one he had identified in Napoleon III. In both cases an individual succeeds in asserting his personal power by dispossessing parliament and establishing a direct relationship with the people. For Marx, Lord Palmerston's assertion thus represents something more and different than yet another peripeteia of the complicated British parliamentary history of the nineteenth century. It expresses a specific tendency inherent in the power of government, which becomes actual at the moment when the social power that certain subjects express prevents the stable definition of political power. At the moment of the double internal and external crisis, political and military, Palmerston manages to assert himself against parliament, threatening it from the columns of the *Morning Post* to appeal directly to the people. "He threatens to dissolve the House should it dare 'not to bestow on him the esteem which he enjoys outside the Palace of Westminster, amongst the public'. This 'public' is restricted to the journals half or wholly belonging to him". In this way he manages to "dictate to Parliament" as he did to the Queen (Marx, 1855a: 646). Palmerston does not simply appeal to the people but builds them up by practicing a specific politics of opinion, which makes him a power capable of influencing institutions. "Lord Palmerston has again become a popular favorite", and although he is by no means a new man, he succeeds in imposing himself in the transition that Britain is experiencing. Indeed, he is a seasoned politician who has been through every season of British politics since 1806, when he first stood for election. "So extraordinary a phenomenon is the Palmerston mania that one is tempted to suppose it to be of a merely fictitious character, got up not for home consumption, but as an article of export, destined for foreign use" (Marx, 1853: 345). Palmerston succeeds in showing the people as the public, i.e., not as the foundation and reference for political decision-making, but as spectators who must almost necessarily approve the decisions the executive makes for their own good. Despite the contempt he repeatedly declares, Marx is clearly fascinated with Henry John Temple, Third Viscount Palmerston, whose foreign policy actions of the preceding decades he analysed, publishing a number of articles later collected in a pamphlet that was a considerable editorial success (Marx, 1853c), to the point of his developing the extravagant conviction that "for several decades Palmerston has been in the pay of Russia" (Marx to Engels, 2/11/1853: 395). If Marx almost erases Napoleon III's personal merits, he cannot fail to emphasize Palmerston's personality, although here too it is not so much his ability to imprint his own mark on realities as his ability to continually adapt to circumstances that he aims to bring out. In Marx's eyes Palmerston, like Napoleon III, is confirmation that the past can constantly reappear in the present as something new; Lord Palmerston is also the embodiment of tradition as a silent power that influences and determines choices in times of crisis. And this is truer in a country like Great Britain, which explicitly makes the reference to tradition a political argument for dealing with the present.

Palmerston makes tradition an instrument of government, reconciling the opposing tensions that, precisely because of their social positioning, traditional parties are unable to address. He is unquestionably the most "extraordinary phenomenon" in official England because he can "conciliate a democratic phraseology with oligarchic views" (Marx, 1853: 347). He alone seized the opportunity of the crisis of the British constitution. "But what is the British Constitution? Does it essentially consist of a representative system and a limitation of the executive power?" Marx's answer is negative. It is not these formal features that establish that essence, because they are now as much present in the American constitution, and thus can no longer be considered a British peculiarity, as they are in every joint-stock company, and thus cannot define the specificity of a political constitution. "The British Constitution is indeed nothing but an antiquated, obsolete, out-of-date compromise between the bourgeoisie, which *rules not officially* but in fact in all decisive spheres of civil society, and the landed aristocracy, which *governs officially*". This compromise is showing its limits in the face of trade crises, working class pressure, and the compulsions of imperial politics, to the point where it can be said that "the crisis is permanent, the government only provisional" (Marx, 1855b: 53, 54).

If the constitution should in some way constantly indicate the possibilities and limits of government, its crisis brings to the forefront the need to govern the movements of a society that escape the usual mediations. Palmerston consistently succeeds in producing a mediation between the variegated congeries of British imperial interests and the class struggle that threatens it. At the same time, Marx is confronted with a dimension of the crisis that is not primarily economic, nor does it come primarily from economic dynamics. Crisis now takes on a more complex political meaning than that which still appears in the documents of the International Association. The commercial and industrial crisis has been there since September of the previous year, but it does not trigger a revolutionary explosion. Instead, it attempts to reform the administration even while remaining within the traditional representative system. The Association for Administrative Reform, an expression of radical intellectual circles and some City circles, tries to move between conservatism that focuses exclusively on the efficiency and competence of civil servants and Chartist projects of comprehensive reform (Anderson, 1965). For Marx, the Association with its meetings has the "the merit of novelty, the merit, rare in England, of having no precedent" (Marx, 1855c: 167).

Without harbouring excessive illusions about the relevance of the *Association,* but nonetheless emphasizing the relationship it is seeking to establish with the Chartists, Marx notes that its critics fail to realize that its meetings have in any case already highlighted three decisive points: "1. The breach between the ruling class *outside* Parliament and the governing class *within* it; 2. a dislocation of those elements of the bourgeoisie that have hitherto set the tone in politics; 3. the disenchantment with Palmerston" (Marx, 1855c: 167). In spite of the all too vague nature of its project, the Association makes clear the social dynamic that invests the political system and the government's difficulties in bringing it back into order. This dynamic cannot be contained in the classical opposition between Tory and Whig, who represent for Marx two competing modes of aristocratic and oligarchic government to control the middle class and popular masses. "By their friendship the Whigs have constantly prevented the middle classes from moving; by their friendship the Tories have always thrown the masses into the arms of the middle classes, who put them at the disposal of the Whigs" (Marx, 1855d: 187).

For Marx, there is clearly no dialectic within the British political system that really aims at the inclusion of those who have always been left on the margins of the social system. Rather, in the first half of the century it was the Whigs who took all those measures culminating in the factory and poor law that established and continually confirmed that social hierarchy. When Marx speaks of the working-class masses, he is not using a generic reference. He means all those who are progressively included even if in different positions in the relationship of capital. This is why he finds the proposals for electoral reform put forward by the Association for the Reform of Administration inconclusive, while he unreservedly supports that of the Chartists. Collaborative projects between the two movements inevitably fail (Marx, 1855e), but two important elements emerge from Marx's chronicles that explain his attention to all these events. First, he is interested in parliamentary vicissitudes for what happens outside parliament, for the debates, meetings, and agitations that take place, yes, with a view to parliamentary reform, but not among the protagonists of parliamentary life. What interests him is how the whole debate on suffrage reform can open up a space for communication and organization that is different from that of the British political tradition. The Association moves "*within* the limits of the *legal* (as Guizot called it), the official England". Instead, Marx's problem is the "*pressure from without*, by mass meetings and the like", capable of mobilizing the "non-official, non-enfranchised masses in motion so as to influence the privileged circle of electoral districts" (Marx, 1855f: 209). Second, this space is not simply the openness to the equal and universal participation of all citizens, but is clearly determined by the demands contained in the Charter as a program of the British working class.

"The *Charter* is a very laconic document". Its demands have nothing revolutionary about them: voting by ballot, no property required of candidates, payment of the elected, annual sessions of parliament, equality of electoral districts. Despite this evidently minimal character of the demands, those on the Continent who, after the events surrounding universal suffrage in France in 1848, underestimate "the importance and meaning of the English *Charter*" are wrong. Marx reiterates that, unlike in France, in Britain it is not that "political ideologists put forward this demand", that is universal suffrage is not based on an abstract principle. On the contrary, "it is a distinguishing feature roughly separating the aristocracy and bourgeoisie on the one hand, and the people, on the other. There it is regarded as a political question and here, as a social one". This is precisely why it is a demand that has grown historically, whereas in France its history has been that of the implementation of a theoretical-political intuition. In Britain it is "the *Charter* of the people and implies the assumption of political power as a means of satisfying their social needs". Because of this social content, the Charter has a revolutionary significance, to the extent that some may even argue that it wants to "break the representative system" (Marx, 1855g: 242–243).

Despite his ability to rally some limited sectors of the labour movement to his politics (Taylor, 1994; Saunders, 2008), Lord Palmerston is an ardent opponent of the enlargement of suffrage. This position is certainly not secondary to Marx's judgement of him. What interests him even more, however, is the supremacy that Palmerston manages to establish over the entire configuration of power in Britain by playing popular legitimation against parliamentary mediation. Imperial politics is the central terrain of that configuration and to defend his choices Palmerston redefines the relationship between parliament and government in depth.

> It is no longer Parliament that condemns the Cabinet on the grounds of treachery or incompetence. It is the Cabinet which accuses Parliament of hindering the conduct of the war, of jeopardising the French alliance and of abandoning Turkey. The Cabinet no longer appeals to the country to absolve it from Parliament's condemnation. It appeals to the country to condemn Parliament.
> MARX, 1855h: 367

It is no coincidence, however, that in making this judgement on Palmerston, his foreign policy, and his tendency to divest parliament of its authority, Marx reconstructs the "physiology of the ruling class of Great Britain", showing that the effects of alcohol prohibition, food adulteration, and industrial accidents are in fact ignored despite the fact that they are revealed by institutional figures such as parliamentary commissions and factory inspectors. The resulting picture is one of substantial indifference to the authority of parliament and commissions. The disempowerment of parliament is thus not only due to the pursuit of power by a single individual, but rather depends on the profound transformation that British society is experiencing. Parliament resists the ongoing change very weakly because it is still unable to represent the conflict between the different interests of the British society-world. Within this framework of precarious parliamentary legitimacy, the defence of British policy in China, despite the Canton massacre, allows Palmerston to accelerate his own government policy. Colonial policy thus shows itself to be a fundamental source of power within the British configuration, which in the same way as Chartism contributes to questioning that constitutionalism which, in both France and England, is showing signs of its futility for Marx. In both countries an expropriation of parliament by the executive is taking place; in both countries it is possible because Napoleon III and Palmerston establish a direct relationship with the 'people'.

Palmerston announces the end of the parliamentarism of the notables. It is no coincidence that it is the freethinkers and aristocrats who harshly attack "the late Doctor, now Sir John Bowring, the pet disciple of Bentham" (Marx, 1857a: 209). There seems to be an obscure symmetry between political philosophy and British colonial rule. Indeed, if in addition to being the governor of Hong Kong, Bowring is the editor of the complete works of Jeremy

Bentham, the radical philosopher Sir William Molesworth, after having been Commissioner of Works in the Aberdeen Cabinet, becomes Colonial Secretary in Palmerston's Cabinet (if only for a few months) and is the editor of the first edition of the complete works of Thomas Hobbes. Hobbesian and Benthamian democratism produces the intensification of domination in the colonies.[5] This connection between democracy and empire is immediately grasped by Marx, as is clear from his account of the parliamentary attack on Bowring led by

> the Earl of Derby, the chief of the hereditary aristocracy of England … pleading for humanity against the professional humanitarian; defending the real interests of nations against the systematic utilitarian insisting upon a punctilio of diplomatic etiquette; appealing to the 'vox populi vox dei' against the greatest-benefit-of-the-greatest-number man; the descendant of the conquerors preaching peace where a member of the Peace Society preached red-hot shell.
>
> MARX, 1857a: 209

Although he had also been secretary of the Peace Society, which aimed for universal peace and disarmament, Bowring manages the British iron fist in China, showing how the triumph of the executive serves to govern the contradiction between the assertion of the sovereign people of the metropolis and the establishment of the necessary political and economic hierarchies within the world market.

5 Colonial Power

Military and financial policy, the two issues that the *New York Daily Tribune* asks Marx to address, show that the turn towards the executive corresponds to the processes of financialization of the economy, the need to respond to global competition, and the equally necessary control of the class struggle. In Britain this configuration seems to experience a crisis when, following the motion of censure on his executive's actions in China, Palmerston "punishes the Commons by sending them home". Once again Marx emphasizes not only the heated parliamentary debate, but also the equally heated discussions of the crowd assembled outside Parliament. The reason for such participation is, according to him, that "Palmerston's administration was not that of

---

5 On Benthamian democratization, see Rudan (2013).

an ordinary Cabinet. It was a dictatorship". The war had established the conditions for a change in the structure of parliament caused by the inability of parties and factions to perform a politically autonomous function. "The war helped to incarnate in the omnipotence of a single individual, who, during half a century of political life, had never belonged to any party, but always used all parties" (Marx, 1857b: 213).[6] For Marx, this is a crisis that involves both the material constitution of British society and its institutional expressions. The neutralization of parliamentary contradictions did not benefit the masses, least of all those who were disenfranchised and thus lacked representation.

> Instead of the political emancipation of the British people, we have had the dictatorship of Palmerston. War was the powerful engine by which this result was brought about, and war was the only means of insuring it. War had therefore become the vital condition of Palmerston's dictatorship.
> MARX, 1857b: 214

The implicit recording of the Chartists' defeat on the ground of suffrage enlargement makes Marx hope that the vote of no confidence in Palmerston is not part of the normal parliamentary dialectic. It should be the sign of a rebellion against an entire system of personal power.

Instead, the concentration of power becomes the real character of a system that represents itself as plural and balanced. In a situation where the opium war and the tea trade are the underlying motivations of each side, "the imminent elections have, therefore, to decide not only whether Palmerston shall engross all the power of the State, but also whether *The Times* shall monopolize the whole manufacture of public opinion" (Marx, 1857c: 220–221; see also, Fenton, 2012). What is emerging reveals for Marx a far from hidden analogy with events in France.

---

6   Marx's judgement of Palmerston is undoubtedly different from, if not opposite to, that of liberal historiography. For instance, Steele (1991) is characterised by a fair dose of methodological nationalism and consequently makes him an exporter of constitutionalism, an innovator of liberalism and a forerunner of democracy in Britain. Ziegler (2003) makes him a consistent interpreter of nascent English nationalism while ignoring any consideration of British colonialism. Brown (2010) argues that Palmerston's commitment to freedom was genuine: power was to be wielded for the benefit of the people, but by a moderate, enlightened, and progressive elite, thus absolving him of the nationalistic excesses that his policies produced.

> The new Parliamentary majority would owe their existence to the explicit profession of passive obedience to the minister. A coup d'état might then, in due course of time, follow Palmerston's appeal from the Parliament to the people, as it followed Bonaparte's appeal from the *Assemblée Nationale* to the nation.
>
> MARX, 1857C: 222

For Marx, the political homology between Palmerston and Bonaparte is also a self-evident fact in light of the former's constant support for the latter. However, it is not the degeneration of two political systems due to the behaviour of their rulers. For Marx, both are not an exception, but the expression of a change in the state structure that is at the most advanced point of capitalist development and that also includes a decisive struggle for the construction of public opinion. While Bonaparte promises to save France from its social problems, Palmerston does so for international ones. "Palmerston, like Bonaparte, is to vindicate the necessity of a strong executive against the empty talk and the intermeddling importunity of the legislative power" (Marx, 1857d: 226). Underlying this very possibility is certainly a lapse in political mores, which allows both to play on the alternative between princes and their personal embodiment. Bonaparte is an unprincipled man who promises the nation what it needs, Palmerston presents himself as the one and only true embodiment of British colonial and imperial politics, to which he demands the sacrifice of all the principles that have hitherto governed it. The fundamental difference between the two is that Bonaparte first makes the coup and then appeals to the nation, whereas Palmerston must appeal to the nation to legitimize his personal rule and this establishes his specific weakness. Moreover, Palmerston actually wins the 1857 election. The *Whigs* gain 57 seats and achieve a landslide victory with 64.77% of the vote from an electorate of 716,552 out of a population of over 22 million.

Palmerston's victory coincides with the defeat of the free-trade faction and thus their integration within the political system. This faction is literally swept away even in its Manchester stronghold. Palmerston's victory is the nation's victory over the class struggle and thus also over the priority given to industrial interests. In the United Kingdom too, the hypothetical revolutionary parable of the bourgeoisie that could have wiped out the whole of the past comes to an end, to hand over to the proletariat a society dominated by money and therefore without any tradition of power (Marx, 1857e). Palmerston's victory is the affirmation of the primacy of imperial colonial politics over domestic politics and thus also of the dominance of tradition over the abstract dominance of money.

Colonial rule in Britain is indeed an integral and decisive part of a configuration of power that, in the constitutive asymmetry between the metropolis and the colonies, also shows elements of clear continuity. As early as 1853, Marx wrote that for better or worse the "poor Hindoo" would be the subject of the "quarreling of the aristocracy, the moneyocracy and the *millocracy*", that is, the aristocracy, the power of money and that of capitalist industry (Marx, 1853d: 141).[7] The colonial domination fits with its own autonomous characters within this constellation, because it is not simply the outcome of ruthless economic exploitation; it is also the practice of bureaucratic and military power, because the "the real Home Government, &c., of India are the permanent and irresponsible *bureaucracy*", which over time makes the government of India "one immense writing-machine" that transcribes, writes, and describes India's past and present at all times. The British colonial dominion thus serves to reproduce the British configuration of power, thus guaranteeing the material balances of its constitutionalism. "The oligarchy involves India in wars, in order to find employment for their younger sons; the moneyocracy consigns it to the highest bidder; and a subordinate Bureaucracy paralyse its administration and perpetuate its abuses as the vital condition of their own perpetuation" (Marx, 1853e: 183–184). The peculiar character of British rule in India lies not only in its despotic traits, which it shares with all other colonialisms, but rather in having "broken down the entire framework of Indian society, without any symptoms of reconstitution yet appearing". Marx characterizes British colonialism as a series of changes that result from the erasure of the past, which is programmatically and systematically intended for producing the future in a different location, without providing for any innovation. This spatial caesura of time prevents any revolt against anachronism, because it claims to establish a society without history by making the colonized the present and unchanging embodiment of the same anachronism. Forced erasure from history prevents any work on the past. It results in a constantly confirmed brutal laceration that "imparts a particular kind of melancholy to the present misery of the Hindoo" (Marx, 1853f: 126).

In the colonial dominions, the government is based on a violence that is constantly applied and legitimized in the name of a claimed difference in civilization, even if, as Marx notes, "actual accounts of Delhi evince the imagination of an English parson to be capable of breeding greater horrors than even the wild fancy of a Hindoo mutineer" (Marx, 1857f: 355). That is, it is not a question of violence produced in a clash of cultures, but of a specific form

---

7 On the Marxian position on colonialism, see Anderson (2010).

of government in which the centrality of the executive is asserted precisely through violence and, for this very reason, calls into question the very consistency of British constitutionalism (see Sammadar, 2007: 19–58). For Marx, both the government of the colonies and Palmerston's political centralization are clear signs of the crisis of British constitutionalism. There is undoubtedly a difference in the modes of government. In the metropolis, "The dull compulsion of economic relations completes the subjection of the labourer to the capitalist. Direct force, outside economic conditions, is of course still used, but only exceptionally" (Marx, 1867: 726). In India, as in China, violence is not only an everyday occurrence, revealing "the profound hypocrisy and inherent barbarity of bourgeois civilization", but is the evidence of colonial rule (Marx, 1853g: 222). This different recourse to violence, however, does not prevent us from seeing that it is the beneficiaries of the same social domination who govern the mechanisms of exclusion that the mass of the population suffers in the metropolis as much as in the colonies. "The East India Company excluded the common people from the commerce with India, at the same time that the House of Commons excluded them from Parliamentary representation" (Marx, 1853h: 149).

The government of India thus exhibits an internal movement within the Marxian concept of domination concerning its relationship with violence, which characterizes it in different times and spaces of its exercise.[8] At the same time, however, domination itself, precisely because of the globally social character of its diffusion, constantly re-proposes the question of its relationship with political power. Moreover, for Marx, the crisis of the East India Company does not only affect a model of economic exploitation, but directly the overall form of government (Piccinini, 2004–2005). Its restructuring, which effectively subjugates it to the executive, would therefore, according to Marx, need a "democratic weight to counterpoise it" (Marx, 1858: 588). However, the enlargement of suffrage would only take place after Palmerston's death in 1865. As the parliamentary debate on the third war in China shows, colonial politics continues to be, for Marx, "not only an international question, but also a constitutional question", because of the supremacy it grants to the executive and because it consequently demonstrates "the political crisis which the representative institutions of England are rapidly approaching" (Marx, 1860: 335–336). The democratic movement, whose legitimacy and necessity Marx continues to

---

8   These Marxian writings on India have as their polemical target the American economist H.C. Carey, who had a large space in the *New York Daily Tribune* and who attributed the imbalances and violence of the global expansion of capitalism to British rule alone. See Lubasz (1984).

advocate, is evidently unable to find its realization in parliaments. For Marx, "imperialist usurpation in France and ministerial usurpation in England" (Marx, 1860: 339) are the instruments that, through their monopoly of political power, also perpetuate social domination. Despite their specific differences, their rehabilitation of sovereignty is a blockade to the full unfolding of the world market, i.e., to the "encroachment [*Übergreifung*] of bourgeois society over the State" (Marx, 1857–1861a: 195) to the point of establishing the conditions for the crisis of both. In this context, only the struggle for suffrage could lead to an expansion of political rights that would change state relations, but this did not happen.

CHAPTER 4

The Domination of Capital

1   The Government of Difference

Inaugurating the First International in 1864, Marx turns to recognize "the failure of the revolutions of 1848". He describes the British situation in particularly harsh tones. Echoing his judgement of the French proletariat, which has renounced being a "conquering power", Marx writes that "the English working class" had never before seemed to have been "so thoroughly reconciled to a state of political nullity", content with minimal economic advantages. At the same time, however, "after a thirty years' struggle" that same working class managed to get the law on the reduction of the working day to 10 hours passed. This is not only a great practical success, freeing up the time of hundreds of thousands of people, but also "the victory of a principle; it was the first time that in broad daylight the political economy of the middle class succumbed to the political economy of the working class" (Marx, 1864a: 10–11).[1] This annotation is polemical towards one of Marx's favourite sources, Andrew Ure, who, criticizing the working-class belief that a reduction in working hours could lead to an increase in prices and thus to wage growth, had written: "Here their political economy was grievously at fault" (Ure, 1967: 304). At the same time, it restores the profound sense of Marx's interest in political economy and its critique as the dominant social science. If the "economical subjection of the man of labour to the monopoliser of the means of labour" is the basis of "all ... political dependence", every "political movement" must aim to emancipate the workers, knowing that this is "neither a local nor a national, but a social problem" (Marx, 1864b: 14).[2] The political emancipation of the proletariat is only possible if its action encompasses the overall space of its subjection, which is not determined by territorial boundaries, but is the set of movements and rules that constitute society.

For Marx, society is the old name for a new thing. According to Niklas Luhmann, Marx's conception of society acknowledges for the first time its capacity to thematize itself, as well as its ability to produce its own abstractions and the categories that define it. There is thus no longer any need for

---

1   On Marx's overall commitment to the Working Men's International Association, see Bravo (1979) and Musto (2018a).
2   On the British affair, see Roberts (1960: 310 ff).

a "transcendental consciousness" superior to and different from society itself (Luhmann, 2005). Also grasping this novelty, Hauke Brunkhorst observes that the Marxian concept of society attributes a material content to the Hegelian concept of *mind* "and thus puts it on its feet". It abolishes the dualism between transcendence and immanence typical of the ancient estate-based society and replaces it "with differences *within* the continuum of immanence" (Brunkhorst, 2013: 418).[3] It is precisely the centrality that differences assume that makes it possible for there to be a critique of society through society, which is ultimately only comprehensible from the differences that cooperate within it. This fundamental insight also marks the definitive abandonment of the anthropological framework that characterized the writings of the 1940s (Rancière, 1976). Society now ceases to be the place where human nature should manifest itself beyond the miseries of the present, just as the conflicts that take place within it can no longer be interpreted as struggles for the restoration or reintegration of any common essence.

The never-ending dispute with Proudhon and the Proudhonians, which runs through the *Grundrisse* and blatantly emerges in the internal confrontations of the First International, is motivated by Marx's conviction that politics as a critique of society reveals that the latter is literally constituted by the thresholds of power which traverse it. As Marx had grasped following the Crédit mobilier affair, interest is not a historical residue of a past social epoch, but a constitutive element of capital. Financial activity cannot be considered a degeneration of economic relations otherwise characterized by reciprocity and solidarity. For Marx, circulation itself produces a specific subordination to the societal might of money that is the necessary precondition for the overall domination of capital. When Proudhon argues that the centralization of credit is a "duty of society, a right of the citizen" (Bastiat et al., 2022: 66; see also, De Boni, 2016: 21–38),[4] because only in this way could interest be eliminated, he claims to reform circulation "without abolishing the production relation itself which is expressed in the category of money" (Marx, 1857–1861a: 61). Just as the contract does not make Adam Smith's 'commercial society' egalitarian, so free credit cannot make Proudhon's anarchic order mutualistic and supportive. Marx thus ends up working with a non-sociological concept of society in the sense that, despite the centrality that is effectively acknowledged to it,

---

3 Trenchantly in Marx (2007: 157), Brunkhorst writes: "The mind, the reflection, the thinking is always already the mind, the reflection, the thinking of society. The history of mind also becomes the history of society". On the problems of immediate overlap of Marxian capital with the Hegelian mind, see Finelli (2018: 134 ff).

4 On the theoretical and political differences between Proudhon and Marx, see Roberts (2016).

it always ends up being determined by processes such as the production of wealth, the movement of money, the capital ratio, or class antagonism that constantly demonstrate its instability and possible inconsistency. It is precisely for this reason that Marx can state that "this so-called consideration from the point of view of society means nothing more than to overlook precisely the *differences* which express the *societal relation*". Society rather expresses "the sum of the relationships and conditions in which these individuals stand to one another" (Marx, 1857–1861a: 195). It cannot therefore even be considered as a unitary complex, perhaps even pluralistically articulated, because historically it is not conceivable outside the capital relation that appears "originally not as containing within itself the moment of wage labour, antagonistically" (Marx, 1857–1861a: 255).

According to Marx, Proudhon's position is practically resolved in indifference to the real conditions in which individuals find themselves and, precisely for this reason, can imagine a society of free and equal people despite the presence of money (Marx, 1873). Indifferent should be understood here in the literal sense of taking exception to differences, so that the renunciation of the power struggle is also the negation of the different position that some find themselves assigned within society. Precisely because it moves from different individuals, Marx sees power as the symptom of the antagonism that constitutes society: it is the process of a cooperation that takes place under the domination of capital, in which the political relations of power aim to prevent the antagonism that characterizes it from leading to a cooperation removed from that domination. Antagonism is thus not only part of the evolutionary dynamic of society, but also the hidden engine that allows, and indeed forces, its continuous movement. Marx does not simply arrive at a conflictual sociology. Antagonism is a clash of power that prevents society from presenting itself as a homogeneous space and, precisely for this reason, "to consider society as a single subject is wrong; a speculative approach" (Marx, 1857–1861a: 31). The processes and positions that define themselves in society as a historical-political process establish thresholds of power that are constantly imposed, respected, or contested. When Marx writes that "society must always be envisaged as the premiss of conception even when the theoretical method is employed" (Marx, 1857–1861a: 39), he does not only mean that the concepts and representations that organize social relations are produced in society itself, but also that within them the pressure of difference must be determined, which imposes their constitution and practically contradicts their existence.

The specificity of bourgeois society is its peculiar historical character, which does not place it at the apex of the evolution of previous forms of society. Its history manifests an "essential difference" (Marx, 1857–1861a: 23) from the past, the "contradictory form [of its] development", to the extent that previous societal forms may persist as its internal anachronisms (Marx, 1857–1861a: 42). The need to understand the historicity of the present is not only a fundamental indication of method (Hall, 2003; see also, Wacquant, 1985; Brown, 1986: 94 ff; Smith, 2004), but the recording of a persistence of the past in the present that contradicts any linear conception of historical development and is essential for the understanding and eventual contestation of society itself.

> Just as generally in the case of any historical, social science so also in examining the development of economic categories it is always necessary to remember that the subject, in this context modern bourgeois society, is given, both in reality and in the mind, and that therefore the categories express forms of being, determinations of existence – and sometimes only individual aspects – of this particular society, of this subject, and that *even from the scientific standpoint* it therefore by no means begins at the moment when it is first discussed *as such*.
>
> MARX, 1857–1861a: 43

The historicity of society thus makes it necessary to consider its movement politically, i.e., by establishing the impact of past elements on the constitution of the present. "It would therefore be inexpedient and wrong to present the economic categories successively in the order in which they played the determining role in history". Economic categories must be arranged from the perspective point that still motivates their action, i.e., that which makes anachronisms politically active. If "in the forms in which capital rules supreme, the societal, historically evolved element predominates", it is therefore because "capital is the economic might [*Macht*] that dominates everything in bourgeois society" (Marx, 1857–1861a: 44). The antagonism to which Marx constantly refers is summed up in the two perspectives that ultimately determine it: that of capital as the dominant societal might and that of the class struggle as an equally constant contestation of the societal relation. In other words, the present contradiction retroacts on the history of society, continually redefining the very process of its evolution, because its movement does not move from the past to the present. On the contrary, it is the action of the present and active subjects that determines the historicity of society.

The 'essential difference' of this society consists in the production of an abstraction that determines the possibilities of action of its various members. Society itself establishes the position of an object – money – whose ownership is the tangible sign of the social character of production. "With the growth of the latter grows the power of *money*, i.e. the exchange relation establishes itself as a might [*Macht*] external to and independent of the producers". Money ends up establishing a general dependence of all individuals on exchange, to the point that its might is "apparently transcendental" (Marx, 1857–1861a: 84), whereas it is actually the product of their own activity. "Since money is the universal equivalent: the *general power of purchasing*, everything is purchasable, everything is convertible into money" (Marx, 1857–1861b: 215). Once again Marx takes up Adam Smith's definition, showing, however, that this power is anything but neutral both in the relationship between the state and individuals and in that of individuals among themselves (see De Brunhoff, 1976: 43–44; Rosdolsky, 1977: 99–108). As the representative of wealth, money establishes a completely abstract universality, which from an empirical point of view not only confirms existing differences, but also places individuals in the positions of command and subordination necessary for the reproduction of society. By virtue of the mediation it constantly operates, money "violently … establishes" the unity of society that would otherwise have to openly confront its antagonism. Money is the material instrument of the capitalist societal synthesis based on equality and indifference. It acts according to the most classical representational scheme, namely by producing a unity otherwise absent in the "mass of antagonistic forms of the societal unity" (Marx, 1857–1858: 159).

2   Societal Might

In the exchange system based on money, every government is a government of difference that presents itself as a government of the universal. Money constantly performs a political operation, bringing about a transformation in the very constitution of power which, thanks to the universality provided by the cover of money, can present itself as indifferent to individuals and their position.

> The absolute mutual dependence of individuals, who are indifferent to one another, constitutes their societal connection. This societal connection is expressed in *exchange value*, in which alone his own activity or his product becomes an activity or product for the individual himself. He must produce a general product – *exchange value*, or exchange value isolated by itself, individualised: *money*.
>
> MARX, 1857–1861a: 94

We are no longer faced with a simple intermediary of exchange, but with an object that, like law or religion, functions as a true *vinculum societatis* that nevertheless does not oblige its possessor to any particular discipline other than that which permits the continuity of its use. Money thus erases the specificity and particularity of the possessor, becoming the measure of all things and of every man. "He carries his societal might [*gesellschaftliche Macht*], as also his connection with society, in his pocket". The constant possibility of transforming the possession of money into societal might does not institutionalize a personal bond of subordination, as was the case between peasant and territorial lord during the Middle Ages and in ancient estate-based society. In other words, money does not establish an immediate relation of lordship, since the relationship that is established between individuals does not depend on "their relationship to each other", but instead presents itself "as their subordination to relationships existing independently of them and arising from the collision between indifferent individuals" (Marx, 1857–1861a: 94). Societal might relates to society as a whole and individuals can use the part of it allowed by their position within the exchange. The societal might of money thus reduces individuals to fragments of society and its circulation is the real power that restrains the assertion of the overall worker.

Money thus allows a specific societal synthesis based on the distance that each individual can establish and maintain with respect to others. This is a distance without *pathos* that allows individuals to establish relationships that do not involve them globally. Money is the measure of the duration and intensity of that distance and of the silent preference to depend on a "thing" rather than directly on another person. Marx is aware that this is ultimately the reason for the social success of money and it is no coincidence that he concludes: "Take away this societal might from the thing, and you must give it to persons [to exercise] over persons" (Marx, 1857–1861a: 95). What might appear as a simplification of social relations, a drastic reduction in their complexity, would in fact resolve itself in the reintroduction of relations of personal domination. On the contrary, money is the maximum production factor of a social complexity that, by apparently transforming indifference into independence, reveals the material content of the conceptual pair formed by equality and freedom which, as we have seen, is for Marx the true ideological foundation of bourgeois society. For Marx to define money as a primarily ideological object means that it is historically a constitutive factor of bourgeois society. It renders material that domination of relations that Marx terms alienation, albeit with meanings that vary over time (which we will return to later in connection with the domination of capital).[5] The circulation of money is not, however,

---

5   Reichelt writes that when money emancipates itself from all its historical and material determination, becoming the expression of commodity value, it "presents itself as a power-holding

comparable to the circulation of ideas. Taking up the analogy already used in *The Eighteenth Brumaire of Louis Bonaparte*, for Marx money is rather like those "ideas which must first be translated from their mother tongue into a foreign language in order to circulate and to become exchangeable would provide a better analogy; but then the analogy is not with the language but with its foreignness" (Marx, 1857–1861a: 99). The gap between the current language and the mother tongue represents the effort required of individuals to be able to think in the language of money. The translation that each individual must make may occasionally allow someone to change their social position, but the politically relevant character of money is that it is an individualizing object that produces mass domination. Precisely because it invests all individuals as individuals, it dissolves personal relations of dependence into the domain of abstractions, of ideas that appear independent of the positions of superiority occupied by other individuals. This "domination of relationships ... appears in the consciousness of individuals themselves to be the rule of ideas, and the belief in the eternal validity of these ideas, i.e. of those objective relationships of dependence, is *of course* in every way reinforced, sustained, drummed into people by the ruling classes" (Marx, 1857–1861a: 101). Thus emerges the specific tension between societal might and domination that runs through Marx's semantics of power (Renault, 2013: 170–185), which must also be traced back to the analytical difference between money as money and money as capital.

Both moments are determined by an antagonism based on reciprocal otherness, because if "the real non-capital is *labour*" (Marx, 1857–1861a: 204), then it is equally true that "the existence of capital as against labour requires that capital in its being-for-itself, the capitalist as *not-worker*, should be able to exist and live" (Marx, 1857–1861a: 243). This tension would be irresolvable if there were not a specific power that is produced in that sphere of circulation, which Marx describes by taking up the terms previously used to define the *Verkehr*, traffic, and which here find a further conceptual clarification. What is in the foreground is not only the inexhaustible movement of men and goods, but the subordination of individual actions to the overall framework they determine. "Their own collisions [*Aufeinanderstoßen*] give rise to an *alien* societal might [*fremde gesellschaftliche Macht*] standing above them. Their own interaction [appears] as a process and force [*Gewalt*] independent of them" (Marx, 1857–1861a: 132). This ability of money to present itself as impersonal might and coactive power is a veritable "*tautology for power*" (Negri, 1991: 35). Precisely

---

abstraction, as the material objectification of all the forces of the human species, which ... must likewise manifest themselves in an inverted form alienated from men" (1973: 208).

because of its being the point of conjunction of different expressions of power, i.e., its being the presupposition and outcome of the possibility of the production of surplus value, money establishes the equivalence between the inequalities that constitute society. "Circulation itself does not establish inequality, but is an equalisation, a transcendence of the merely imagined difference" (Marx, 1857–1861a: 177). Money fulfils this function not only as an economic object, but also, as we have seen, as an ideological object capable of presenting material dependence as the domain of relations. It is only thanks to this ideological supplement that it succeeds in sustaining what would otherwise be a weak connection between individuals who, despite producing "for and within society" (Marx, 1857–1861a: 95), can in no way come to control social production, being only able to rely on the contingency of exchange to modify their condition. Since, however, as we have seen, he is not aiming at the reduction of social complexity, Marx identifies in the development of the exchange economy itself an extension and intensification of connections such that the limits and possible overcoming of that same economy can be glimpsed. "In the *world market* the *connection of the individual* with all others, but at the same time also the *independence of this connection from the individuals*, has itself developed to such a point that its formation already contains the conditions for its being transcended" (Marx, 1857–1861a: 98; see also, Espinoza Pino and Mezzadra, 2018). The empirically universal individuals we have already mentioned find here the material basis of their development, at the moment when, within the world market, they encounter the possibility of breaking down the obstacles to the construction of their full individuality. In this space of movement, the universality of the individual cannot be understood "as an imaginary concept, but the universality of his real and notional relations". For Marx, this is a possibility of liberation because the individual can break through his isolation and the indifference that isolates him from others, producing the "comprehension of his own history as a *process*" (Marx, 1857–1861a: 466).

Only by bearing in mind this tendency that the world market introduces into the money economy can one understand why the purely objective link it establishes between individuals is for Marx nevertheless "to be preferred to the lack of any connection or to a purely local connection based on primitive blood ties, nature, and relationships of lordship and bondage" (Marx, 1857–1861a: 98). The freedom it grants is undoubtedly apparent, and "this appearance leads democracy astray" (Marx, 1857–1861a: 100), exchanging the mobility governed by money for free movement and thus becoming the political form most appropriate to the government of indifferent individuals. Money thus establishes the legitimate characteristics of democratic individuality, determines its constitutive limits, and is based on a freedom whose "possession is not the development of any one of the essential aspects of his individuality, but rather possession of something devoid of individuality" (Marx, 1857–1861a: 154). Ferdinand Tönnies defined democracy as a 'surface life' (Tönnies, 1927: 16) and it is indeed only absolute impersonality that allows access to the "general domination over society, over the whole world of enjoyments, labour, etc". (Marx, 1857–1861a: 154). Unlike the slave and serf, the wage labourer is thus guaranteed potential access to the entire world of goods. His position as a consumer subject is in fact part of the societal might that money expresses as its universal character. By other means, money thus operates in the same direction as bureaucracy. It is the complement that contributes to the realization of what universal ideas show as the necessary normativity of society. If bureaucracy is the factory of the universal, money is "the *real community*, in so far as it is the general material of existence for all, and also the communal product of all" (Marx, 1857–1861a: 158).

Society is therefore not possible without money, and politics as a critique of society and its sociology must necessarily take its starting point from the specific power dynamic it determines, defining the very stable rules of the apparent mobility of each position. Interaction among individuals can thus obtain its legal sanction by which each is recognized "as men". All individuals are free, they "recognise each other as owners, as persons, whose commodities are permeated by their will. Accordingly, the juridical concept of the person comes in here, as well as that of freedom in so far as it is contained therein. ... Each serves the other in order to serve himself; and makes reciprocal use of the other as his means" (Marx, 1857–1861a: 175). This reduction of the other to a means is not the manifestation of a moral limit that must be overcome, but the consequence of the very constitution of modern individuality that Marx had already criticized in 'On the Jewish Question'. Individuals are free and equal because they can exchange, not because they can act freely in any context, nor because they can demand an equality other than that which guarantees exchange. This is the specificity of the money relation and the reason why it must be analytically distinguished within the capital relation, although then both must be differentiated from slavery, understood as direct and personal dominion over the worker's body. For Marx, the question of the extent to which slavery and, more generally, forced labour were an "anomalous necessity" for the global establishment of the capital relation (Miles, 1987: 196 ff; see also, Moulier Boutang, 1998) is not a historical question, but concerns the current modes of labour power domination. If "to present the laws of the bourgeois economy, it is not necessary therefore to write the *real history of the production relation*" (Marx, 1857–1861a: 389), then the problem of slavery remains as a political question within wage labour, once one considers it not simply as a lack of self-ownership (Mezzadra and Neilson, 2013: 260 ff), but as a relation of mass subordination. Marx therefore defines the condition of black slaves as "a purely industrial form of slavery" (Marx, 1857–1861a: 157), thus emphasizing its connection to the capitalist mode of production.

For Marx, slavery is certainly an anachronism, but on the other hand even wage labour, which in the United States still manages to enjoy high wages, owes its position of strength to the "the reproduction of earlier modes of production and [forms of] property on the basis of capital" (Marx, 1857–1861a: 500), such as the possibility of becoming direct farmers. Rather than establishing a kind of pure model of capitalist development, for Marx the condition of the United States is marked precisely by the coexistence of forms of oppression and spaces of freedom. Slavery in particular presupposes that there is someone who can freely buy the goods produced by slaves and finds its limit when it attempts to escape from the territories in which it is dominant. In other words, slave labour exists internally within the world market, as a hidden face, insofar as it does not challenge the global dominance of money relations, of which it can also be a significant part. It is in fact the money relation that establishes the specificity of the wage labourer, since "the range of his enjoyments is not limited qualitatively, but only quantitatively. This distinguishes him from the slave, serf, etc" (Marx, 1857–1861a: 213). His subordination to capital is mediated by money and his being a limited agent within the circulation. In fact, when he returns to describe the subordination of wage labour, Marx recovers words and concepts that in the *Grundrisse* he reserves exclusively for slavery as a relation of lordship or domination [*Herrschaftsverhältnis*].

Precisely because he has access to money, each worker is nonetheless a "consumer and one who posits exchange value"; he is part of the system of circulation, one of the infinite centres "in which his specific character as worker is extinguished" (Marx, 1857–1861a: 349). In this specific capacity he represents a limit to the autonomy of the capitalist organization of production and this makes it different from any previous economy based on slavery or patriarchal domination. The slave "does not come into consideration at all as an *exchanger*", whereas the wage labourer "is himself an independent centre of circulation, someone who exchanges, posits exchange value and maintains exchange value by means of exchange" (Marx, 1857–1861a: 345–346). In other words, the wage-earner has a social power that, however individually limited it may be, can produce a mass effect within the movements of capital itself (Hampton, 2013). If, in fact, each individual capitalist can regard his workers as labour power to be exploited with the greatest intensity for as long as possible, "the total mass of all workers ... appears not as workers but as consumers" (Marx, 1857–1861a: 346). This participation in the societal might of money is not simply the outcome of a structural necessity of capital, but also and above all the political effect of the struggle that the overall worker conducts for his own valorization. While it is true that that might tends to be compressed, it is also true that it cannot be completely erased globally. For Marx, slavery cannot therefore be the horizon of the capital relation, because it presents itself as an absolute difference incompatible with the reproduction of society. In the capital relation, "the two sides confront each other as persons" and, however illusory their opposition may be and however much it may only exist from a legal point of view, it is necessary, so that each individual labour power does not only belong to the individual capitalist who employs it, but potentially to all capitalists. Thanks to money, the wage-earner must only refer his labour availability to himself. The slave, on the other hand, "is nothing but a living labouring machine" (Marx, 1857–1861a: 392–393), because "the appropriation of another's *will* is presupposed in the relationship of domination" (Marx, 1857–1861a: 424). Conceptually, however, there is for Marx no succession and thus no evolution of forms of subordination through labour. If the historical context in which slavery is imposed can change until it disappears, or can re-propose it in transformed forms within the world market, then the relations of lordship and servitude "are reproduced in capital, in a mediated form, and hence they also constitute a ferment in its dissolution, and are emblems of its limitations" (Marx, 1857–1861a: 425).

On the other hand, according to Marx, the slave and the wage labourer do not have a different attitude towards work. Both see it as a condemnation, as an imposition, made so only by the power relation in which they are placed. "Labour capacity relates to it as to something alien, and if capital wanted to pay it *without* setting it to work, it would make the bargain with pleasure". The otherness of labour power with respect to its systematic employment is the constant tendency to escape the coercive elements present in the domain of capital that continually reactivate the anachronism of slavery. Marx amusedly explains this by quoting from an article in *The Times* which laments the fact that the inhabitants of Jamaica "don't give a damn about sugar and the fixed capital invested in the *plantations*, but rather react with malicious pleasure and sardonic smiles when a planter goes to ruin, and even exploit their acquired Christianity as a cover for this sardonic mood and indolence" (Marx, 1857–1861a: 390). These Jamaicans do not accept going from slaves to wage earners and producing only the bare minimum for their livelihood. "Capital as capital does not exist for them, because wealth made independent in general exists *only* either through *direct* forced labour, slavery, or through *mediated* forced labour, *wage labour*" (Marx, 1857–1861a: 251). As we shall see even more clearly later, slavery becomes the political truth of wage labour, thanks precisely to the mediation of money that allows inequality and unfreedom to present themselves in their opposite. Money is thus not only the instrument of the infinite expansion of capitalist relations of production, but also their internal and inviolable limit.

The *Grundrisse* is an investigation into the forms and figures of this limit, and thus into the obstacles that prevent the full enjoyment of the wealth produced in society. It is certainly no coincidence that wealth is also the first word in *Capital*, even though it is immediately traced back to the realm of appearances that dominates commodity society. In the *Grundrisse*, however, Marx asks: "If the narrow bourgeois form is peeled off, what is wealth if not the universality of the individual's needs, capacities, enjoyments, productive forces, etc., produced in universal exchange"? To erase that limit means first of all to erase the historical-political anachronism that establishes the domination of past labour, of dead labour, over living labour and its labour power. To escape the domination of anachronism, man "does not seek to remain something he has already become, but is in the absolute movement of becoming". Instead, bourgeois wealth is the normative repetition of an anachronism that it cannot renounce because it is an integral part of the very movement that produces it. The comparison with antiquity that Marx proposes in these pages does not reveal any nostalgia for the fullness of the ancient world although, somewhat anticipating Nietzsche's sarcasm towards the last men, that world is recalled to show that it produced "satisfaction from a narrow standpoint; while the modern world leaves us unsatisfied or, where it does appear to be satisfied with itself, is merely *vulgar*" (Marx, 1857–1861a: 411–412).

3   Value and Law

Das Kapital, as we have anticipated, begins by stating that "the wealth of those societies in which the capitalist mode of production prevails, appears [*erscheint*] as 'an immense accumulation of commodities'" (Marx, 1867: 45). Understanding society as a mode of production leads Marx to a radical reconfiguration of societal power that reserves the real ownership of action for commodities and assigns to individuals the rank of executors of the movements they dictate. Marx's sarcasm towards the Robinsonades is not only due to the rejection of a methodological assumption of economic science with its habit of taking its starting point from the isolated individual. It is at the same time a recording that the sovereign individual is not the foundation of society and thus not even of its political organization, as Robinson Crusoe himself claims to be. The character invented by Daniel Defoe, in fact, is the representation of the individual who, by his deliberate and purposeful action, struggling against nature to build his own free world destined for progress, embodies a specific power exercised over other men through a sequence of hierarchies. Significantly, taking stock of his actions, Robinson indulges in this reflection:

> First of all, the whole Country was my own mere Property; so that I had an undoubted Right of Dominion. *Secondly*, My People were perfectly subjected: I was absolute Lord and Law-giver; they all owed their Lives to me, and were ready to lay down their Lives, *if there had been Occasion of it*, for me.
> (DEFOE, 2007: 203; see also, JUNG, 2003).

Marx's rejection of this anthropological and political model expresses the conviction that the unfolded form of the capital relation cannot be conceived as a society of individuals. Indeed, within it, the commodity, the elementary form of wealth, prevents the hierarchies and differences that constitute the societal relationship itself from being grasped but is unable to erase them. Nor does the fact that wealth appears in the form of commodities mean that the real relationships between men are concealed, but that their very constitution occurs precisely by virtue of that appearance that makes a relationship between classes of individuals a relationship between individuals.

The apparently paradoxical form of this relation is not the effect of its linguistic formulation, because "these contradictions are innate in the subject-matter, not in its verbal expressions". In the fundamental category of the societal relation, Marx reconstructs a constitutive asymmetry that is inherent to the relation itself and not the result of the utterances that describe it. This priority assigned to the material situation over the linguistic formulation emerges clearly in the polemic with Samuel Bailey, who considers "the independent existence of value", and thus capital, as an invention of economists, as the outcome of the construction of verbal paradoxes contradicted by the immediate perception of things. For Marx, on the other hand, the difference in power is materially produced within the relationship itself. Money, or rather "*money in process*, as it goes through a series of processes in which it preserves itself, departs from itself, and returns to itself increased in volume", is the expression of a relationship in which power seems to disappear in the infinite series of relations, while the same object that changes hands also practically measures the difference in power of the contracting parties (Marx, 1861–1863a: 324).[6]

---

6 The specific political status of the Marxian concept of the 'societal relationship' emerges by way of difference from what was affirmed in France in the same period (see, Macherey, 1992).

Despite the contractual form that their relationships regularly take, individuals must more or less frantically chase the propensity of commodities to be exchanged. Exchange is no longer the sign of their freedom and equality, but the irresistible effect of their belonging to the world of commodities. The latter are the protagonists of a society that assumes them as its constituent subjects. Freedom, which law presupposes and defends, is revealed as a necessary precondition of the inexhaustible movement of commodities. At the same time, equality, which, as we have seen, is for Marx the other fundamental pillar of modern individuality, also shows itself to be the necessary presupposition of the dominance of the 'value form', which establishes the connection between individuals and their labour and society and the process of its production. "The secret of the expression of value, namely, that all kinds of labour are equal and equivalent, because, and so far as they are human labour in general, cannot be deciphered, until the notion of human equality has already acquired the fixity of a popular prejudice" (Marx, 1867: 70). From a political point of view, what Marx calls the 'value form' is the authentic sovereign structure of society through which individual labour is made equal and measurable. Their very equality now appears not as an abstract principle, but as the necessary precondition of society's production and reproduction. While establishing the monetary measure of all social action, value mediates and reproduces the differences of individuals who continue to present themselves as universally equal. Their equality in principle is overwritten by that resulting from the work of equalization conducted through the exchange of commodities. "The equalization of the most different kinds of labour can be the result only of an abstraction from their inequalities, or of reducing them to their common denominator, viz., expenditure of human labour power or human labour in the abstract" (Marx, 1867: 80). The dialectic between equality and indifference that we have already seen with regard to money thus returns. Here, however, indifference is also the paradoxical link between commodities and individuals, who do not develop any substantial reciprocal bond, because "by virtue of the form of its value, [each commodity] is now stands in a societal relation, no longer with only one other kind of commodity, but with the whole world of commodities. As a commodity, it is a citizen of that world" (Marx, 1867: 73–74). This universal citizenship overlaps with that of individuals without erasing it, but redefining its boundaries and content, i.e., establishing criteria that are removed from the immediate power of political authority.

It is evidently not only the national limitation of that authority, but the establishment of a specific dynamic whereby relations between individuals appear to be governed exclusively by an impersonal mechanism that is ultimately uncontrollable for them. Value is the most obvious expression of the domination of the past over the present; it is anachronism as a movement that reproduces itself over and over again. Although it imposes itself as an objective, seemingly impersonal, and impolitic force, only the dynamics of value make the domination of capital possible. "On the one hand, the value, or the past labour, which dominates living labour, is incarnated in the capitalist. On the other hand, the labourer appears as bare material labour power, as a commodity" (Marx, 1894: 49). *Herrschaft*, which we have translated as domination, dominion, dominance or even lordship, occupies a specific and decisive position in Marx's semantics of power. It refers to the overall capacity of capital to subordinate the whole of society to its movements. It is presented as an objective systemic necessity to which everyone must submit, although it produces differentiated effects. The domination of capital is exercised over all but to the exclusive benefit of a few. For Marx, its critique can only take place by collectively contesting its existence, thus showing how it is possible to escape the individualistic depoliticization of social relations. For Marx, the capital relation is characterized by the predominance of unintentional action[7] which confirms the untimeliness of the individual subject of will who claims to be the author of his own actions in both the economic and political spheres. As we shall see, there is for Marx no possibility of reintegrating the individual's capacity for action, which necessarily functions as a bearer [*Träger*] for the movements of capital. It is only possible to respond to this practical impossibility with the affirmation of collective power, i.e., by becoming power, to return to the terms he used in his polemic with Heinzen. The opposition between societal [*gesellschaftlich*] and private largely reformulates the traditional one between public and private, wanting to avoid placing political action in a single sphere. What must be overcome is that specific autonomy of the commodity form, whereby

> in it the social character of men's labour appears to them as an objective character stamped upon the product of that labour; because the relation of the producers to the sum total of their own labour is presented to them as a societal relation, existing not between themselves, but between the products of their labour.
> MARX, 1867: 82–83

---

7 Spivak rightly speaks of "the fundamental critique of the intending subject that sustains all Marx's thought" (1999: 77).

What Marx calls commodity fetishism is the unfolded form of a societal power that has the capacity to make people accept historical social relations as objective and necessary and that ends up producing individual adherence to the existence of things that seem to have a life of their own, independent of the will of the men who produce them (Ripstein, 1987). This societal power appears as a systemic necessity and constitutes the foundation of what Balibar has significantly called the "social contract of commodities", thanks to which "society is the true 'subject', or rather the *set of* individual practices that, without knowing it, satisfy the necessities of its existence" (2011b: 325). In this commodity society, individuals appear as "their guardians [and] must place themselves in relation to one another, as persons whose will resides in those objects" (Marx, 1867: 95; see also, Campbell, 2009; Merlo, 2023). Individuals are thus represented as commodities that guarantee the societal sovereignty of the value form. Precisely because they end up being the personification of commodities, confirming the universally binding character of the value form, the appropriation of wealth can take place without violence, i.e., remaining within the relationship that indissolubly binds money and the value of the individual commodity. This relationship seems to reproduce itself in an automatic manner because, "in any case the market for commodities is only frequented by owners of commodities, and the power which these persons exercise over each other, is no other than the power of their commodities" (Marx, 1867: 171).

In fact, this automatism shows its limit at the moment Marx poses the question of where capital is born, asking how money is transformed into capital. The paradox of capital in its movement is that "it must have its origin both in circulation and yet not in circulation" (Marx, 1867: 176). In other words, the exchange of equivalents, the necessary equivalence of the power of each individual involved in the exchange, does not allow us to explain how capital arises historically and how it constantly reproduces itself as a relation. To explain this, Marx introduces labour power, which is a "special commodity", not only because of its peculiar characteristic "of being a source of value", but also because it is inseparable from the individual who possesses it, from his "living self" (Marx, 1867: 179). Since the "the value of each commodity is determined by the quantity of labour expended on and materialised in it, by the working time necessary, under given social conditions, for its production" (Marx, 1867: 196–197), value is not only what makes indifferent commodities comparable, but at the same time it is the societal power required for labour power to continue to supply its time with regularity and constancy. In the ordered and impersonal system of the value form, however, labour power introduces a difference that is at the same time a power differential, which cannot be grasped unless one considers that, for there to be a capital relation, it must be provided in a social context and not as a purely individual relationship. Although, like any other subject of exchange, the possessor of labour power is formally free when according to law he surrenders what he possesses, it is his material condition that obliges him to the surrender. We are thus confronted with a relationship between individuals that produces consequences that go beyond the individual condition, precisely because the exchange serves primarily to reproduce capital and only mediately labour power.

> How, then, does any amount of commodities, of exchange values, become capital? By maintaining and multiplying itself as an autonomous societal might [*selbständige gesellschaftliche Macht*] that is, as the might *of a portion of society*, by means of its *exchange for direct, living labour*. The existence of a class which possesses nothing but its capacity to labour is a necessary prerequisite of capital. It is only the domination of accumulated, past, materialised labour over direct, living labour that turns accumulated labour into capital.
>
> MARX, 1849d: 213

The individual power differential is resolved in a collective subordination that remains completely obscure if one considers only the commodity exchange relation mediated by money. When the worker and the capitalist face each other, they are individuals who exchange their respective commodities and who must necessarily conclude their encounter by respecting the fundamental principles of society: freedom, because each formally acts according to his legally protected will; equality, because their exchange takes place between equivalent values; property, because each can only exchange what is his, and, Marx adds, "Bentham, because each looks only to himself. The only force that brings them together and puts them in relation with each other, is the selfishness, the gain and the private interests of each" (Marx, 1867: 186). However, it is precisely on the terrain of profit that the society of commodities that must necessarily be transformed into capital requires an imbalance of power, a constitutive asymmetry between the individual and the collective. Marx makes ample use of Mandeville's corrosive irony as an *ante litteram* critique of the Benthamian maxim that assumes as the principle of utilitarianism the greatest happiness for the greatest number, to show that "the process of accumulation itself increases, along with the capital, the mass of 'labouring poor', i.e., the wage labourers", who precisely because they are forced to sell their labour power, "eternise their dependent relation on their own product, as personified in the capitalists" (Marx, 1867: 610–611).

Poverty is evidently a state of more or less relative deprivation in access to enjoyments, to which corresponds the continuing impossibility of exercising any collective power. In his lengthy quotation from *The Fable of the Bees*, Marx adds that the necessary presence of the poor causes society to be reduced to the "non-workers" who, despite Bentham, are not the greatest number and still enjoy the greatest possible happiness. The interpolation is significant because it signals that poverty introduces a cleavage, and thus a political element, within the societal relationship, as it is an integral part of the calculation of the value of labour power, i.e., the labour time socially required to reproduce it. Indeed, unlike that of other commodities, that value includes "a historical and moral element" (Marx, 1867: 181), which exists prior to the exchange between capitalist and worker. Poverty is part of this historical precondition of the value of labour power. Just as for Durkheim there are notoriously pre-contractual conditions of contractualism that make it possible and legitimize it, so for Marx poverty is a pre-wage condition of the wage-labour relationship. It can certainly be traced back to the absence of employment, or to low wages, but it is first and foremost the condition that requires a part of society to enter the wage-labour relationship, just as the 'non-workers' are not simply the idle, but those who do not enter that relationship as wage earners. The value of labour power thus ends up being the expression of a societal relationship that is political because it is founded on a division that 'classifies' a multitude of individuals. As we have seen, the form of value as societal power takes charge of constantly fractioning the mass dimension of that relationship, making it appear as an impersonal mechanism of systemic reproduction. The individualization that characterizes the sphere of circulation is, from this point of view, the condition of possibility for the governance of the cooperation that takes place within the sphere of production, in which, however, the collective dimension necessarily emerges since here the process of valorization is also inevitably a labour process. Capital can no longer valorize itself by exchanging with itself in the form of money but must expose itself to the risk of direct contact with non-capital, showing itself as the most important and fundamental of anachronisms, as past labour aiming to dominate living labour power.

> By turning his money into commodities that serve as the material elements of a new product, and as factors in the labour process, by incorporating living labour with their dead substance, the capitalist at the same time converts value, i.e., past, materialised, and dead labour into capital, into value big with value, a live monster that is fruitful and multiplies.
> MARX, 1867: 205

Within this process, time is the material of which the domain of capital is made. The worker in fact surrenders the temporary use of his labour power, the value of which depends on the socially necessary labour-time for the reproduction of that labour power, while the valorization of capital depends on the time in which the dead labour objectified in it comes into contact with the living labour of labour power. In the face of this economy of time, the societal might of money that commands exchange shows all its limits, because labour power is not merely a commodity, and its very concept is wholly incomplete if one stops at the mere determination of exchange (Dummer, 1997; Kuczynski, 2009). The struggle over time that, starting from the British and American experience, Marx describes when speaking of the battle for the reduction of the working day thus goes beyond those concrete historical episodes and outlines an ineliminable clash within the production of surplus value. In fact, it reveals the constant presence of an element of ungovernable uncertainty in a process that pretends to be increasingly automatic and systematic, still showing the aporias of law when it has to regulate the working day. At first, the clash of two rights: that of the buyer of the labour power, who wants to intensify and extend to the maximum degree the utility of what he has purchased, and that of the seller, who for the money he receives wants to surrender the minimum possible quantity of his goods. Both parties legitimately demand to maximize their own profit. "There is here, therefore, an antinomy, right against right, both equally bearing the seal of the law of exchanges. Between equal rights force [*Gewalt*] decides" (Marx, 1867: 243). Marx here takes up almost literally the formula he had used to defend himself in court against the charge of organizing the tax strike. At that time, he had spoken of the opposition between two powers, but even this clash of unenforceable rights ends up showing the opposition between two powers, because it cannot in fact be mediated by the law that has already legitimized the individual claim of the contracting parties. The reference to force-violence indicates the limit point reached by the societal capital relation, which can no longer correspond to the natural right of capital. The recording of this failure paves the way for factory legislation, which is for Marx the prelude to the moment "when the working class comes into political power [*politische Gewalt*], as inevitably it must" (Marx, 1867: 491). Indeed, it makes it possible for the workers to acquire more and more knowledge about the production process and thus about how to reproduce their existence. This confirms that conquering power is not an act, but the effect of a subversion of knowledge that overcomes the division between intellectual and manual labour and the social hierarchy it imposes. On the other hand, the clash between two rights reveals that if the extraction of surplus value does not take place "merely by the violence [*Gewalt*] of economic relations", but also with the "help of the power of the State [*Staatsmacht*]", at the same time the latter is invested by the class struggle, becoming a specific area of contention, a politically contestable area precisely because its connection to the movements of society is called into question (Marx, 1867: 276).

4 The Law and the Exception

The return of *Gewalt* as violence and power thus opens up a glimpse into the original scene, when capital was "in embryo" (Marx, 1867: 276) and, as we shall see, precisely with the decisive help of the state began to impose its laws as if they were natural, concealing the fact that at their origin law and violence acted in concert. The process of expropriation, which now takes place according to the symmetries of the contract, began and continues to carry within it the violence with which it came into being, the original sin that should not be remembered. It is no coincidence that in *Capital,* Marx only resorts to theological metaphors on three occasions: to speak of commodity fetishism, to introduce so-called original accumulation (*urprüngliche Akkumulation*), and to explain, as already within it, the importance of public debt in the modern state. In the first two cases they point to constant movements of which, despite their evidence, men seem unaware. Property is legitimized as the result of a past sacrifice that some have made and whose just fruits they now enjoy. Violence is reduced to an exception, denying that it can and does play any role in the capital relation.[8] As we have already said, for Marx, private property, or rather the private appropriation of the social product, is the expression of a power relation that is only possible through the violence that founded and sustains it. The violence that Marx affirms as a constant and decisive historical emergence has a dual presence: first in the long and troubled processes from which capitalism arose, then it is incorporated into the production relation itself even when it appears to function in its normality guaranteed by law, becoming an essential part of the social condition that forces some individuals to sell their labour power (Rudan, 2023). With the clash between the overall capitalist and the overall worker, a violence erupts that revokes the validity of the natural law of capital, showing the social relation as a clash of powers.

---

8 "The theme of force [*Gewalt*], if we look carefully, is so persistent in *Capital* (particularly in Volume I), that this whole work could be read as a treatise on the structural violence that capitalism inflicts (and as a treatise on the *excess of violence* inherent in the history of capitalism), described in its subjective and objective dimensions, of which the critique of political economy provides the red thread" (Balibar, 2009: 109). See also, Basso (2016).

Gewalt primarily signals the presence of a subject that law does not provide for within it. It shows the incompetence of law to give form to a relation that finally exhibits the very content it purports to neutralize.

This paradoxical societal limitation of the law emerges with particular clarity for Marx in the Factory Acts, the labour legislation that, on several occasions from 1833 onwards, first aims to limit the use of child labour, then that of women, and finally the working day as a whole. Marx is not interested in the struggle for the limits of the working day because of the state's ability to intervene in societal relations,[9] but because it reveals the existence of an unforeseen subject, a collective and organized subject that both the commercial society in Britain and the Le Chapelier law in France had long banished (see Marx, 1867: 730–731).[10] It is in fact "a struggle between overall capitalist [*Gesamtkapitalist*], i.e., the class of capitalists, and overall worker [*Gesamtarbeiter*], i.e., the working class" (Marx, 1867: 243).[11] However, the force that should decide this struggle between two collective subjects does not immediately establish the basis for a new order, because "boundless thirst for surplus labour" (Marx, 1867: 244) cannot be contained by law. Free competition, in fact, is a superior right that acts on capitalists "as external coercive laws" (Marx, 1867: 276), enforcing "the immanent laws of capitalist production" (Marx, 1867: 588). For capitalists and economists, the law of supply and demand represents a kind of natural law of capital. So there is not only the struggle between two rights, but also the clash between two laws that do not coincide, and within this clash, the state cannot claim any absolute superiority. The Factory Acts are the expression of this contradiction and, at the same time, the mediation between two legislations that have different bases of legitimacy: the former seems to respond to a pre-legal necessity, while the latter should rely on the sovereign ability to decide outside any constraint, to be *legibus soluta*. They must therefore moderate "the passion of capital for a limitless draining of labour power, by forcibly limiting the working day by state regulations, made by a state that is ruled by capitalist and landlord" (Marx, 1867: 247). This is a legislative intervention in the very laws of accumulation that the state carries out as the representative of the overall

---

9   On the historical context and effects of that legislation see Lieven (1988), who reproaches Marx and Engels with a fundamental misunderstanding of the capacity for political intervention that it manifests.

10   "It is one of the most important truths resulting from the analysis of manufacturing industry, that unions are conspiracies of workmen against the interests of their own order, and never fail to end in the suicide of the body corporate which forms them" (Ure, 1967: 41).

11   "The collective capitalist is the form assumed by the power that is in the hands of social capital – capitalist society's power over itself, capital's government of itself and therefore of the capitalist class" (Tronti, 2019: 45).

capitalist and thus also against the particular interests of certain capitalists. The class struggle has invested the state, breaking the spell of its autonomy from society, showing that society is unable to regulate itself. The class struggle forces it to intervene to remedy what are considered accidents of production, whereas for Marx "the establishment of a normal working day is the result of centuries of struggle between capitalist and labourer" (Marx, 1867: 276).

As the examples he gives show, Marx can affirm the centuries-old character of this struggle because he also includes slave struggles and even others conducted under servile conditions, in the conviction that "capital has not invented surplus labour" (Marx, 1867: 243). At first Marx interprets the demand for the working day to have a "normal" character as the search for a ratio of wages to time that allows the worker to resist the dominance of surplus labour. However, when analysing the legislation passed in Britain and France, he emphasizes that to claim its "normal" character is to deny that of "exceptional legislation [*Ausnahmegesetzgebung*]" (Marx, 1867: 303) which the capitalists seek to attribute to it, thinking they can return to the previous normality, i.e., to the usual and therefore normal forms of exploitation, as soon as possible. Marx had already made it clear that "the material factors of the process are of normal quality" (Marx, 1867: 206), i.e., the competitiveness of all those conditions that permit the employment of labour power and thus the valorization of capital, depends on the capitalist, who, however, also claims to establish the "average efficacy" of labour power itself. That is, he claims to be able to exploit it without interruptions or hiccups that would cause him to lose or waste part of his investment. In order to 'normalize' labour power, he "has a penal code of his own" (Marx, 1867: 207) that disciplines and punishes all individual workers who do not abide by that normality. The working class, the overall worker, is the exception to this order that does not provide for a collective presence, an exception that does not simply break the norms, but claims to reformulate them according to "his political economy". It is thus a subjective exception, which poses not so much the question of what the exception is from a political-normative point of view, but of who the exception is within society. From this point of view, the exception concerns neither the decision nor the system, but the material subject who cannot assert his difference in society. In order to eliminate the "exceptional character" of the regulations on the working day, it becomes necessary "to declare any house in which work was done to be a factory". The legislation, which exceptionally protected certain workers from overexploitation, must progressively recognize that even "that manufactures with more or less obsolete methods, ... that old-fashioned handicrafts, like baking, and, finally, even that the so-called domestic industries ... had long since fallen as completely under capitalist exploitation as the factories themselves"

(Marx, 1867: 303). In this way, the law's space of intervention is made to coincide with that of the capital relation. In other words, the terrain of law can only encompass the workers' exception by further extending the domination of capital: the factory thus becomes the societal space of every capitalist production process regardless of how labour power is specifically employed.

At the moment when legislation goes so far as to regulate relations in this enlarged and tendentially all-encompassing sphere, contractual freedom and the individual that it delineated show signs of their own crisis, highlighting the historical limitation of the category of interest declined on an exclusively individual level. On the other hand, for Marx the fact that legislation can hardly ensure the normality of the working day in a lasting way is demonstrated by the fact that against the 10-hour legislation of 1833, British capitalists had for years carried out a "proslavery rebellion in miniature", refusing to implement it. In the following decade, however, "Capital preluded its revolt by a step which agreed with the letter of the law of 1844, and was therefore legal" (Marx, 1867: 290–291). The terrain of law is traversed by processes that are always reversible, because "the creation of a normal working day is, therefore, the product of a protracted civil war, more or less dissembled, between the capitalist class and the working class" (Marx, 1867: 303). This "civil war of half a century" (Marx, 1867: 300), as Marx calls it, does not take place over the power of the state, nor is it the sign of a contest over the state. The collision between capital and labour reveals the antagonistic nature of their relationship and ends up showing itself as a constant clash that affects the material constitution of society. Civil war, as we have already said, is not the exception, nor does it take place on the boundary of the state but in society, which thus becomes the political space of a division between collective subjects. It is precisely this struggle that reveals that "the isolated worker, the labourer as 'free' vendor of his labour power" does not have the means to oppose the domination of capital. It evidently follows for Marx that workers must struggle "as a class", but what is more interesting is that the law for the limitation of the working day serves not so much for the normality it imposes, but rather as "an all-powerful social barrier that shall prevent the very workers from selling, by voluntary contract with capital, themselves and their families into slavery and death" (Marx, 1867: 306).

Marx does not think of factory legislation as an enlargement of the sphere of rights, but as the removal of the individual from his destiny as a solitary contractual individual. It is the insurance against the workers' tendency to compete with each other which, as Engels and Marx wrote in the *Manifesto*, determines the provisional character of their eventual victories, constantly calling them into question. Moreover, showing once again his indifference to what we have previously termed the Stein hypothesis, Marx does not see factory legislation as the product of the state's ability and right to mediate class confrontation. It would the "first conscious and methodical reaction of society against the spontaneously developed form of the process of production" (Marx, 1867; 483). Being an expression of society, state power is certainly also the instrument that, in the face of the intensification of the class struggle, intervenes in the inseparable historical nexus between society and the capitalist mode of production in order to guarantee its reproduction in any case. That law expresses the opening of a conflict within society, but it is at the same time the condition of possibility of a dividing line that "shall make clear 'when the time which the worker sells is ended, and when his own begins'" (Marx, 1867: 307; see also, Didry, 2018).

This victory of the political economy of the working class is "the modest Magna Charta" against capital's constant tendency to make its political presence a collective exception to be limited as much as possible (Marx, 1867: 307). The "normal working day" cannot erase a condition that is not established by legal norms or political decisions, but by a domination exercised simultaneously over individuals and their cooperation, which is the real object of its action, because the "social productive power which arises from cooperation is a *free gift* [*unentgeldlich*]" (Marx, 1861–1863b: 260). Yet despite its apparently minimal results, the struggle over the limitation of the working day is a struggle that establishes the specifically political character of the workers' social movement, because it is not defined by the individual goals it sets itself, but by the overall, mass dynamic that characterizes it. Marx wrote a few years later:

> The *political movement* of the working class naturally has as its final object the conquest of *political power* for this class, and this requires, of course, a *previous organization* of the *working class* developed up to a certain point, which arises from the economic struggles themselves. but on the other hand, every movement in which the working class comes out as a *class* against the ruling classes and tries to coerce them by *pressure from without* is a *political movement*.
> MARX to BOLTE, 23/11/1871: 258

Here we return to the terms Marx used to describe the Chartists' struggle for suffrage, while at the same time he makes it clear that claims against an individual capitalist are economic claims, but actions such as the one aiming to impose an eight-hour working day for all establish a political movement, "that is to say a movement of the *class*, with the object of achieving its interests in a general form, in a form possessing general, socially [*gesellschaftlich*] binding force". Opposing the "the collective power [*Kollektivgewalt*], i.e. the political power, of the ruling classes" (Marx to Bolte, 23/11/1871: 258) is the only way to avoid being subservient to the game of the ruling classes. The collective power of the workers, which is organized power, is the only one that can oppose the silent compulsion of the evolution of capitalist society (Merlo, 1999).

5   Cooperation and Command

It is therefore a matter of following the process of the constitution of capitalist domination within the increasingly broader and more intense ones of cooperation, because the latter for Marx are both the maximum unfolding of a determinate capacity to subjugate society, but also those where the concrete possibilities of overcoming this condition can be grasped. As we have already seen, for Marx the world market is one of these transitional formations, not because it automatically or spontaneously opens up spaces of freedom, but because within it move those empirically universal individuals who with their connections and movements materially show the possibility of going beyond the characteristics of abstract modern individuality.[12] In the transitional formations, the power and domination of capital in turn show their provisional character, clashing with the practical possibilities of overcoming the conditions of subordination that they determine. On the other hand, for Marx, if this possibility were not already present in the existing condition of subordination and exploitation, "all attempts to explode it would be quixotic" (Marx, 1857–1861a: 97). What is relevant, however, is that overall, the Marxian concept of power is built around its provisionality. It corresponds to a politics that does not consist in limiting nor in conquering it in order to use it for other ends but aims to establish the conditions for a part of society to become itself the social process capable of dissolving the specific configuration of power based on the capital relation. There is thus no fundamental anthropology in Marx that leads one to consider power as a historical invariant and thus to fear it or seek it out. There is a semantics of power that connotes relations that arise and change within a historical process of cooperation that Marx critiques to show its non-natural and therefore contingent character. On the other hand, the Marxian critique aims not only to investigate its object to show the internal logic of its operation but also to dissolve it by showing its historical character, that is, the

---

12   To use the conceptual pair proposed by Berki (1983: 76–79, 144–149), in the transitional formations, communism is present both as insight and vision, either as a complete transcendence of capitalism or as a continuation of capitalism itself.

product of a past from which it is possible to liberate oneself. The critique of society itself thus has the sense of showing its provisionality, its unfinished character, the historical character of the hierarchies that it produces and that sustain it.

Following the events of this cooperation requires us to start from what Marx calls the manufacturing age. At that moment, the practical existence of the overall worker begins to take shape, which, although composed of partial workers hierarchically placed within the production process, is also the first manifestation of the cooperative possibilities of labour as a socialized activity and not merely individual or subject to the external command of capital. The age of manufacturing introduces radical changes on a political and ideological level (Borkenau, 1971; Borkenau et al., 1978), because it is the dawning moment of both what Marx calls "socialised labour" [*vergesellschaftete Arbeit*] and the process of expropriation that brings workers "face to face with the intellectual potencies of the material process of production, as a foreign property, and as a might that dominates them [*sie beherrschende Macht*]" (Marx, 1867: 366). We will return shortly to the characters Marx assigns to this power. The factory is a composite reality in which there is the "life-long annexation of the labourer to a partial operation, and his complete subjection to capital". "Detail labourers" coexist with the presence of the overall worker (Marx, 1867: 361), and they are neither alternative nor successive figures, just as the latter does not definitively erase the former. The overall worker is not simply a figure of the labour process, he is a political figure that shows the possibility of a cooperation not directed by capital. The socialized character of production that he introduces is not simply a mode of production for Marx. He uses the term *Vergesellschaftung* in this regard, which is difficult to translate but has become increasingly important in German sociology since Marx (Lichtblau, 2011).[13] In this context it has been rendered with 'societalization'[14] but what is important for us is that it refers to a social process and not to the statics of society as an established relationship. It is the condition of a possibility of both collective and individual action, which does not simply add up to those provided by the discourse of modern individualism. We are therefore not faced with the production of a

---

13 Charles Fourier (1829) used the adjective referring specifically to society; for Marx, however, *vergesellschaftet* has a further meaning.
14 See Massimo Pianta's Foreword to the new Italian translation of Weber (2005: cxxix). More recklessly, but perhaps also more clearly, Pierangelo Schiera in his Italian translation of Böckenförde (1970) rendered it as 'societarization'. On the different English translations of the German term *Vergesellschaftung* see Schmidt (2020).

new man with all his predictable tragedies (Cioli et al., 2020)[15] but rather with the identification of a possibility to produce and reproduce society that does not move from individual action but from the collective environment in which it is located. The reference to the *Vergesellschaftung* does not appear in the *Grundrisse*, whereas in the first volume of *Capital* it identifies one of those transitional formations in which Marx glimpses the material possibility of the overcoming of the capital relation. That term and its adjective are used alternatively to *sozial*, which Marx seems to reserve for the specific, and thus commanded, sociality of the capital relation. In a less imaginative manner than in the famous 'Fragment on Machines' of the *Grundrisse*, in the first volume of *Capital* Marx continues to affirm the contradictory character of the machinery which, while it imposes capitalist power, also shows that it functions "only by means of associated [*vergesellschaftet*] labour, or labour in common" (Marx, 1867: 389). The socialized worker, and thus the individual, is not characterized by a new and different anthropology, nor does he add any new qualities to those previously ascribed to the liberal individual, i.e., he is not the holder of certain social rights to which individual rights can or must be added. For Marx, he is clearly neither the principle nor the predestined victim of technology, but rather the figure who, by eliminating the isolated worker through machinery, radically changes the cooperation in which he is embedded.

The machine is political precisely because it shows the presence of this split between the use that capital makes of it and the cooperation that it can help to establish. Marx does not argue for the neutrality of technology, as if it were possible to conceive of it in an ahistorical manner and outside the power relations within which it develops, but rather also places the machine within the process of the tendential sociability of labour.[16] At the moment when the mode of production "which rests on exploitation of the nominally free labour of others" is definitively established, any possibility of tracing private property back to personal labour is overcome, ushering in the era of specifically capitalist private property. In this situation, "the further societalization of labour and further transformation of the land and other means of production into socially [*gesellschaftlich*] exploited, and, therefore, common [*gemeinschaftlich*] means

---

15 Already Marx replied to those who accused the communists of "wanting to improve the human race" by saying: "Let it calm down! Fortunately, we Germans are not unaware that since 1640 the *Congregatio de propaganda fidei* has had the monopoly in improving the human race. We are too modest and too few to want to compete with the reverend fathers in that humanitarian industry" (Marx, 1847d: 403).

16 Wendling (2009: 108–117) shows how for Marx machines can represent a challenge to the "capitalist logic of exhaustion".

of production, as well as the further expropriation of private proprietors, takes a new form". For Marx, the societalization of labour is produced and at the same time intensifies the transformation of property from a private institution to an overall societal function in view of the valorization of capital. The centralization of capital and the full development of the world market are the most obvious conditions of this transformation. The simultaneous growth of "the revolt of the working class" should mark the moment when "centralization of the means of production and societalization of labour at last reach a point where they become incompatible with their capitalist integument" (Marx, 1867: 750). It is a matter of achieving a practical condition of freedom which, unlike the modern tradition, is not the condition of the liberal individual vis-à-vis society and its state, for whom in the private sphere the societal rules are almost suspended. Nor is it about liberty understood as the citizen's participation in the *res publica*. Finally, it is not about the realization of the idea of freedom that leads to the fulfilment and thus the end of history. "The realm of freedom actually begins only where labour which is determined by necessity and mundane considerations ceases". For Marx, this practical freedom can only have as its subject "socialised man [*vergesellschaftetes Mensch*], the associated producers" (Marx, 1894: 807; see also, Lebowitz, 2003: 197 ff), who collectively regulate their own activity for not "being ruled by it as by a blind might". Marx reiterates that even for this redefinition of freedom the "the shortening of the working day is its basic prerequisite" (Marx, 1894: 807). It is therefore not a question of successive moments, but of a determinate relation to time that is appropriated or not appropriated by capital. The realm of freedom is not placed in the future but is the product of the present struggle over working time, when this same struggle is collective and removes labour from its function as the foundation of society.

The tendency Marx identifies within these transitional formations is relevant because, as we have said, it shows the provisional character he attributes to the domination of capital. These formations show the possibility of overcoming a condition of subordination and exploitation that Marx otherwise describes with great punctuality. On the other hand, it is precisely the ever-present possibilities opened up by the societalization of labour that impose the capitalist's command and despotism as its determinate form. The wealth produced by the overall worker becomes primarily the property of those who govern his cooperation; machinery becomes established within the production process thanks to the separation of intellectual labour from manual labour, which becomes the basis for the establishment of large-scale industry; science becomes a factor in the production to which it is overall applied. Machines incorporate the relationship of subordination within which they are used and, precisely because they become an overall system that extends to the entire production process, they become a constitutive part of "the power of the 'master'" (Marx, 1867: 426). The machine not only acts as a competitor who gets the better of the workman, and is constantly on the point of making him superfluous. It is also a power inimical to him, and as such capital proclaims it from the rooftops and as such makes use of it. It is the most powerful weapon for repressing strikes, those periodical revolts of the working class against the autocracy of capital (Marx, 1867: 438).

In the machine system, the antagonistic character of capitalist production and thus the opposition of the overall worker to the times and methods established by that system, is thus expressed. Marx applies the same criterion to the power of machines as he does to the normal working day, reaffirming that what is at issue is the saving of labour time that they might allow, whereas their capitalist use is a function of the intensification and lengthening of labour time and thus of exploitation. In this case, when they are not at the service of the "collective labourer", but subordinate him to their rhythms, reducing the workers to the rank of their "conscious organs", then a power relationship becomes evident whereby the machine presents itself as "an autocrat" (Marx, 1867: 421–422).

Since the machine evidently has no interest of its own, the power it wields puts a value for the capitalist on the fact that "the combined worker or overall worker [*der kombinierte Arbeiter oder Gesamtarbeiter*] has hands and eyes both before and behind, and is, to a certain degree, omnipresent" (Marx, 1867: 332). The working day of this worker can extend indefinitely in space and time, becoming a global working day that unfolds in nonhomogeneous spaces and at diversified times, being the fruit of the cooperation of a multitude of partial workers, for which the "*simultaneity* of action" (Marx, 1861–1863a: 263) is no longer necessary. Capitalist cooperation thus becomes the foundation of any 'contemporaneity of the non-contemporary', although the time of the combination of labour constantly eludes its perpetrators, who find themselves completely subsumed in a process in which they have lost all independence, to the point that "their labour becomes *compulsory labour* [*Zwangsarbeit*] because once they enter into the labour process it belongs not to them but already to capital, is already incorporated in capital. The workers are subjected to the *discipline* of capital and placed in completely changed conditions of life" (Marx, 1861–1863a: 269). Yet it is precisely within this cooperation that the overall worker who is indifferent to the different tasks he can perform shows himself to be the other face of the empirically universal individual whose emergence within the world market Marx foresees. It is precisely the control of that indifference that makes "the command of capital ... a requisite for carrying on the labour process itself, into a real requisite of production" (Marx, 1867: 335). Marx distinguishes between direction [*Leitung*] and command [*Kommando*]: the former is the generic need to organize the cooperation of many individuals, the latter is a necessity of the capitalist process of valorization, and thus a political necessity, which guarantees the reproduction of a hierarchy that allows the differentiated appropriation of the social product. Command is thus directly motivated by the antagonism that pervades the process of valorization and is ultimately dictated by the need to establish the conditions of exploitation.

Command certainly encompasses the process of discipline, which Marx describes punctually, showing how it served and serves to produce the 'normal' labour power necessary for the capitalist to withstand competition. However, it cannot be relegated to the dawning moment of capitalist production when, as Michel Foucault writes, factory discipline was the condition for achieving the division of labour, just as for Marx it is not one power among others that establish society as an "archipelago of different powers" (Foucault, 1981). As demonstrated by the reference to the factory *code pénal*, used to describe the daily discipline of working time, for Marx as well "the supervision-punishment couple is imposed as an indispensable power relationship for fixing individuals to the production apparatus, for the formation of productive forces" (Foucault, 2015: 196; see also, Pandolfi, 2016). It is equally true that, as we have seen on several occasions, Marx also investigates different configurations of power, within which, however, the command over labour and the discipline that innervates it are not just a local technique and, above all, are for him already political, because their function is not so much to individualize power, but to enforce and make productive on a social scale the relationship that establishes it.[17] Exploitation defines a specific subordination that gives society its equally specific historical capitalist determination. Within this mode of production, different processes of subjectivation are certainly possible and present that continuously violate the different thresholds of power that constitute society. As we have seen from his analysis of English and French constitutional history, however, the capital relation is for Marx the 'apparatus' that establishes the conditions that determine the practical ways in which all other power relations are also suffered and contested (Mezzadra, 2018). The capital

---

17 A growing literature investigates the relationship between Marx and Foucault (see Marsden, 1999; Leonelli, 2010; Dardot and Laval, 2012: 225–226; Laval et al., 2015; Macherey, 2015; Negri, 2016). In my opinion, rather than attempting to highlight the convergences that do exist, it would be more a question of showing the productivity of the constant tension that, as it were, brings them closer together and distances them apart also in relation to the analysis of power.

relation does not rank the different subjugations on a scale of importance, but determines the regime of historicity (Hartog, 2015) of the different forms of their subjugation, making it unthinkable to overcome them separately without questioning the overall form of capitalist domination. Several feminist theorists have clearly grasped this historical and systematic connection between capitalism and patriarchy, a form of subjection that historically preceded it, but which exists by constantly renewing the intertwining of subjection and exploitation (Spivak, 1996a, 1996b; Mies, 1998; Mohanty, 2003).

On the other hand, criticizing Adam Smith, Marx argued that capital

> is not only ... the command over labour. It is essentially the command over unpaid labour. All surplus value, whatever particular form (profit, interest, or rent), it may subsequently crystallise into, is in substance the materialization of unpaid labour. The secret of the self-expansion of capital resolves itself into having the disposal of a definite quantity of other people's unpaid labour.
>
> MARX, 1867: 534

Command emphasizes a split and a separation and is the presupposition by virtue of which the link between individuals at work – their social bond – is expropriated so that they find it opposed as an extraneous force that constrains their cooperative action. "Their union into one single productive body and the establishment of a connexion between their individual functions, are matters foreign and external to them, are not their own act, but the act of the capital that brings and keeps them together". Their reciprocal connection is opposed "in the shape of a preconceived plan of the capitalist, and practically in the shape of the authority of the same capitalist, in the shape of the might of a foreign will, which subjects their activity to his aims" (Marx, 1867: 336–337; see also, Lohmann, 1991: 127–129). Through command, this indifferent power establishes the conditions for the exploitation of cooperation and not only of the performance of the individual worker and, precisely for this reason, it must take on a form that Marx calls despotic.

CHAPTER 5

Despotism and Difference

1   Authority and Slavery

For Marx, authority does not derive from a process of authorization. Rather, it is the position of supremacy established by the ownership of the means of production that allows for the monopolization of the decision on cooperation. It is not defined by the personal qualities of those who have it, but by the position they find assigned to them within the process of the reproduction of society. It is the personal moment of a systemically produced domination. "The idea of some socialists that we need capital but not capitalists, is therefore completely false" (Marx, 1857–1861a: 436). The capital relation requires the presence of a personalization of ownership and thus of command that is subjectively opposed to the worker. Despite the bureaucratization of management functions that Marx clearly recognizes within it, this relationship cannot evolve into an impersonal system based solely on functional differentiation.[1] For Marx, domination is not a contingent social deficiency that society can eliminate by evolving:[2] it is a constitutive element of it and societalization is the process that shows the already present unsustainability of what Marx calls the subsumption of labour to capital. The two forms of subsumption that Marx distinguishes correspond to the two competing modes that capital assumes as a specific configuration of power. While formal subsumption is characterized by the command that individually invests everyone who is put to work, real subsumption is capital as global domination, which determines the whole movement of society. Marx writes very clearly that "the capitalist supervises the worker, controls the functioning of labour power as an action belonging to him" (Marx, 1861–1863b: 93). He supervises each stage of the labour process and ensures that the most profitable combination of labour and means of production is achieved. "In all these aspects, the labour process and thereby labour and the worker himself come under the control of capital, under its command. I call this the *formal subsumption* of the labour process under capital". This is the power relation that distinguishes the capital relation from earlier ones, for

---

1 Without any reference to Marx, this perception also seems to surface in the later Luhmann (1999).
2 Dardot and Laval (2012: 592–595) rightly see in this opposition the "strategic sense" of the Marxian concept of civil war.

instance that between the shop master and his apprentices, because here it is still the valorization of capital that is in the foreground and not the production of some more or less sought-after use-value. With respect to this condition, the specifically capitalist mode of production presents itself as the subsumption of individuals in society as a whole, as their subsumption based on the extraction of relative as well as absolute surplus value. What is important for Marx is that "the concrete social character of labour present itself as the character and quality of capital", and this "changes the mode of production itself" (Marx, 1861–1863b: 261–262).

In this process, the presence of technological and organizational innovations, as well as the increasingly decisive presence of science within the production process, do not establish a new configuration of power. Both forms of the subsumption of labour to capital are in fact "a *relation of compulsion*, … which does not rest on any personal relations of domination and dependence, but simply arises out of the difference in economic functions" (Marx, 1861–1863c: 426). They cannot therefore be separated and opposed, nor are they stages in the internal evolution of the capital relation. First, every individual put to work prioritizes and necessarily experiences formal subsumption, however much his existence may be increasingly dominated by real subsumption. Moreover, the formal subsumption of labour to capital signals once again the constitutive action of anachronism within the capitalist mode of production. Its constant presence as poor labour is not a remnant of the past destined to be overcome by the movement of capital itself. As we have already seen with regard to Marx's method, it must be reiterated that here "even categories belonging to earlier epochs of production receive a specifically distinct character – an historical character – on the basis of a different mode of production" (Marx, 1861–1863b: 313).[3] The specific historicity of capital is established precisely in the governance of these different temporalities (Bensaïd, 2002),[4] in which the constitutive anachronism – the dominance of dead and past labour over living and present labour (Neocleous, 2005: 47 ff) – determines the fundamental sign of the epoch and for Marx the necessity of its overcoming. The movements of labour power constantly challenge the ability of capital to present itself as "an automatically active character" (Marx, 1867: 164), counteracting the tendency

---

3 "The operation of formal subsumption set up the temporal structure of every present, through its mission to appropriate what it found useful in prior practices and procedures" (Harootunian, 2015: 13).

4 By contrast, Tomba (2013) contrasts a pre-modern problematic with the unresolved problems of even Marxian modernity. Negri (1982: 253 ff) contains considerations that are still relevant today although he overemphasizes the weight of real subsumption.

whereby "capital must increase in value and assume social dimensions; hence it must shed any individual character" (Marx, 1861–1863c: 440).

This tendency towards the fading of the individual as an almost irresistible movement accompanying the reproduction of capital is clearly present in Marx's analysis of the capitalist mode of production. It is no coincidence that, with regard to the second volume of *Capital*, Engels wrote that there is "nothing at all out of which to fabricate catch-words and orations" (Engels to Karl Kautsky, 18/09/1883: 58), because Marx describes the tendency of capital to make itself autonomous from the relationship that produces it and to present itself as "value generating value" (Marx, 1885: 88; see also, Arthur and Reuten, 1998; Fine and Saad-Filho, 2004: 61 ff; Bihr, 2010). It continues to depend both on the societal might of money and on the command by which, with or without the supplement of law, labour power produces value but seems to exceed both in order to present itself as the "übergreifendes Subjekt", which means either the "subject that leads back to unity" or the "dominant subject", the sole sovereign subject of the whole process – roughly translated in English as "the active factor" (Marx, 1867: 165). The enlarged reproduction of capital shows that power as violence and the discipline of the working day do indeed serve the immediate ends of those who exercise them, but are above all instrumental for a domination through which productive capital presents itself in forms that are not immediately productive of value yet functional to valorization. In any case, what matters is the discovery of capital as an autonomous movement so complex and articulated that it can forget the labour power that keeps it in motion. "Capital as self-expanding value embraces not only class relations, a society of a definite character resting on the existence of labour in the form of wage labour" (Marx, 1885: 110). It is also a cyclical process that, with an inexhaustible and unrelated movement, not only tends to autonomize itself from the relationship with labour power, but also ends up being indifferent to the fate of individual capitalists. The more frequent and violent are what Marx calls

> revolutions in value become, the more does the automatic movement of the now independent value operate with the elemental force of a natural process, against the foresight and calculation of the individual capitalist, the more does the course of normal production become subservient to abnormal speculation, and the greater is the danger that threatens the existence of the individual capitals.
> MARX, 1885: 111

Capital thus shows itself to be indifferent to any individual expression, even though evidently the split that constitutes it distributes the risk of this indifference in radically different ways. Actually, the capital that moves is surplus value accumulated despite the antagonism of labour power. It materially consists of money, stocks, and machinery that make participation in society otherwise profitable for those who can access it.

As we have already pointed out, Marx uses the term *Träger* to refer indifferently to people and things that literally become bearers for the movement of capital. Being a "partial individual, [a] bearer [*Träger*] pure and simple of a detailed societal function" makes a considerable difference, however, whether one has access to money only as a consumer or instead as a bearer of capital. Through the accumulated surplus value, capital reproduces its domination over society in an extended manner despite and sometimes also because of its contrast to labour power. From this point of view, accumulated surplus value is an autonomous reserve of power that can be invested in new and different spheres against all opposition. "Surplus value thus congeals into a hoard and in this form constitutes latent money capital" (Marx, 1885: 84). The problem is constantly to value this reserve, i.e., to establish conditions of domination such that it can actually be productive. This is precisely why in the extended reproduction of capital its power turns against all individual expression to become domination, capital's hegemony over the whole of society and its reproduction.

Marx clarifies the relative autonomy of capital with respect to the social relation that produces it by speaking of a double relation between capital and surplus value and between capital and profit. These are clearly not different and separate relations, but in the first case capital and labour immediately appear in their mutual tension and constitutive antagonism, whereas in the second, "*the capital* appears *as a relation to itself*, a relation in which it, as the original sum of value, is distinguished from a new value which it generated" (Marx, 1894: 52). The capitalist now does not have to deal with labour power, but necessarily with other capitalists, or rather with the commodities they have produced, selling his commodities "at prices which yield the average profit, i.e., at prices of production. In this form capital becomes conscious of itself as a *societal might* in which every capitalist participates proportionally to his share in the total societal capital" (Marx, 1894: 194). Thus, a situation is produced in which different tensions are added together that are difficult to govern. Labor power finds before it only the indifference of money as capital, which has no substantial interest in the quality of its reproduction. Capitalists live among themselves in a regime of competition that ultimately determines the amount of their profits. In this situation, of which interest-producing capital, the primal form of finance capital, is the highest expression, both fundamental figures of the capitalist mode of production are obliged to relentless movement. Capital is forced to constantly move to the sectors and places where the profit margin is highest, just as labour "must submit to being transformed in accordance with the requirements of capital and to being transferred from one sphere of production to another" (Marx, 1894: 194). The mobile condition of both individual capital and labour power is constitutive of the society of capital, which, however, is established at the crossroads of two indifferences, that of the capitalists towards labour power and that of the latter towards the concrete conditions of its employment. It is precisely this situation, however, that brings capital back to the fore as a specific power relation, because each individual capitalist is necessarily interested in the reproduction of the general conditions that allow for the realization of his profit. It is thus shown that "the individual capitalist, as well as the capitalists as a whole, take direct part in the exploitation of the total working class by the totality of capital and in the degree of that exploitation, not only out of general class sympathy, but also for direct economic reasons" (Marx, 1894: 195).

This depersonalization based on the increasingly evident evanescence of the individual is the specific form of the domination of capital. Society presents itself in the paradoxical form of a society without individuals. "Capital comes more and more to the fore as a societal might, whose agent [*Functionär*] is the capitalist. This societal might no longer stands in any possible relation to that which the labour of a single individual can create" (Marx, 1894: 263). This bureaucratization of capital, about which in his description Marx seems to echo what he had written about Napoleon III's administrative machine, does not so much concern procedures as the substance of the relationship. It does not erase the antagonism, because it is already present in material wealth, in its private appropriation, which immediately "commands the labour of others, claims to appropriate the labour of others" (Marx, 1894: 354), showing that command is a constitutive part of the overall configuration of power, being both its condition and its consequence.[5] Precisely at the moment when the capitalist pretends to present himself as an official of capital, as one who applies its natural law, carrying out a simply organizational activity, Marx identifies in this apparently neutral relationship a specific expression of domination. Resorting once again to Aristotle, he emphasizes that mere surveillance work adds nothing to the relationship, while the slave owner "proves himself such not by obtaining slaves ... but in employing slaves". It is this latter position that is decisive for the power that is exercised.

---

5 "Command interacts with power, but it is not power but is its consequence and condition at the same time. ... Private property also appears to be a condition of command" (Alquati, 1977: 82).

Aristotle says in just so many words that domination [*Herrschaft*] in the political and economic fields imposes the functions of government [*Herrschen*] upon the those in power [*Gewalthaber*], and hence that they must, in the economic field, know the art of consuming labour force.[6]

For Marx, the availability of labour power is thus inseparable from its government and, precisely for this reason, as we have anticipated, slavery is once again affirmed as the political truth of wage labour as well, despite the difference in the modalities of exploitation. This is done by significantly linking ancient slavery to American slavery, through the words of the slave lawyer Charles O'Conor, who claims that rule over the slave is legitimate as compensation due to the master "for the labour and talent employed in governing him and rendering him useful to himself and to the society". The deep conviction that the slave is incapable of independently understanding his own usefulness thus serves to legitimize a separate function that is ostensibly performed for the overall good of society. Governing labour power thus means doing the society's good even while sacrificing the immediate profit of the individual. It is precisely for this reason that Marx considers this paradigm not limited to personal slavery alone, since "the wage labourer, like the slave, must have a master who puts him to work and rules over him [*regieren*]. And assuming the existence of this relationship of lordship and servitude [*Herrschafts- und Knechtschaftsverhältnis*], it is quite proper to compel the wage labourer to produce his own wages and also the wages of supervision" (Marx, 1894: 383–384).

The expression that in the *Grundrisse* was reserved for slave and servile labour now becomes the presupposition of wage labour, while the depersonalization of capitalist command, whose increasing relevance Ure had already identified, does not change the capital relation, but shows that the governance of labour does not concern the activity to be performed, but arises "out of an antithesis, out of the domination of capital over labour" (Marx, 1894: 384), i.e., that it is class behaviour and the movement of capital itself that imposes the presence of figures in which the function of command and control becomes autonomous to the point of rendering the very figure of the capitalist operationally superfluous. Although they are not instrumental for the immediate

---

6 Haug (2006: 102) speaks of "powers of determination" that establish the range of action of subjects, and indeed subjugate them while making them act. "The first is the relatively 'gentler' power of the immanent laws of capitalist production that allows the individual's capacity to act to be shown because one understands those laws. This power acts from within. The second power comes from outside, from market competition, and is the 'hard power' that ultimately threatens economic demise".

production of profit, they are nevertheless increasingly indispensable for governing that antagonism, to the point that in the industrial system the fundamental figures are no longer "the industrial capitalists, but the industrial *managers*" (Marx, 1894: 386). The separation of "the wages of management" and "the profits of enterprise" becomes a constant that, once again, points to both the bureaucratization of production and the possibility of deepening the reasons for antagonism by moving into non-capitalist modes of production. Such a transformation does not have exclusively technical-organizational causes. To explain it, Marx resorts to an analogy and a completely political vocabulary that not only reveal its irresistibility, but also its continuity with the configuration of power that imposes itself on society as a complex.

> Just as in despotic states, supervision and all-round interference by the government involves both the performance of common activities arising from the nature of all communities, and the specific functions arising from the antithesis between the government and the mass of the people.
> MARX, 1894: 382

Just as political despotism with its eagerness to rule is the model of capital despotism, so slavery becomes for Marx the political truth of wage labour, this does not produce an overlap either between the political economy of slavery and the capitalist economy or between their respective configurations of power. In the capitalist mode of production, for the immediate producers their own production

> is confronted by the social character of their production in the form of strictly regulating authority and a social mechanism of the labour process organised as a complete hierarchy – this authority reaching its bearers [*Träger*], however, only as the personification of the conditions of labour in contrast to labour, and not as political or theocratic rulers [*Herrscher*] as under earlier modes of production – among the bearers of this authority, the capitalists themselves, who confront one another only as commodity owners, there reigns complete anarchy within which the social interrelations of production assert themselves only as an overwhelming natural law in relation to individual free will.
> MARX, 1894: 867–868

It is thus made clear that the anarchy of the commodity world is only possible because of its political complement, namely the hierarchy of authority inherent in this mode of production, a hierarchy that further belies the claim of the fundamental equality of all individuals. Moreover, the centrality Marx attributes to economic relations is such because it has an immediately political character for him (Mezzadra and Ricciardi, 2002), although authority is not founded according to the classical criteria of history or authorization but depends directly on the position occupied within the societal process of production. The societal character of this authority does not establish its specific sign in relation to that of political authority, but locates its foundation in the material relations between individuals. Finally, since these individuals do not have the possibility of individually modifying the relations in which they are embedded, the form of the latter presents itself as despotic, because it is the result of the expropriation of a collective intelligence that now opposes individuals and their knowledge (Iacono, 2018: 19).

2   Western Despotism

The concept of despotism occupies a central position in Marx's semantics of power. It is the fruit of a complex accumulation of meanings derived from different moments of his political and intellectual militancy and ends up identifying a particular configuration of power in which forms and figures differing in temporality and geographical origin operate to block the processes of subjectivation, that is, to prevent the autonomous action of the subjects to which the history and anthropology of capital is constantly opposed. Although the materials used come from different parts of the globe and have different histories, the Marxian concept of despotism does not aim to establish a hierarchy of 'systems of power', but rather to show the presence of that past and those decentralized geographies in the present history of capital's despotism. Even when naming "Oriental despotism", Marx is fundamentally interested in how a specific relationship prevents the assertion of autonomous power by denying access to history. As a political and polemical term, it is first used by Marx in the knowledge that its obsessive presence in the political debate of eighteenth-century France was a kind of discursive pre-condition for the revolution. This explains his use of it in 1843, when the hopes aroused by Frederick William IV's accession to the throne of Prussia and the consequent confirmation of German backwardness were dissipated. In March of the same year, Marx wrote to Ruge that "the mantle of liberalism has been discarded and the most disgusting despotism in all its nakedness is disclosed to the eyes of the whole world" (Marx, 1843b: 133). Patriotism can no longer mask disappointment in the face of a government that demeans any hope of change. The language used shows all the debt to Feuerbach, as he describes despotism as a system and as personal power that prevents the expression of the universal that should be recognized in every man. "Despotism's sole idea is contempt for man, the dehumanised man, and this idea has the advantage over many others of being at the same time a fact. The despot always sees degraded people [*entwürdigt*]" (Marx, 1843b: 138).

However, it is again in the clash with Hegel that Marx begins to attribute a more immediately political meaning to despotism, increasingly shifting its scope from the state to society. For Hegel, "despotism signifies the condition of lawlessness in general, in which the particular will as such … counts as law (or rather replaces law)". Thus, despotism is not the partial or occasional perversion of state action, but the negation of sovereignty, "specifically under lawful and constitutional conditions as the moment of ideality of the particular spheres and functions" (Hegel, 1991: § 278). Marx reverses this conception. "*Sovereignty* – the idealism of the state" does not only derive from the integration of all existing interests, but depends on the "direct influence from above". Despotism is not a deficiency of the state, the state failing to live up to its concept, but the intensive and non-contingent manifestation of representation. In other words, it is the consequence of the autonomy granted to the representative, who not only produces the unity of the state, but also has the power to act with measures that can be imposed against any opposition and are not defined as despotic simply because they are traced back to the constitutional framework in which they are inscribed. "This ideality", Marx writes, "finds its 'own proper actuality' only when the state is in a 'condition of war or emergency' so that its essential nature is expressed here in this 'condition of war and emergency' of the actual, existing state; whereas its 'peaceful' conditions are just the war and misery of selfishness" (Marx, 1843a: 22). Thus, despotism is inscribed in a sovereignty that finds its ultimate legitimization in the suspension of law in cases of necessity. Marx not only brings despotism back into sovereignty, establishing a continuity between the external war and the war that is 'fought' daily within the state, but also, as the reference to egoism reveals, makes it an ever-available form to be exercised over the conduct of individuals.

In the following decades, however, it becomes clear that Marx's concept of despotism brings together a broader set of meanings largely already present in its complex use in the eighteenth century, when it is constructed at the intersection of different discursive regimes that at once invest the state constitution, the definition of the mode of production, colonial command, the patriarchal family, and racism. Marx traverses practically all of them, with the significant exception of the last one, which is, however, absolutely clear in Montesquieu, who explicitly posits a lack of rationality at the basis of despotism due to a lack of understanding of the laws that govern both society and nature: "When the savages of Louisiana want fruit, they cut down the tree and gather the fruit. There you have despotic government" (Montesquieu, 1989: 59; see also, Boesche, 1990). Throughout the eighteenth century and beyond, if Montesquieu is an almost obligatory point of reference for the discourse on despotism and its critique, then Kant announces the connection between the form of the state and the mode of production. Reflecting on the power of analogy and symbol, he in fact writes that

> a monarchical state is represented by a body with a soul if it is ruled in accordance with laws internal to the people, but by a mere machine (like a handmill) if it is ruled by a single absolute will, but in both cases it is represented only symbolically. For between a despotic state and a handmill there is, of course, no similarity, but there is one between the rule for reflecting on both and their causality.
> KANT, 2000: 226

The analogy reveals the intimate political intention that presides over the discourse on despotism, i.e., its constituting the opposite of the regime it is intended to indicate as legitimate. The analogy establishes a criterion of legitimacy that can be based on time, when despotism is relegated to the past of social production, or on the opposition between a political body that is alive because it possesses a 'soul', as popular laws evidently are for Kant, and another that functions instead mechanically thanks to a natural force. The driving force of the state thus becomes the foundation from which to judge the state itself, as the cause of its constant movement. If, therefore, the "worst conceivable *despotism*" is that constitution that "cancels every freedom of the subjects, who retain no rights at all" (Kant, 1974: 59), this is possible by virtue of the simultaneously physical and political semantics of the concept of force. Thanks to it, in fact, it is possible to distinguish the constellation given by "law and force without freedom (despotism)" from that which Kant attributes to civil constitutions proper to the republic: "force with freedom and law" (Kant, 2006: 235).

The concept of force is also central to Marx, who however does not use the reference to driving force as an analogy of political form, but as a kind of metonymy to characterize different social forms. "The hand-mill gives you society with the feudal lord; the steam-mill, society with the industrial capitalist" (Marx, 1847b: 166). Although without an explicit reference to Kant, this constellation also remains central to Marx, for whom despotism is a combination of law, force, and freedom, although these three moments are arranged differently depending on the contexts in which it is analysed. In the production process, despotism presides over the application of the 'natural laws' of capitalism thanks to the capitalist's force, which is expressed in his command or autocracy through contractual freedom. However, it is once again the societal dimension that shows the global deployment of a concept that, despite often taking as its reference the so-called 'Oriental despotism', ends up indicating a form of subjugation that is not specific to Asia, but which, through the description of social and political relations in the colonies, manifests itself globally in the capitalist mode of production and in the power relationship that extends from the factory to the whole of society. In short, the Marxian concept moves from West to West, passing through the East, where it is loaded with political content rather than reference to a specific anthropology. Indeed, he soon abandons even the idea that power in the East is characterized by the rule of a single individual to whom all others are subservient. For Marx, despotism becomes the very form of social relations and not simply the state or government. This conclusion is expressed in the most incisive way by Lemercier de la Rivière's statement: "by the very fact that man is intended to live in a community, he is intended to live under a despotism", which Marx takes up, thus confirming his interest in the integration of state power within society advocated by the Physiocrats (Marx, 1861–1863b: 373). Moreover, it is the latter who, seeing in the centralization and irresistibility of power the only possibility of affirming the necessary reforms, contest Montesquieu's description of Oriental despotism (Zamagni, 2002). Marx is familiar with these critiques, but even more important to him is that of Simon Linguet, who uses the category of despotism in an entirely original way to oppose the centrality now granted to private property, understood as the paradigm of a government that systematically excludes a part of society (Ricciardi, 2012a). According to Linguet: "The spirit of the laws is property" (Marx, 1867: 611; Linguet, 1767: 236), and it is not by chance that law is the first register on which Marx's confrontation with the concept of despotism is articulated.

This is clear in Marx's comparison in 1848 between the Prussian *Landrecht* and the *Code pénal* that emerged from the French revolution. The former is based on a "patriarchal-schoolmasterly despotism" that claims to instruct the citizen in every moment of his life, over which it arrogates the right to constant and unlimited power. Considered a minor, the citizen is faced with an official to whom, like a priest, is owed a respect and submission that goes far beyond his office. By contrast, the situation is completely different in France, where "Napoleonic despotism" strikes to the extent that the power of the state is actually obstructed, if only by offending an official in the exercise of his functions. Outside his office he is "an ordinary member of civil society, without privileges, without special protection" (Marx, 1848m: 309). In any case, for Marx, law lays the foundations for a bureaucratic despotism of which he emphasizes the differences rather than the unbroken continuity, since otherwise it would only lead to the sanction that the "sad result of revolutions" is that "despotism remains despotism" (Marx, 1849e: 356). Despite the undeniable innovations introduced by the revolution, it is clear to Marx that modern sovereignty is not the opposite of despotism. The post-revolutionary French codification itself reveals within it this double genealogy: "a Sovereign who was a democrat commenced, and a Sovereign who was a despot completed" (Marx, 1974: 336). Legal command is thus presented as despotic because the formulation and application of its rules are removed from the possibility of challenge by those who are merely an object of the law.

This specific character Marx attributes to law re-emerges within the despotic exercise of command in the labour process, which is regulated "like a private legislator", so that capital can exercise its "autocracy over his workpeople, unaccompanied by that division of responsibility, in other matters so much approved of by the bourgeoisie" (Marx, 1867: 427). However, the despotism of capital goes beyond the mere discipline imposed on the labour process, showing its societal dimension, so that the relationship on which it is based is made necessary by the very conditions that impose it. The necessity of surrendering one's strength to the conditions occurring in the market "completes the despotism of capital" in the sense that it makes the condition of workers, who are completely dependent on the law of supply and demand to reproduce their existence, "more and more precarious". What Marx calls the "natural law of capitalistic production" is for him the true constitution of the capital relation (Marx, 1867: 634). It establishes a kind of unquestionable fundamental norm that legitimizes the cogency of both autocracy in the labour process and societal domination, creating a subordination to such an extent that Marx used the term *Hörigkeit* (servitude), which invests the person as a whole.

It is also evident that for Marx, it is not possible to produce such subordination solely from the labour process. The process of capital valorization has a societal dimension precisely because it must produce the conditions of its own power far beyond the workplace. For Marx, this implies a constant focus on the mobilization of the mode of production that cannot be considered as the mechanical effect of its structural conditions. It is thus the centrality accorded to social forms that makes it necessary to include in the reference to despotism a broader historical experience that, in keeping with Marx's 'method', although located in the past ends up reappearing even within the capitalist mode of production.[7] In this perspective, when Marx uses the formula "the Asiatic mode

---

7 See Wolin (2016) who, however, points out as a limitation of Marx's discourse the integration of the political and the social, which for Marx is the historical novelty of the capitalist mode of production.

of production" (see Krader, 1975), he is referring to real Indian or Asian events, in order to derive a historical model of domination that unifies ancient despotism with contemporary despotism and which, precisely for this reason, can reappear in European political events and in capitalist domination itself. It is therefore no coincidence that, reconstructing Spanish constitutional history, Marx states that Spanish absolutism represents a particularity within the more general process of centralization of power that takes place in Europe during the early modern age. Monarchical absolutism in Spain does everything to prevent the growth of common interests, thus ending up breaking up society instead of unifying it. It is precisely for this reason that it can be put on the same level as the "Asiatic forms of government", but it cannot be compared with the remaining European absolutism, which for Marx is clearly not comparable with a form of despotism. Despite its despotic trait, however, Spanish absolutism fails to prevent the provinces of the kingdom from maintaining and developing an autonomous political life in the provinces, maintaining their own distinctive symbols, their own laws and customs, their own tax systems. This indifference to the processes of autonomous organization developing in society characterizes what Marx calls Asiatic despotism to indicate a model of organization of government and administration and not a regional specificity based on a particular history or anthropology. "The oriental despotism attacks municipal self-government only when opposed to its direct interests, but is very glad to allow those institutions to continue so long as they take off its shoulders the duty of doing something and spare it the trouble of regular administration" (Marx, 1854: 396). Spain experienced this specific despotism that allowed the survival of those autonomous instances within Spanish society, which Napoleon had to experience painfully and which for Marx are at the heart of the series of revolutionary cycles that still follow one another.

3   Domination and History

Marx is thus interested in a configuration of power, in which the ancient and spatially distant 'model' acts as a metaphor – or rather, acts in a way that Spivak uses the rhetorical figure of catachresis to describe – and ends up determining and clarifying the current form of a relationship of supra- and subordination, in which the drive for recognition tends to be obliterated because what counts is the material difference in power and the distance it establishes. And this also applies to the factory command, in which the "power [*Macht*] of Asiatic and Egyptian kings, Etruscan theocrats, &c, has in modern society been transferred to the capitalist, whether he be an isolated, or as in joint-stock companies, a overall capitalist" (Marx, 1867: 339). This impossible recognition is another constitutive feature of Marx's concept of despotism. From this point of view, it aims to produce and maintain a kind of detachment from history in its subordinates, which must unfold without their involvement. They are enclosed in a restricted sphere with certain rules that do not, however, challenge the general domain within which they move. The absence of recognition is possible precisely because they lack this tension to assert their position. So not even in India is Oriental despotism a reality any longer, since it is now the result of "European despotism, planted upon Asiatic despotism, by the British East India Company" (Marx, 1853f: 126). There is thus a caesura in the seemingly unbroken continuity of the historical conditions of the Indian subcontinent, which essentially coincides with its forced insertion into the world market. What "the British intruder" has broken is what Marx calls the "village system" (Marx, 1853f: 128), i.e., a specific system of communities on which Marx's judgement is politically merciless, because

> we must not forget that these idyllic village-communities, inoffensive though they may appear, had always been the solid foundation of Oriental despotism, that they restrained the human mind within the smallest possible compass, making it the unresisting tool of superstition, enslaving it beneath traditional rules, depriving it of all grandeur and historical energies.
> MARX, 1853f: 132[8]

For Marx, so-called 'Oriental despotism' is possible because there is a tension to alienate oneself from history, to deny oneself the possibility of acting as individuals on the world-historical plane, and this is why he argues that village communities not only tolerated castes and slavery, but also that "subjugated man to external circumstances instead of elevating man the sovereign of circumstances, [and] transformed a self-developing social state into never changing natural destiny". One can certainly discuss the historical relevance of Marx's judgement and how well-founded the link between community and despotism in India is,[9] but it does not manifest a particular Orientalism of discourse, not least because it assumes that only "a fundamental revolution in the

---

[8] On Marx's sources and the internal movement of his research in relation to Asia and the constitution of the world market, see the valuable work by Pradella (2015).

[9] Chakrabarty (2000: 47 ff) imputes to the Marxian project the tension to homogenize differences. Kaiwar (2014) has a radically opposite assessment.

social state of Asia" will make the global transformation of the capitalist mode of production possible (Marx, 1853f: 132).

However, Marx is anything but inattentive to the profound changes sweeping India, as we can witness in the series of articles in 1857 that he dedicates to the Great Mutiny, in which the reference to despotism disappears in the face of the attention with which he follows the revolt of the sepoys that shakes the British colonial power, forcing the reconfiguration of the political power. On the other hand, Marx's judgement of the Indian communities is taken up again in *Capital*, albeit less emphatically, as an example of a prehistory of the division of labour, when the aim was to reproduce daily life in an orderly way, without creating the conditions in which "each bee has freed itself from connexion with the hive" (Marx, 1867: 339). These communities are the basis of despotism for Marx because they are the opposite of the social form of independent cooperating individuals. They are the opposite of the "'social' movement [that] has been started both in the West and in the East" in the 1860s with the anti-slavery revolts in the United States and the push for the emancipation of the peasantry in Russia (Marx to Engels, 11/01/1860: 4). Without being directly linked to the factory regime, this movement opposes despotic rule, its tendency to make the past the dominant historical dimension despite its constant dynamic. In the specific Marxian understanding, despotism is not an Oriental peculiarity, as is clear from the similar considerations he makes both in relation to premodern communities in Europe and even more incisively with regard to the organization of labour in medieval guilds. The latter, according to Marx, were constitutively the place of a "special development", oriented towards its own inexhaustible reproduction and consequently denied "the need for universality, the tendency towards an integral development of the individual begins to be felt. The automatic workshop wipes out specialists and craft-idiocy" (Marx, 1847b: 190). The Greek word *idiotes* stands for private man, one who thinks only of his own, indifferent to what happens in the larger world. As much in relation to the Indian communities as to the medieval guilds in Europe, Marx seems to have in mind this 'privatization of life'[10] as a constitutive element of a despotism in which the adjective Asian ends up decaying in the face of the global phenomenon being described.

It is no coincidence that the reference to despotism based on the distinction between public and private, between collective and individual, returns in Marx's last writings, when he studies the origin of the family and property and criticizes the position of Sir Henry Sumner Maine, who recognizes

---

10 With little more than occasional reference to Marx, Curtis (2013) identifies this process.

paternal power as the personal and necessary core of all power. The modern monogamous family is primarily based on the exclusion of women from the possibility of ownership, and for Marx it "contains the germ not only of servitus (slavery) but also serfdom ... It contains in miniature all the antagonisms within itself which are later broadly developed in society and its State" (Marx, 1974: 120). Marx's overall reconstruction takes place around two fundamental points. First, the Jewish and Roman patriarchal family is a historical exception and therefore the model of social relations it outlines cannot be considered invariable and absolute. Consequently, precisely because private appropriation and personal domination are only present in germ in that type of family, they cannot be regarded as a kind of universal anthropological necessity. For Marx, historically there is neither an urge to dominate nor an instinct to possess. Instead, monogamy as an institution ensures the orderly transfer of property from the father to the children, since with the dominion he exercises over the mother, the father also exercises the power to determine who the legitimate children are. In fact, Marx often criticizes reconstructions that deny any freedom for women within these relationships, emphasizing the degree of freedom they could enjoy even in the Roman family. Likewise, he is not interested in reconstructing the absolute character of the right to property. As is already evident in the pages of the *Grundrisse* devoted to the so-called "forms preceding capitalist production" (Marx, 1857–1861a: 399–439), Marx's interest is not so much directed towards identifying a path that dialectically ensures the overcoming of the present state of things. Rather, it aims to identify the historical existence of other modes of possession that were not based on private appropriation. The importance of the *Ethnological Notebooks* lies precisely in this use of anthropology as the material history of humans (Patterson, 2009) to show the radically historical character of what seems to have always existed. Only in this way can the antecedents of the present not be used to legitimize it, just as they do not represent improbable alternatives in the past, but show the 'dead ends', the defeated and obliterated institutions, the modes of possession that persist as traces within a mode of production that claims to be universal and homogeneous.

At the same time, this work of historical unravelling of anthropology shows how despotism is not a residue that can be confined to the past, but the fully societal form of an alienation that can no longer be conceived as alienation from a generically human essence, because it is the effect of submission to a domination that prevents access to a wealth that every worker also contributes to producing. Through his own action he "creates wealth as a *power* alien to him and ruling over him" (Marx, 1861–1863b: 171). This specific societal dimension of alienation as submission to an overall power is already present in the private appropriation of social wealth, i.e., in the possibility of exercising individual power over that same wealth (Cowling, 2006). Marx's anthropological research thus investigates the social process of constituting this relationship of societal power that necessarily passes through its private moments, showing its historicity and thus its contingency. Private property is affirmed at a certain point in societal evolution, but the fact that there have historically been alternative forms of appropriation establishes for Marx the condition of possibility that further different ones will also be possible in the future. "*The element of property*, which has controlled society to a great extent *during* the *comparatively short period of civilization*, [gave] mankind *despotism, imperialism, monarchy, privileged classes* [and] finally *representative democracy*" (Marx, 1974: 233). Thus, property as a societal relationship underlies forms of political power that, while varying significantly over time, never manage to emancipate themselves from their generative core.

The question is therefore what this core of power – which Sir Henry Sumner Maine claims to find in both Roman and Hindu families – actually does to preserve both property and the political patriarchalism that goes with it.[11] And this is an absolutely crucial issue for Marx, because Maine, as it were, reverses the disposition of despotism by making it the attribute of collective forms of property and social relations, so that the emergence of modern individuality is seen as the slow emancipation from the despotic domination that the group exercised over the individual in times that automatically predate civilization. For Maine, the power of the father is the natural one: "this quite natural function of the Chief of the gens, further of the tribe, natural because he is its chief, (and is theoretically always 'elected') appears as 'artificial' and 'mere administrative authority', whereas the arbitrariness of the modern paterfamilias is just as 'artificial' as the private family itself from the archaic standpoint" (Marx, 1974: 42). And, precisely because the private family is the model, it is also equally consequential for Maine to show that women are excluded from ownership in all social formations that have reached a certain degree of development. When the "philistine Englishman Maine conceives of the whole primitive question as 'despotism of groups over the members composing them'" (Marx, 1974: 326), he simultaneously establishes two intertwining lines of evolution: civilization consists in the progressive affirmation of the individual described by Bentham in his utilitarian relationship with others, while at the same time the paternal

---

11   Various studies now show that the ways in which women are present in Marx's texts are at least more complex than what may appear from some expressions in which he seems to legitimize sex roles in an ahistorical and therefore impolitic way. See Brown (2012), Carver (2013), Cappuccilli and Ferrari (2023).

power that opposes and individualizes itself with respect to the group also becomes the model for every possible form of political power. According to Marx, this inversion by Maine is instrumental for his idea of sovereignty as an exclusive power from which the mass of individuals must be systematically excluded.

"Hobbes wants to fathom the origin of the state (*Government* and *Sovereignty*)" (Marx, 1974: 329) because he needs to provide an urgent response to the struggles of his time. His science, like that of Machiavelli and Linguet for Marx, responds to a political necessity. Maine, on the other hand, by separating science and politics in the wake of John Austin, ends up taking the presence of the state for granted, somehow naturalizing it, making it the necessary manifestation of public power (Piccinini, 2003: 112 ff). Separating science and politics literally means abstracting the state from the conditions of its production and thus making it something external and superior to society, while the "apparently supreme and autonomous existence of the state itself is only apparent" (Marx, 1974: 329). The state is thus not a historical object, although its history is told, because the state's past is always regarded as the obvious and natural presupposition of the present.[12] The consequence of this process of abstraction is to relegate despotism to a different space and time of the configuration of power of the capitalist mode of production, whereas for Marx it arises from societal relations and is therefore necessarily also present in the state and in the law that represents the universal structure of its order. It is no coincidence that Marx had opposed empirical collisions to the Hegelian claim to mean the whole of reality from the very law of the state. In a statement that is in many ways programmatic, he writes in the *Grundrisse*: "the really difficult point to be discussed here is how the relations of production as legal relations enter into uneven development" (Marx, 1857–1861a: 46). The example given by Marx is the United States and Europe, but the argument can evidently also apply to other areas in which legal relations express differential power relations. When the capitalist mode of production becomes globally dominant, law is constantly able to mediate the differences within it. And this is clearly not an occasional and transitory fact, but constitutive of this social formation (Wainwright, 2008).

---

12   On the State as a historical object, see Schiera (2004; 2007).

4   The Subversion of Power

Already in *Capital*, Marx had explained the historical origin of these differences as part of the process of establishing the capitalist mode of production, showing how this process was not the result of an ordered system of individual merits. It is not determined by trade as a mechanism of order between different nations, by the savings and diligent labour of some individuals that established the legal title to their ownership, but by the violence that accompanied the so-called original accumulation. Once again, however, for Marx, law is not the opposite of violence, i.e., that which prevents its action. Rather, violence is the complement of law, i.e., that which enables its systematic vigour, so that the history of power as *Gewalt* takes place on a double stage that is both conceptual and geographical. Not unlike what happens between the spheres of circulation and production, the violent coercion that dominates in the latter is possible precisely because law regulates the former. While for the "the tender annals of political economy", the means that legitimize the accumulation of wealth have always been "right and 'labour'", it is indisputable that "in actual history ... conquest, enslavement, robbery, murder, briefly, force, play the great part" (Marx, 1867: 705). This double process of consolidation of law and violence took place in Europe to produce the formally free labourer with an additional burden of violence in the portions of the globe placed by the Treaty of Cateau-Cambresis beyond the so-called line of friendship, beyond which no peace was envisaged (Mattingly, 1963). Beyond this line, there was no need for the legally obliged free labourer and therefore force applied, not as an exception to the law, but as a normal condition of its global validity. Exception and normality referred to the different conditions that had to be subsumed into the capitalist mode of production.

For Marx, the constellation of power from which capitalism arises on the global level is established by a unitary process traversed by differences: for the first time in seventeenth-century England "the colonies, the national debt, the modern mode of taxation, and the protectionist system" (Marx, 1867: 739) are really presented as subsystems of a global social system that exists for the exploitation of labour power, for the "usurpation of the common lands" and thus for the assertion of "private property, as the antithesis to social, collective property" (Marx, 1867: 748). In the colonial system, violence is used as "brute force", but all subsystems make use of "the might of the state [*Staatsmacht*], the concentrated and organised violence [*Gewalt*] of society" (Marx 1867: 739), which originally serves to impose the domination of capital, but which always remains a viable option precisely because it is not a product of state action, but one of the ways in which society imposes the power relationship that historically determines it. Rather than the famous vaguely historicist definition of violence as the midwife of history, the historically very precise idea that it is an "economic power", used "exceptionally" and in places legally defined as "exceptional" such as the colonies, while "in the ordinary run of things, the labourer can be left to the 'natural laws of production'" (Marx, 1867: 726). Violence is not merely a state monopoly, but a societal production for the management of which the state, immediately integrated into the overall cycle of capital, acts to guarantee both the different right and the natural right of capital. It is therefore also the protagonist of the substantial connection between exploitation in the colonies and exploitation in the metropolises, just as there is an economic nexus in what otherwise appear to be mere power relations between states. If "the veiled slavery of the wage workers in Europe needed, for its pedestal, slavery pure and simple in the new world" (Marx, 1867: 747), then states were charged with making this societal necessity possible. It is no coincidence that, while British society disciplined labour power by all available means so that it would not escape the command of capital, with the 1713 Treaty of Utrecht the United Kingdom pledged to supply the Spanish colonies with 4800 slaves per year until 1743. For Marx, the historical and systematic character of societal violence establishes a kind of invariant of capitalist accumulation and, at the same time, an ever-available instrument of capital's despotism.

Then, suddenly, the Commune seems to be the unexpected verification of the possibility of affecting this long history. Marx defends the gamble of the Communards who from 18 March to 28 May 1871 dared to challenge the orderly reproduction of society.[13] On 15 April 1871, Ludwig Kugelmann wrote to him predicting a dramatic defeat of the experiment, which would weigh heavily on the struggle of the proletariat, which in his opinion had more "need of enlightenment [*Aufklärung*] than of armed struggle" (Marx, 1976: 165). The failure could not have been blamed on chance, because it was exactly the attitude that Marx had stigmatized as petit-bourgeois in *18 Brumaire*. In his reply, Marx denies that this historical parallel is possible, but above all states "world history would indeed be very easy to make if the struggle were taken up only on condition of infallibly favourable chances". This attitude would only be the result of a mystique of history that claims to annul all randomness. Instead, for Marx there are contingencies of a different kind that condition the evolution of universal history in one sense or another: "acceleration and delay" both depend on personal variables, such as the occasional quality of the leaders of a movement, and on objective factors, such as the situation created by the

---

13   On the events leading up to the Commune see Cervelli (2015).

Franco-Prussian war that the Communards exploited. What is not contingent is for Marx the significance that the Commune will have in any case because, regardless of its outcome, it represents a turning point in the history of the class struggle. With the Commune "a new point of departure of world-historic importance has been gained" (Marx to Kugelmann, 17/04/1871: 136–137). With it also begins a phase of Marx's political reflection that grasps the political as an interruption of the capitalist process of the subsumption of labour to capital. The case and opportunity seized by the Parisian revolutionaries show the political as a practical critique of society.

As early as 1868, in another letter to Kugelmann, Marx already criticized Wilhelm Liebknecht's use of the conceptual pair 'state and society'. Throughout the nineteenth century in Germany, thanks to Lorenz von Stein, it had been not only one of the most important points of arrival of the new science of society (Chignola, 2004) but also one of the constituent articulations of the German 'bourgeois laboratory' (Schiera, 1987). Marx thus wonders how one can "have such things published as, for instance, *Society and State*, in which '*the societal*' [*das Gesellschaftliche*] (and that's a fine category too!) is treated as the secondary, and '*the political*' [*das Politische*] as the essential" (Marx to Kugelmann, 5/12/1868: 175).[14] Marx denies the separate and autonomous character of the two spheres, showing and criticizing the ways in which that distinction is articulated in the modern state. The struggle of the Commune is important precisely because it goes beyond the state sphere, showing the possibility of breaking the link between political power and societal might. For this to be possible, it is necessary to rethink the modes of politics so as to change the conditions under which economic confrontation occurs in society. It is no coincidence that Marx repeatedly speaks of the economic emancipation of labour, that is, of changing the objective structures that produce the proletariat. In his analysis of that experience, which is also a political defence against everything that was written against it in Europe after its defeat, Marx takes up the title of his first writing on 1848, but now the *Class struggles in France* become a *Civil War* that is part of that secular war for the reconfiguration of power that culminated in the struggle for the limitation of the working day. At the same time, the Commune is one of the occasions in which Marx, as he will do throughout the last decade of his life, returns to reflecting on the societal dimension of the state, completing the rectification of the position formulated with Engels in the *Manifesto*, in which, as we have seen, the indication was expressed that

---

14   On the constitutive connection of the social and the political in Marx, see Negri (1992: 287–306).

each national proletariat should conquer its own state in order to use it for its own benefit (Balibar, 1974: 65–102). The tension between the international action of the communists and the national conquest of the state is tested by the nationalism that emerged even among the socialists on opposing sides in the Franco-Prussian war. Now the Marxian conviction is that "the *working class* alone could offer active resistance to the national swindle" (Marx to Engels, 3/8/1870: 31). The Commune thus catalyses a whole series of tensions accumulated in Marx's reflection on power, allowing them to be brought into focus in the face of the subjective contestation of the objective structures of society that that same reflection had identified.

"What is the Commune, that sphinx so tantalizing to the bourgeois mind?" In the Commune, power is directly at stake, "but the working class cannot simply lay hold of the ready-made State machinery, and wield it for its own purposes". To verify this impossibility, Marx traces the entire history of the modern state in France from the Great Revolution to the Second Empire, showing how the different configurations of power produced its ever-deeper integration into society. This means that the "political character" of the state changes and it becomes the instrument through which the ruling classes try to respond to the antagonism that increasingly characterizes society itself (Marx, 1871a: 328–329). Already in the *Manifesto*, Engels and Marx had written that in a classless society "public power will lose its political character" (Marx and Engels, 1848: 505). Now Marx reiterates that this character corresponds to a line of disunity that runs through and constitutes society, and that it has historically marked the history of the state. It is precisely for this reason that the "State power assumed more and more the character of the national power of capital over labour, of a public force organized for social enslavement, of an engine of class despotism". This same state, however, was also to perform the function of regulating the internal conflicts of the classes in whose name it acted. This double movement culminates in the Second Empire, which creates the political unity by acting as the representative of the overall capitalist. The capacity to dominate its political character is precisely what gives "the State power apparently soaring high above society". The Commune breaks this appearance and shows the political as the interruption of a fictitious unity, the representation of which it prevents. It is thus "the direct antithesis to the Empire" because it is the "positive form" of the social republic of 1848, without, however, the illusions and compromises that had accompanied it. It shows that political unity itself is an illusion (Marx, 1871a: 329–331; see also Althusser, 1978: 416–486).

Instead of what in the *Manifesto*, with full awareness of their limited practical impact, were termed "despotic inroads" (Marx and Engels, 1848: 504), Marx now values measures that practically deconstruct the bureaucratic constitution of the state, first and foremost the abolition of the standing army and its replacement by the National Guard. "This fact was now to be transformed into an institution". It is therefore a matter of making continuous over time all those measures that indicate a different configuration of the relationship between individuals and the power they establish. The bureaucratic machinery of the state should therefore cease to be the *boa constrictor* that prevents autonomous movements from society. Elected and revocable officials show that there is no utopia of a simplified society that can exist without a common administration. The key point is the elimination of government as a separate function: "the destruction of the State power which claimed to be the embodiment of that unity independent of, and superior to, the nation itself, from which it was but a parasitic excrescence" (Marx, 1871a: 331–332). For Marx, the separation of state and administration alludes to a radical transformation of the political-organizational articulation of society. Already in his critique of Bakunin, he made it clear saying that "the distribution of general functions has become a routine matter [*Geschäftssache*] which entails no domination" (Marx, 1874–1875: 519). It thus loses its historically political character.

5   The Power of Difference

This raises the question of what the Commune is not. For Marx, it is not a re-edition of the old federalist municipalism cherished by the Proudhonians. "The antagonism of the Commune against the State power has been mistaken for an exaggerated form of the ancient struggle against over-centralization",[15] which is nothing more than the decentralized reconfiguration of state power, whereas the Commune "breaks the modern State power". If it is not the victory of the commune over the state, neither is it merely the "cheap government", although, by abolishing the army and bureaucracy, it ends up realizing what at least free-trade propaganda had claimed as a political project (Marx, 1871a: 333–334). In fact, a few years earlier Marx had shown how, as the global domination of capital asserts itself, the state becomes if not a commodity like any other, at least a politically valuable one. Public debt, in fact, shows that the state must be at the service of capital and not vice versa. "National debts, i.e., the alienation of the state – whether despotic, constitutional or republican – marked with its stamp the capitalistic era". The state is sold off in pieces, allowing it to make

---

15   By contrast, Dardot and Laval (2012: 309 ff) interpret the Commune precisely in this sense, criticizing Marx for wanting to combine it forcibly with his own theory. Their federalist reading is reiterated in Dardot and Laval (2014).

a profit and in fact authorizing its activities in a way that exceeds its specific political authority. "And with the rise of national debt-making, want of faith in the national debt takes the place of the blasphemy against the Holy Ghost, which may not be forgiven" (Marx, 1867: 742). The legitimation of the state thus finds a mercantile foundation and the public debt becomes the material form of the integration of the state into society, the tangible sign that it is the state of society. For Marx, breaking the power of the state thus also means the breaking of the constitutive link between state and market.

The Commune also "was a thoroughly expansive political form, while all previous forms of government had been emphatically repressive". This annotation is particularly relevant because it signals the breakdown of the relationship that, in the *Jewish Question*, describes a political form conceived as a necessary limit to both individual and collective action. This state is for Marx a paradoxical community of enemies, in which repression is the necessary complement to a freedom that sits dangerously on the border of the freedom of others. For Marx, the Commune is the reversal of this institutionalization of enmity, being "the political form at last discovered under which to work out the economical emancipation of Labour" (Marx, 1871a: 334). It is thus the political form that a social process takes, which does not erase antagonism but redetermines the field of tension in which it occurs. In line with what we have seen regarding Marx's perspective on the dictatorship of the proletariat, the Commune cannot erase the class struggle, but it can redefine the social hierarchies that establish its direction. From this perspective as a specific political-institutional form, it was possible for Marx because "plain working men for the first time dared to infringe upon the Governmental privilege of their 'natural superiors'" (Marx, 1871a: 336). The innovation of the political form thus implied a revolt against the social hierarchy that becomes political power, against the duty of deference that establishes a mechanically accepted nexus between social power and political power. The Commune indicated this possibility of an institutionalization of power also based on the redefinition of social roles, and this is also why, despite the fact that the workers won "only for a time" (Marx and Engels, 1848: 493), "the great social measure of the Commune was its own working existence. Its special measures could but betoken the tendency of a government of the people by the people" (Marx, 1871a: 339). The "working existence" of a different political form replaces the unity of the workers which was referred to in the *Manifesto* as the success they could still achieve despite the temporary nature of their victories.

The formula "government of the people by the people" clearly echoes the speech given by Abraham Lincoln at Gettysburg on 19 November 1863. Compared to the original, it lacks the statement that it also comes "from the people", which would be at least problematic in a government of the working class, the different subject. While this confirms Marx's distance from the people as the foundation of the political order, it also confirms the great impact that the liberation of the slaves had on him already in the writing of *Capital*. Marx drafted the letter that the International sent to Lincoln himself to congratulate him on his re-election as president in the closing phase of the Civil War. In it, it is forcefully argued that the struggle waged against the "Slave Power" must continue until it is wiped out, because in the first place it is a question of whether the immense American territories will be enriched by the "labour of the emigrant or prostituted by the tramp of the slave-driver". The liberation of the slaves, the defeat of "an oligarchy of 300,000 slave-holders", is thus a necessity of the workers, "the true political power of the North". As long as they had considered it a privilege to be able to choose their own master, they had neither been able to access "the true freedom of labour" nor "support their European brethren in their struggle for emancipation" (Marx, 1864c: 19–20; see also, Battistini, 2023). The people that Marx has in mind by quoting Lincoln is composed of the multitude of exploited people who become empowered and as a working-class rebel against the condition of 'slavery' whose historicity capital establishes. Already in *Capital*, he had argued that the freeing of the slaves would lead to the impetuous spread of the struggle to limit the working day to eight hours in the United States (Marx, 1867: 305). It is therefore no coincidence that Marx calls those who, under the leadership of Thiers, bloodily repressed the Commune as "enslavers" (Marx, 1871a: 351), which, as he writes in the first draft of the paper, "does not [do] away with the class struggles … but it affords the rational medium in which that class struggle can run through its different phases in the most rational and human way. It could start violent reactions and as violent revolutions" (Marx, 1871b: 491). It does not mark the end of a history but establishes the political environment in which class struggles can be fought outside the despotism of capital. This is precisely why it must destroy state power which has always been the "the power for the maintenance of order, i.e., the existing order of society, and … as long as this order was accepted as the uncontrovertible and uncontested necessity, the state power could assume an aspect of impartiality" (Marx, 1871b: 534).

Beyond its empirical limits,[16] the Commune interests Marx as a form of transition, in which the reconfiguration of power displays elements of both rupture and continuity with the political and statual organization of the capital

---

16 Marx's judgement on the Commune varies significantly over time, see Thomas (1997) and Basso (2015: 177–188).

relation. Thus, the question of the disarticulation of capital as order is practically raised by the Commune. As we have seen, this is a problem that runs through all of Marx's thought and lies beyond the opposition between order and disorder. Difference and its power are not simply elements of disorder, nor are they the immediate prefiguration of a new order destined to replace the existing one. The Marxian rejection of political theology is resolved in the rejection of order thinking, a rejection that emerges in the critique of law as a necessary form of social relations. The Marxian critique of the Gotha program itself eschews the alternative between reform and revolution, between state politics and state contestation, rejecting rather the idea that democracy is really the power of the people and that it is therefore possible to use it to oppose the domination of capital over society (Ricciardi, 2012b). Instead, the Marxian critique insists on thinking of the political as an interruption of the political relation of capital, producing the points of rupture that make this interruption evident, revoking the legitimacy of the past that burdens the present. This is precisely why, even when denouncing the contradictions of the social democratic program, Marx does not oppose a future to be achieved to the limits present in that project. Marx does not really clarify what that 'communist society' (Musto, 2018b: 243–252) should look like, which here, with a semantics that is convoluted to say the least, he also defines as a "collective [*genossenschaftlich*] society based on common ownership [*Gemeingut*] of the means of production" (Marx, 1875: 85). As we have often said, this depends on the weight he and Engels give to the past over the present. And it is not so much a matter of clearly separating, with a single decision, the two temporalities, but of traversing their tangle, knowing that

> alongside of modern evils, a whole series of inherited evils oppress us, arising from the passive survival of antiquated modes of production, with their inevitable train of social and political anachronisms [*zeitwidrig*]. We suffer not only from the living, but from the dead. *Le mort saisit le vif!*
> MARX, 1867: 9

Resolving the political anachronism of capital and its state organization means living with these two historical times. However, it is not only a matter of escaping the grip of what is dead, because the past also shows the incompleteness of the present, its only partial and apparent legitimacy.[17] On the other hand, Marx argues that the living are the ones who use the past to their advantage, and

---

17 See also Rancière (1996), who, however, values anachronism as a critique of the present.

that their power can only be subverted by a revolution that shows the present possibility of configuring it differently. All this emerges in Marx's reflection on the relationship between law and individuals, which should still persist in the first phase of communism, when the conditions of production have not yet completely changed, in which, however, one can see how the clash with the past is part of the present and its possibility of showing itself as an opening to the future. In this phase, bourgeois law continues to apply with its universality, which in reality is indifference to the empirical individual, but only applies to the average individual. Staying within that right means establishing an equality that is only produced by evaluating individuals through a common measure, and this measure is labour. But already with regard to work performance, individuals differ physically and intellectually. Thus, "this *equal* right is an unequal right for unequal labour" (Marx, 1875: 86). Law in other words makes equal, or if you like, law equalizes individuals who are not only different in themselves but who are also placed in materially different positions with respect to societal production. Law establishes an order precisely because it imposes a homogeneous plane on which 'social traffic' can flow without individual impediments.

> *It is, therefore, a right of inequality, in its content, like every right.* Right by its nature can exist only as the application of an equal standard; but unequal individuals (and they would not be different individuals if they were not unequal) are measurable by an equal standard only insofar as they are made subject to an equal criterion, are taken from a certain side only.
> MARX, 1875: 86–87

Therefore, law subjects each individuality to a measurement that claims to be universal precisely because it ignores differences, both those that make each a singularity and those that accrue within the order of production. Quite paradoxically, law makes a difference, i.e., the different share of the social product that everyone manages to appropriate to themselves, the measure of equality, because it makes that share the very measure of individuality. "To avoid all these defects, right would have to be unequal rather than equal" (Marx, 1875: 87). It should not only be the law of different individuals, but also of different situations, which for Marx, bourgeois law clearly cannot do. He undoubtedly places law on a superstructural level, but this does not mean, of course, that he underestimates its ability to establish the form of production itself. Far from being merely a reflection of objective relations, it also establishes the position of individuals outside of those relations and, like ideology, establishes the way in which they conceive their antagonisms and fight to resolve them (Marx, 1859: 263; see also, Hall, 1977b).

The Marxian critique of law, therefore, is directed not so much at legal theories, but at the normative structures that prevent or authorize struggles, at the space of action that through law is delimited.[18] The very formula "from each according to his abilities, to each according to his needs" (Marx, 1875: 87) identifies such a normative field and should not be understood as the promise of an equalization of all individuals within communist society. It does not refer to the recognition of their equality in need, as Marx imputes to Bakunin, whose main concern would instead be "levelling out" (Marx, 1874–1875: 507). This, moreover, is also the outcome of the rule of law with its indifferent production of equality. The fact that law, as Maine argues, simultaneously expresses order and force is for Marx a historical fact and as such limited to specific organizations of politics. Since he closely connects the possibility of freedom to the end of the reign of necessity, i.e., to the possibility of everyone enjoying the common wealth, the constellation formed by order, force, and law identifies for him much more realistically than the Kantian normativity of a society in which the despotism of capital is inscribed. To assert a different but historically produced individuality is to allude to a social relationship that escapes the compulsion imposed by that constellation. If the Marxian political presents itself as an interruption of domination, its overcoming, assuming this is possible while remaining within a juridical logic, can only be achieved by affirming a 'right of difference' of empirically universal individualities on the world-historical level. The Marxian paradox of this right of different individuals is that it can only be the product of a common action, of their ability to become a power that is not an anthropological necessity, that does not pit their private powers against public power to neutralize both, that is not a power that limits them, but one that must liberate them collectively.

---

18   On the relationship between Marx and law, see Landau (1973), Vincent (1993), and Petrucciani (2018).

Karl Marx Works

Marx K (1842) The Philosophical Manifesto of the Historical School of Law. In MECW (1975), Volume 1: 203–210.
Marx K (1843a) Contribution to the Critique of Hegel's Philosophy of Law. In MECW (1975), Volume 3: 3–187.
Marx K (1843b) Letters from the *Deutsch-Französische Jahrbücher*. In MECW (1975), Volume 3: 133–145.
Marx K (1843c) Aus Historisch-politische Zeitschrift von L. Ranke. Über die Restauration in Frankreich. In Karl Marx Friedrich Engels Gesamtausgabe (MEGA), Vierte Abteilung: Exzerpte – Notizen – Marginalien. Band 2: Exzerpte und Notizen 1843 bis Januar 1845. Berlin: Dietz Verlag: 177–186.
Marx K (1844a) On the Jewish Question. In MECW (1975), Volume 3: 146–174.
Marx K (1844b) Economic and Philosophic Manuscripts of 1844. In MECW (1975), Volume 3: 229–348.
Marx K (1844c) Critical Marginal Notes on the Article "The King of Prussia and Social Reform. By a Prussian". In MECW (1975), Volume 3: 189–206.
Marx K (1844d) Comments On James Mill, Éléments d'Économie Politique. In MECW (1975), Volume 3: 211–228.
Marx K (1847a) The Communism of the *Rheinischer Beobachter*. In MECW (1976), Volume 6: 220–234.
Marx K (1847b) The Poverty of Philosophy. Answer to the *Philosophy of Poverty* by M. Proudhon. In MECW (1976), Volume 6: 105–212.
Marx K (1847c) Moralising Criticism and Critical Morality. A Contribution to German Cultural History Contra Karl Heinzen. In MECW (1976), Volume 6: 312–340.
Marx K (1847d) Remarks on the Article by M. Adolphe Bartels. In MECW (1976), Volume 6: 402–403.
Marx K (1848a) The Democratic Party. In MECW (1977), Volume 7: 27–29.
Marx K (1848b) The Programmes of the Radical-Democratic Party and of the Left at Frankfurt. In MECW (1977), Volume 7: 48–52.
Marx K (1848c) The June Revolution. In MECW (1977), Volume 7: 144–149.
Marx K (1848d) The Crisis in Berlin. In MECW (1977), Volume 8: 3–4.
Marx K (1848e) A Decree of Eichmann's. In MECW (1977), Volume 8: 37–38.
Marx K (1848f) State of Siege Everywhere. In MECW (1977), Volume 8: 53.
Marx K (1848g) The Bourgeoisie and the Counter-Revolution. In MECW (1977), Volume 8: 154–178.
Marx K (1848h) The Public Prosecutor's Office in Berlin and Cologne. In MECW (1977), Volume 8: 50.
Marx K (1848i) News from Paris. In MECW (1977), Volume 7: 128.

Marx K (1848j) The Crisis and the Counter-Revolution. In MECW (1977), Volume 7: 427–433.

Marx K (1848k) The Revolutionary Moment in Italy. In MECW (1977), Volume 8: 101–105.

Marx K (1848l) Speech on the Question of Free Trade Delivered to the Democratic Association of Brussels at Its Public Meeting of January 9, 1848. In MECW (1976), Volume 6: 450–465.

Marx K (1848m) The First Trial of the *Neue Rheinische Zeitung*. In MECW (1977), Volume 8: 304–322.

Marx K (1849a) The Trial of the Rhenish District Committee of Democrats. In MECW (1977), Volume 8: 323–340.

Marx K (1849b) Montesquieu LVI. In MECW (1977), Volume 8: 254–267.

Marx K (1849c) The Revolutionary Movement. In MECW (1977), Volume 8: 213–215.

Marx K (1849d) Wage Labor and Capital. In MECW (1977), Volume 9: 197–228.

Marx K (1849e) The Division of Labour in the *Kölnische Zeitung*. In MECW (1977), Volume 8: 354–359.

Marx K (1850a) The Class Struggles in France 1848–1850. *Neue Rheinische Zeitung*, January–November. In MECW (1978), Volume 10: 45–146.

Marx K (1850b) Meeting of the Central Authority. September 15. In MECW (1978), Volume 10: 625–629.

Marx K (1852) Marx to Weydemeyer, March 5. In MECW (1983), Volume 39: 60–66.

Marx K (1852a) The Eighteenth Brumaire of Louis Bonaparte. In MECW (1980), Volume 11: 99–197.

Marx K (1852b) The Chartists. In MECW (1980), Volume 11: 333–341.

Marx K (1852c) The Elections in England – Tory and Whigs. In MECW (1980), Volume 11: 327–332.

Marx K (1852d) Pauperism and Free Trade – The Approaching Commercial Crisis. In MECW (1980), Volume 11: 357–363.

Marx K (1852e) Political Consequences of the Commercial Excitement. In MECW (1980), Volume 11: 364–368.

Marx K (1853) Marx to Engels, November 2. In MECW (1983), Volume 39: 395–396.

Marx K (1853a) Revelations Concerning the Communist Trial in Cologne. In MECW (1980), Volume 11: 395–457.

Marx K (1853b) Palmerston's Resignation. In MECW (1979), Volume 12: 543–546.

Marx K (1853c) Lord Palmerston. In MECW (1979), Volume 12: 341–406.

Marx K (1853d) English Prosperity – Strikes – The Turkish Question – India. In MECW (1979), Volume 12: 134–141.

Marx K (1853e) The Turkish War Question – The *New-York Tribune* in the House of Commons – The Government of India. In MECW (1979), Volume 12: 174–184.

Marx K (1853f) The British Rule in India. In MECW (1979), Volume 12: 125–133.

Marx K (1853g) The Future Results of the British Rule in India. In MECW (1979), Volume 12: 217–222.
Marx K (1853h) The East India Company – History and Results. In MECW (1979), Volume 12: 148–156.
Marx K (1854) Revolutionary Spain. In MECW (1980), Volume 13: 389–446.
Marx K (1855a) Two Crises. In MECW (1980), Volume 13: 645–648.
Marx K (1855b) The British Constitution. In MECW (1980), Volume 14: 53–56.
Marx K (1855c) On the History of Political Agitation. In MECW (1980), Volume 14: 166–169.
Marx K (1855d) *The Morning Post* versus Prussia – The Character of the Whigs and Tories. In MECW (1980), Volume 14: 186–188.
Marx K (1855e) The Agitation Outside Parliament. In MECW (1980), Volume 14: 194–197.
Marx K (1855f) On the Reform Movement. In MECW (1980), Volume 14: 208–210.
Marx K (1855g) The Association for Administrative Reform – [People's Charter]. In MECW (1980), Volume 14: 240–244.
Marx K (1855h) Palmerston – The Physiology of The Ruling Class of Great Britain. In MECW (1980), Volume 14: 367–370.
Marx K (1856a) Speech at the Anniversary of *The People's Paper* Delivered in London, 14 April. In MECW (1980), Volume 14: 655–656.
Marx K (1856b) The French Crédit Mobilier. I. In MECW (1986), Volume 15: 8–13.
Marx K (1856c) The French Crédit Mobilier. II. In MECW (1986), Volume 15: 14–18.
Marx K (1856d) The French Crédit Mobilier. III. In MECW (1986), Volume 15: 19–24.
Marx K (1856e) The Monetary Crisis in Europe. In MECW (1986), Volume 15: 113–116.
Marx K (1856f) The Economic Crisis in France. In MECW (1986), Volume 15: 130–135.
Marx K (1857a) Parliamentary Debates on the Chinese Hostilities. In MECW (1986), Volume 15: 207–212.
Marx K (1857b) Defeat of the Palmerston Ministry. In MECW (1986), Volume 15: 213–218.
Marx K (1857c) The Coming Election in England. In MECW (1986), Volume 15: 219–222.
Marx K (1857d) The English Election. In MECW (1986), Volume 15: 226–231.
Marx K (1857e) The Defeat of Cobden, Bright and Gibson. In MECW (1986), Volume 15: 238–242.
Marx K (1857f) The Indian Revolt. In MECW (1986), Volume 15: 353–356.
Marx K (1857–1861a) Economic Manuscripts of 1857–1858. In MECW (1987), Volume 28.
Marx K (1857–1861b) Economic Manuscripts of 1857–1858. In MECW (1987), Volume 29: 1–256.
Marx K (1858) The Indian Bill. In MECW (1986), Volume 15: 585–588.
Marx K (1859) A Contribution to the Critique of Political Economy. In MECW (1987), Volume 29: 257–417.
Marx K (1860) Marx to Engels, January 11. In MECW (1985), Volume 41: 3–5.
Marx K (1860) English Politics. In MECW (1981), Volume 17: 335–340.

Marx K (1861–1863a) Economic Manuscripts of 1861–1863. In MECW (1989), Volume 32.

Marx K (1861–1863b) Economic Manuscripts of 1861–1863. In MECW (1988), Volume 30.

Marx K (1861–1863c) Chapter Six. Results of the Direct Production Process. In MECW (1994), Volume 34: 355–466.

Marx K (1864a) Inaugural Address of the Working Men's International Association. In MECW (1985), Volume 20: 5–13.

Marx K (1864b) Provisional Rules of the Association. In MECW (1985), Volume 20: 14–16.

Marx K (1864c) To Abraham Lincoln, President of the United States of America. In MECW (1985), Volume 20: 19–21.

Marx K (1867) Capital. A Critique of Political Economy. Book 1. In MECW (1996), Volume 35.

Marx K (1868) Marx to Kugelmann, December 5. In MECW (1988), Volume 43: 173–175.

Marx K (1870) Marx to Engels, August 3. In MECW (1989), Volume 44: 30–33.

Marx K (1871) Marx to Bolte, November 23. In MECW (1989), Volume 44: 251–259.

Marx K (1871) Marx to Kugelmann, April 17. In MECW (1989), Volume 44: 136–137.

Marx K (1871a) The Civil War in France. Address of the General Council of the International Working Men's Association. In MECW (1986), Volume 22: 307–359.

Marx K (1871b) Drafts of *The Civil War in France*. In MECW (1986), Volume 22: 435–551.

Marx K (1873) Political Indifferentism. In MECW (1988), Volume 23: 392–397.

Marx K (1874–1875) Notes on Bakunin's *Statehood and Anarchy*. In MECW (1989), Volume 24: 485–526.

Marx K (1875) Critique of the Gotha Programme. In MECW (1989), Volume 24: 75–99.

Marx K (1885) Capital. A Critique of Political Economy. Book 2, in MECW (1997), Volume 36.

Marx K (1894) Capital. A Critique of Political Economy. Book 3, in MECW (1998), Volume 37.

Marx K (1973 [1857–1858]) *Grundrisse. Introduction to the Critique of Political Economy*. Translate with an Introduction of Martin Nicolaus. New York: The Random House.

Marx K (1974 [1880–1882]) *The Ethnological Notebooks of Karl Marx. Transcribed and Edited, with an Introduction by* Lawrence Krader. Assen: Van Gorcum & Co.

Marx K (1976) *Lettere a Kugelmann*. Roma: Editori Riuniti.

Marx K (2007 [1852]) Der achtzehnte Brumaire des Louis Bonaparte. Kommentar von Hauke Brunkhorst. Frankfurt am Main: Suhrkamp.

Friedrich Engels Works

Engels F (1845) The Festival of Nations London. In MECW (1976), Volume 6: 3–14.
Engels F (1847) The Communists and Karl Heinzen. In MECW (1976), Volume 6: 291–306.
Engels F (1848) The Berlin Debate on the Revolution. In MEW (1977), Volume 7: 73–86.
Engels F (1883) Engels to Karl Kautsky, September 18. In MECW (2010), Volume 47: 55–58.
Engels F (1958 [1845]) The Condition of the Working Class in England. Stanford: Stanford University Press.

Marx and Engels Works

Marx K and Engels F (1845) The Holy Family. Or Critique of Critical Criticism. Against Bruno Bauer and Company. In MECW (1975), Volume 4: 5–211.

Marx K and Engels F (1845–1846a) The German Ideology. Critique of Modern German Philosophy According to Its Representatives Feuerbach, B. Bauer and Stirner, and of German Socialism According to Its Various Prophets. In MECW (1976), Volume 5: 19–539.

Marx K and Engels F (1845–1846b) Deutsche Ideologie. Manuskripte und Drucke. In Marx Engels Gesamtausgabe (MEGA), Erste Abteilung: Werke – Artikel – Entwürfe. Band 5. Berlin – Boston, Walter de Gruyter GmbH, 2017.

Marx K and Engels F (1848) Manifesto of the Communist Party. In MECW (1976), Volume 6: 477–519.

Marx K and Engels F (1850) Ansprache der Zentralbehörde an den Bund vom März 1850. In MEW (1960), Volume 7: 244–254.

Marx et al. Works

Marx K, Engels F, and Weydemeyer J (2004) Die deutsche Ideologie. Artikel, Druckvorlagen, Entwürfe, Reinschriftenfragmente und Notizen zu I. Feuerbach und II. Sankt Bruno. Berlin: Akademie Verlag.

Marx K, Schapper K, and Schneider II (1848) Appeal. In MECW (1977), Volume 8: 41.

References

Abensour M (2011 [1997]) *Democracy Against the State: Marx and the Machiavellian Moment*. Cambridge: Polity Press.
Agamben G (2005 [2003]) *State of Exception*. Chicago and London: University of Chicago Press.
Alquati R (1977) *Sindacato e partito*. Torino: Stampatori.
Althusser L (1978) Marx dans ses limites. In Althusser L (1994) *Écrites philosophiques et politique*. Tome I. Paris: Stock-Imec, 357–524.
Althusser L (1993 [1982]) Sur la pensée marxiste. In Althusser L, Berger D, Karsenti B, et al. *Sur Althusser. Passages*. Paris: L'Harmattan, 11–29.
Anceau É (2008) *Napoléon III. Un Saint-Simon à cheval*. Paris: Tallandier.
Anderson KB (2010) *Marx at the Margins. On Nationalism, Ethnicity, and Non-Western Societies*. Chicago – London: Chicago University Press.
Anderson O (1965) The Janus Face of Mid-Nineteenth-Century English Radicalism: The Administrative Reform Association of 1855. *Victorian Studies* vol 8(3): 231–242.
Arndt A (2014) Spazi di libertà. Universalità astratta e concreta nei *Lineamenti di filosofia del diritto* di Hegel. *Giornale di metafisica* vol 1: 19–36.
Arthur ChJ and Reuten G (eds) (1998) *The Circulation of Capital. Essays on Volume Two of Marx's Capital*. Basingstoke: Macmillan Press.
Balibar É (1974) *Cinq études du matérialisme historique*. Paris: Masquero.
Balibar É (1977 [1976]) *On the Dictatorship of the Proletariat*. London: New Left Books.
Balibar É (2009) Reflections on *Gewalt*. *Historical Materialism* vol 17: 99–125.
Balibar É (2011a) Le moment messianique de Marx. In Balibar É *Citoyen sujet et autres essais d'anthropologie philosophique*. Paris: PUF, 234–264.
Balibar É (2011b) Le contrat social des marchandises: Marx et le sujet de l'échange. In Balibar É *Citoyen sujet et autres essais d'anthropologie philosophique*. Paris: PUF, 315–342.
Balibar É (2013) 'Klassenkampf' als Begriff des Politischen. In Jaeggi R and Loïck D (eds) *Nach Marx. Philosophie, Kritik, Praxis*. Frankfurt am Main: Suhrkamp, 445–462.
Balibar É (2020 [2016]) *On Universals. Constructing and Deconstructing Community*. New York: Fordham University Press.
Balibar É and Roulet G (eds) (2001) *Marx démocrate. La Manuscrit de 1843*. Paris: PUF.
Barrow C W (2020) *The Dangerous Class. The Concept of the Lumpenproletariat*, Ann Arbor: University of Michigan Press.
Barthes R (1982 [1970]) *Empire of Signs*. New York: Hill and Wang – The Noonday Press.
Basso L (2012 [2008]) *Marx and Singularity: From the Early Writings to the* Grundrisse. Leiden – Boston: Brill.

Basso L (2015 [2012]) *Marx and the Common: From* Capital *to the Late Writings*. Leiden – Boston: Brill.
Basso L (2016) L'ambivalenza della *Gewalt* in Marx and Engels. A partire dall'interpretazione di Balibar. *Consecutio temporum* vol 1(1): pp. 77–91.
Basso M (2012) Sul concetto di *Herrschaft* in Max Weber. In *Concordia Discors. Scritti in onore di Giuseppe Duso*. Padova: Padova University Press, 25–45.
Basso M (2023 [2020]) On Possession and Property. Marx, Gans and the Law. In Battistini M, Cappuccilli E and Ricciardi M (eds) *Global Marx. History and Critique of the Social Movement in the World Market*. Leiden: Brill, 3–15.
Bastiat F, Proudhon PJ and Chevé CF (2022 [1850]) *Gratuité du crédit: Discussion entre M. Fr. Bastiat et M. Proudhon*. Paris: Guillaumin.
Battistini M (2017) "Revolutions are the Order of the Day". Atlantic Fragments of Thomas Paine, c. 1819–1832. In Edwards S and Morris M (eds) *The Legacy of Thomas Paine in the Transatlantic World*. London: Routledge, 87–106.
Battistini M (2023 [2020]) Between Slavery and Free Labour. Marx, the American Civil War and Emancipation as a Global Issue. In Battistini M, Cappuccilli E and Ricciardi M (eds) *Global Marx. History and Critique of the Social Movement in the World Market*. Leiden: Brill, 3–15.
Bensaïd D (2002 [1995]) *A Marx for Our Times: Adventures and Misadventures of a Critique*. London: Verso.
Berki RN (1983) *Insight and Vision. The Problem of Communism in Marx's Thought*. London – Melbourne: Dent and Sons.
Berta G (1979) *Marx, gli operai inglesi e i cartisti*. Milano: Feltrinelli.
Bihr A (2010) *La Logique méconnue du Capital*. Lausanne: Éditions Page Deux.
Blumenberg H (1976) *Aspekte der Epochenschwelle: Cusaner und Nolaner*. Frankfurt am Main: Suhrkamp.
Blumenberg H (1985 [1966]) *The Legitimacy of Modern Age*. Chicago – London: MIT Press.
Böckenförde EW (1970) *La storiografia costituzionale tedesca nel secolo decimonono*. Milano: Giuffrè.
Boesche R (1990) Fearing Monarchs and Merchants: Montesquieu's Two Theories of Despotism. *Western Political Quarterly* vol 43(4): 742–761.
Bologna S (1974) Moneta e crisi: Marx corrispondente della 'New York Daily Tribune', 1856–57. In Bologna S, Carpignano P and Negri A (eds) *Crisi e organizzazione operaia*. Milano: Feltrinelli, 9–72.
Bongiovanni B (1981) *L'universale pregiudizio. Le interpretazioni della critica marxiana della politica*. Milano: La salamandra.
Bongiovanni B (1989) *Le repliche della storia. Karl Marx tra la Rivoluzione Francese e la critica della politica*. Torino: Bollati Boringhieri.

Borkenau F (1971 [1934]) *Der Übergang vom feudalen zum bürgerlichen Weltbild: Studien zur Geschichte der Philosophie der Manufakturperiode*. Darmstadt: Wissenschaftliche Buchgesellschaft.

Borkenau F, Grossmann H and Negri A (1978) *Manifattura, società borghese, ideologia*. Edited by Schiera P. Roma: Savelli.

Born S (1847) *Der Heinzen'sche Staat. Eine Kritik von Stephan*. Bern: Rätzer.

Bourdieu P (1998 [1994]) Rethinking the State: Genesis and Structure of the Bureaucratic Field. In *Practical Reason: On the Theory of Action*. Stanford: Stanford University Press, 35–74.

Bravo GM (1979) *Marx e la Prima Internazionale*. Bari: Laterza.

Briggs A (ed) (1962) *Chartist studies*. London: Macmillan; New York: St Martin's Press.

Brocker M (1992) *Arbeit und Eigentum. Der Paradigmenwechsel in der neuzeitlichen Eigentumstheorie*. Darmstadt: Wissenschaftliche Buchgesellschaft.

Brown D (2010) *Palmerston: A Biography*. New Haven: Yale University Press.

Brown H (2012) *Marx on Gender and the Family. A Critical Study*. Leiden – Boston: Brill.

Brown ME (1986) *The Production of Society. A Marxian Foundation for Social Theory*. Totowa: Rowan & Littlefiled.

Brunkhorst H (2013) Von der Krise zum Risiko und zurück. Marxistische Revisionen. In Jaeggi R and Loïck D (eds) *Nach Marx. Philosophie, Kritik, Praxis*. Frankfurt am Main: Suhrkamp, 412–444.

Burkett J P (2000) Marx's Concept of an Economic Law of Motion. *History of Political Economy* vol 32(2): 381–394.

Campbell M (2009) L'oggettività del valore *versus* l'idea dell'azione abituale. In *Marx in questione. Il dibattito "aperto" dell'International Symposium on Marxian Theory*. Napoli: La città del sole, 87–116.

Cappuccilli E and Ferrari R (2023 [2020]) The Feminine Ferment. Marx and the Critique of Patriarchy. In Battistini M, Cappuccilli E and Ricciardi M (eds) *Global Marx. History and Critique of the Social Movement in the World Market*. Leiden: Brill, 58–73.

Carver T (1996) Engels and Democracy. In Arthur C I (ed) *Engels Today. A Centenary Appreciation*. Houndmills Basingstoke: Macmillan Press, 1–28.

Carver T (2002) Imagery/Writing, Imagination/Politics: Reading Marx through the 'Eighteenth Brumaire'. In Cowling M and Martin J (eds) *'Marx's Eighteenth Brumaire'. (Post)modern Interpretations*. London: Pluto Press, 113–128.

Carver T (2010) The German Ideology Never Took Place. *History of Political Thought* vol 31(1): 107–127.

Carver T (2013) Marx and Gender. In Jaeggi R and Loick D (eds) *Karl Marx – Perspektiven der Gesellschaftskritik*. Berlin: De Gruyter Akademie Forschung, 193–207.

Cervelli I (2015) *Le origini della Comune di Parigi. Una cronaca (31 October 1870–18 March 1871)*. Roma: Viella.

Cesaroni P (2006) *Governo e costituzione in Hegel. Le "lezioni di filosofia del diritto"*. Milano: FrancoAngeli.
Chakrabarty D (2000) *Provincializing Europe. Postcolonial Thought and Historical Difference*. Princeton: Princeton University Press.
Chase M (2007) *Chartism. A New History*. Manchester – New York: Manchester University Press.
Chauí M (2017) Marx y la democracia (el joven Marx lector de Spinoza). *Papel Máquina. Revista de cultura* vol 9(11): 73–107.
Chignola S (2004) *Fragile cristallo. Per la storia del concetto di società*. Napoli: Editoriale scientifica.
Cioli M, Ricciardi M and Schiera P (eds) (2020) *Traces of Modernism. Art and Politics from the First World War to Totalitarianism*. Frankfurt – New York: Campus Verlag.
Collins H and Abramsky C (1965) *Karl Marx and the British Labour Movement: Years of the First International*. London: Macmillan; New York: St Martin's Press.
Consolati I (2023 [2020]) Breaking the Chain of Time. Marx and the French Historians. In Battistini M, Cappuccilli E and Ricciardi M (eds) *Global Marx. History and Critique of the Social Movement in the World Market*. Leiden: Brill, 16–27.
Cowling M (2002) Marx's Lumpenproletariat and Murray's Underclass: Concepts Best Abandoned. In Cowling M and Martin J (eds) *'Marx's Eighteenth Brumaire'. (Post)modern Interpretations*. London: Pluto Press, 228–242.
Cowling M (2006) Alienation in the Older Marx. *Contemporary Political Theory* vol 5: 319–339.
Curtis N (2013) *Idiotism. Capitalism and the Privatisation of Life*. London: Pluto Press.
Dardot P (2014) Marx 1843. L'émancipation humaine et la question de la démocratie. *Cités* vol 59(3): 19–32.
Dardot P and Laval C (2012) *Marx, prénom: Karl*. Paris: Gallimard.
Dardot P and Laval C (2014) *Commun. Essai sur la révolution au 21. Siècle*. Paris: La Découverte.
De Boni C (2003) Le seduzioni della dittatura: positivismo e bonapartismo. In Ceretta M (ed) *Bonapartismo, cesarismo e crisi della società. Luigi Napoleone e il colpo di Stato del 1851*. Firenze: Olschki, 49–73.
De Boni C (2016) *Liberi e uguali. Il pensiero anarchico in Francia dal 1840 al 1914*. Milano: Mimesis.
De Brunhoff S (1976 [1973]) *Marx on Money*. New York: Urizen Books.
Defoe D (2007 [1719]) *Robinson Crusoe*. Oxford – New York: Oxford University Press.
DeGolyer, M (1992) The Greek Accent of the Marxian Matrix. In McCarthy G E (ed) *Marx and Aristotle. Nineteenth Century German Social Theory and Classical Antiquity*. Savage: Rowman and Littlefield, 107–153.
Demirović A (2006) Kritik der Politik. In Jaeggi R and Loïck D (eds) *Nach Marx. Philosophie, Kritik, Praxis*. Frankfurt am Main: Suhrkamp, 463–485.

Derrida J (1993) Force of Law: The "Mystical Foundation of Authority". In Cornell D, Rosenfeld M, and Carlson D G (eds) *Deconstruction and the Possibility of Justice*. New York – London: Routledge, 3–67.

Didry C (2018) Les factory acts dans Le Capital. Une écologie juridique du travail. *Droit & Philosophie* vol 10. Available (consulted December 1, 2023) at: http://www.droitphilosophie.com/article/lecture/les-factory-acts-dans-le-capital-une-ecologie-juridique-du-travail-254.

Draper H (1972) The Concept of the 'Lumpenproletariat' in Marx and Engels. *Économies et sociétés* vol 6(12): 2285–2312.

Draper H (1978) *Karl Marx's Theory of Revolution, II: The Politics of Social Classes*. New York – London: Monthly Review Press.

Dummer I (1997) *Die Arbeitskraft – eine Ware? Eine werttheoretische Betrachtung*. Hamburg: VSA-Verlag.

Duso G (2013) *Libertà e costituzione in Hegel*. Milano: FrancoAngeli.

Elster J (1985) *Making sense of Marx*. New York: Cambridge University Press; Paris: Editions de la Maison des Sciences de l'Homme.

Espinoza Pino M and Mezzadra S (2018) Cartografie globali. Il concetto di mercato mondiale in Marx tra giornalismo e teoria. In Petrucciani S (ed) *Il pensiero di Karl Marx. Filosofia, politica, economia*. Roma: Carrocci, 177–208.

Farr J (1983) Marx no Empiricist. *Philosophy of the Social Sciences* vol 13: 465–472.

Fenton L (2012) *Palmerston and The Times: Foreign Policy, the Press and Public Opinion in Mid-Victorian Britain*. London: Tauris.

Fernbach D (1973) Introduction. In Marx K, *Political Writings. II: Surveys from Exile*. New York: Random House, 7–34.

Fine B and Saad-Filho A (2004) *Marx's Capital*. London: Pluto Press.

Finelli R (2018) *Karl Marx uno e bino. Tra arcaismi del passato e illuminazioni del presente*. Milano: Jaka Book.

Finelli R and Trincia FS (1983) Commentario. In Marx K (1983 [1843]) *Critica del diritto statuale hegeliano*. Roma: Edizioni dell'ateneo.

Forbes I (1990) *Marx and the New Individual*. London: Unwin Hyman.

Foucault M (1981) As malhas do poder (Les mailles du pouvoir). In Foucault M (1994) *Dits et Écrits, 1954–1988*. Volume 4. Paris: Gallimard 1994, 182–201.

Foucault M (2015 [2013]) *The Punitive Society. Lectures at the Collège de France, 1972–1973*. Houndmills: Palgrave Macmillan.

Fourier C (1829) *Le Nouveau monde industriel et sociétaire ou invention du procédé d'industrie attrayante et naturelle, distribuée en séries passionnées*. Paris: Bossange père.

Galli C (2015 [2008]) *Janus's Gaze. Essays on Carl Schmitt*. Durham – London: Duke University Press.

Gilbert A (1990) *Democratic Individuality*. Cambridge: Cambridge University Press.

Girard L (1952) *La politique des travaux publics du second Empire*. Paris: Colin.

Granjonc J (1989) *Communisme/Kommunismus/Communism. Origine et développement international de la terminologie communautaire prémarxiste des utopistes aux néo-babouvistes 1785–1842*. Trier: Karl-Marx-Haus.

Guastini R (1974) *Dalla filosofia del diritto alla scienza della società. Il lessico giuridico marxiano (1842–1851)*. Bologna: Il Mulino.

Gurney PJ (2014) The Democratic Idiom: Languages of Democracy in the Chartist Movement. *The Journal of Modern History* vol 86(3): 566–602.

Hall S (1977a) The 'Political' and the 'Economic' in Marx's Theory of Classes. In Hunt A (ed) *Class and Class Structure*. London: Lawrence and Wishart, 15–60.

Hall S (1977b) Re-Thinking the Basis and Superstructure Metaphor. In Bloomfield J (ed) *The Communist University of London: Papers on Class, Hegemony and Party*. London: Lawrence and Wishart, 43–72.

Hall S (2003 [1973]) Marx's Notes On Method: A 'Reading' of the '1857 Introduction'. *Cultural Studies* vol 17(2): 113–149.

Hampton M (2013) Money as Social Power. The Economics of Scarcity and Working Class Reproduction. *Capital & Class* vol 37(3): 373–395.

Harney GJ (1850) The Charter, and Something More. In Harney GJ (1968) *The Democratic Review, June 1849-September 1850*. London: Merlin Press, 349–352.

Harootunian H (2015) *Marx after Marx. History and Time in the Expansion of Capitalism*. New York: Columbia University Press.

Hartog F (2015 [2003]) *Regimes of Historicity*. New York: Columbia University Press.

Haug WF (2006) *Neue Vorlesungen zur Einführung in „Kapital"*. Hamburg: Argument.

Hawkings A (1998) *British Party Politics 1852–1886*. Houndmills: Macmillan.

Hegel GWF (1975 [1835]) *Aesthetics. Lectures on Fine Art*. Volume 1. Oxford: Oxford University Press.

Hegel GWF (1991 [1820]) *Elements of the Philosophy of Right*. Cambridge: Cambridge University Press.

Hegel GWF (2010a [1817, 1827, 1830]) *Encyclopedia of the Philosophical Sciences in Basic Outline. Part I: Science of Logic*. Cambridge: Cambridge University Press.

Hegel GWF (2010b [1812–1816, 1831]) *The Science of Logic*. Cambridge: Cambridge University Press.

Heinzen K (1847a) Polemik. Karl Heinzen und die Kommunisten. *Deutsche-Brüsseler-Zeitung*, 26 September.

Heinzen K (1847b) Ein ‚Repräsentant' der Kommunisten. *Deutsche-Brüsseler-Zeitung*, 21 October.

Hindrichs G (2006) Das Erbe des Marxismus. *Deutsche Zeitschrift für Philosophie* vol 54(5): 709–729.

Hobbes T (1998 [1651]) *Leviathan*. Oxford – New York: Oxford University Press.

Hudelson R (1982) Marx's Empiricism. *Philosophy of the Social Sciences* vol 12: 241–253.

Hudelson R (1983) A Reply to Farr. *Philosophy of the Social Sciences* vol 13: 473–474.

Iacono AM (2018) *Studi su Karl Marx. La cooperazione, l'individuo sociale e le merci.* Pisa: ETS.
Iorio M (2003) *Karl Marx – Geschichte, Gesellschaft, Politik. Eine Ein- und Weiterführung.* Berlin – New York: De Gruyter.
Jung S (2003) The Language(s) of Hierarchy in Daniel Defoe's Robinson Crusoe. *Nordic Journal of English Studies* vol 2(2): 265–277.
Kaiwar V (2014) *The Postcolonial Orient. The Politics of Difference and the Project of Provincializing Europe.* Boston – Leiden: Brill.
Kant I (1974 [1793]) *On the Old Say: That May Be Right in Theory but It Won't Work in Practice.* Philadelphia: University of Pennsylvania Press.
Kant I (2000 [1790]) *Critique of the Power of Judgment.* Cambridge: Cambridge University Press.
Kant I (2006 [1798]) *Anthropology from a Pragmatic Point of View.* Cambridge: Cambridge University Press.
Kelley D R (1978) The Metaphysics of Law: An Essay on the Very Young Marx. *American Historical Review* vol 83: 350–367.
Kouvélakis E (2003) *Philosophie et révolution. De Kant à Marx.* Paris: PUF.
Krader L (1975) *The Asiatic Mode of Production. Sources, Development and Critique in the Writings of Karl Marx.* Assen: Van Gorcum & Co.
Krätke MR (1991) Marx und die Weltgeschichte. In *Studien zum Werk von Marx und Engels. Beiträge zur Marx-Engels-Forschung.* Hamburg: Argument-Verlag, 133–178.
Krätke MR (2008a) The First World Economic Crisis. Marx as an Economic Journalist. In Musto M (ed) *Karl Marx's Grundrisse Foundations of the Critique of Political Economy 150 Years Later.* London – New York: Routledge, 162–168.
Krätke MR (2008b) Marx's 'Books of Crisis' of 1857–8. In Musto M (ed) *Karl Marx's Grundrisse Foundations of the Critique of Political Economy 150 Years Later.* London – New York: Routledge, 169–175.
Kuczynski T (2009) Was wird auf dem Arbeitsmarkt verkauft?. In Van Der Linden M and Roth KH (eds) *Über Marx hinaus. Arbeitsgeschichte und Arbeitsbegriff in der Konfrontation mit den globalen Arbeitsverhältnissen des 21. Jahrhunderts.* Berlin – Hamburg: Assoziation A, 362–377.
Landau P (1973) Marx und die Rechtsgeschichte. *Tijdschrift voor Rechtsgeschiedenis* vol 41: 361–371.
Lascoumes P, Zander H (1984) *Marx: « du vol de bois » à la critique du droit. Karl Marx à la « Gazette rhénane », naissance d'une méthode.* Paris: PUF.
Laval C, Paltrinieri L and Taylan F (eds) (2015) *Foucault and Marx. Lectures, usages, confrontations.* Paris: La Découverte.
Lebowitz MA (2003) *Beyond Capital. Marx's Political Economy of the Working Class.* Houndmills: Palgrave Macmillan.
Leonelli RM (ed) (2010) *Foucault-Marx. Paralleli e paradossi.* Roma: Bulzoni.

Leopold D (2007) *The Young Karl Marx. German Philosophy, Modern Politics, and Human Flourishing*. Cambridge: Cambridge University Press.

Levine N (1987) The German Historical School of Law and the Origins of Historical Materialism. *Journal of the History of Ideas* vol 48(3): 431–451.

Lichtblau K (2011) Von der ,Gesellschaft' zur ,Vergesellschaftung'. Zur deutschen Tradition der Gesellschaftsbegriffs. In *Die Eigenart der kultur- und sozial-wissenschaftlichen Begriffsbildung*. Wiesbaden: Verlag für Sozialwissenschaften, 11–36.

Liebich A (1982) On the Origins of a Marxist Theory of Bureaucracy in the Critique of Hegel's "Philosophy of Right". *Political Theory* vol 10(1): 77–93.

Liedman S-E (1986) *Das Spiel der Gegensätze. Friedrich Engels' Philosophie und die Wissenschaften des 19. Jahrhunderts*. Frankfurt am Main – New York: Campus.

Lieven M (1988) Marx and Engels's Account of Political Power: The Case of British Factory Legislation. *History of Political Thought* vol 9(3): 505–527.

Linguet S-N-H (1767) *Théorie des loix civiles ou principes fondamentaux de la société*. Londres.

Lohmann G (1991) *Indifferenz und Gesellschaft. Eine kritische Auseinandersetzung mit Marx*. Frankfurt am Main: Suhrkamp.

Lubasz H (1984), Marx's Concept of the Asiatic Mode of Production: A Genetic Analysis. *Economy and Society* vol 13(4): 456–483.

Luhmann N (1999) Jenseits der Barberei. In *Gesellschaftsstruktur und Semantik. Studien zur Wissenssoziologie der modernen Gesellschaft*. Volume 4. Frankfurt am Main: Suhrkamp, 138–150.

Luhmann N (2005) Selbst-Thematisierung des Gesellschaftssystems. Über die Kategorie der Reflexion aus der Sicht der Systemtheorie. In *Soziologische Aufklärung 2. Aufsätze zur Theorie der Gesellschaft*. Wiesbaden: Verlag für die Sozialwissenschaft, 89–127.

Luporini C (1979) Le politique et l'étatique: une ou deux critique?. In Balibar É, Luporini C, and Tosel A (eds), *Marx et sa critique de la politique*. Paris: Maspero, 53–106.

Luxemburg R (1971 [1899]) Social Reform or Revolution. In Howard D (ed) *Selected Political Writings of Rosa Luxemburg*. New York – London: Monthly Review Press, 52–134.

Macherey P (1992) Aux sources des 'rapports sociaux'. Bonald, Saint-Simon, Guizot. *Genèses* vol 9: 25–43.

Macherey P (2015 [2012]) The Productive Subject. *Viewpoint Magazine*. Available (consulted December 1 2023) at: https://viewpointmag.com/2015/10/31/the-productive-subject/.

Marsden R (1999) *The Nature of Capital. Marx after Foucault*. London – New York: Routledge.

Martin J (2015) The Rhetoric of the Manifesto. In Carver T and Farr J (eds) *The Cambridge Companion to The Communist Manifesto*. New York: Cambridge University Press, 50–66.

Mascat J M H (2018) Marx et le vol de bois. Du droit coutumier au droit de classe. *Droit & Philosophie* vol 10. Available (consulted December 1, 2023) at: http://www.droit philosophie.com/article/lecture/marx-et-le-vol-de-bois-du-droit-coutumier-au-droit-de-classe-252.

Mattingly G (1963) No Peace beyond What Line?. *Transactions of the Royal Historical Society*, Fifth Series, vol 13: 145–162.

Mayer H (1951) Karl Marx und die deutsche Revolution von 1848. *Historische Zeitschrift* vol 172: 517–534.

Merlo M (1999) Il significato politico della critica dell'economia politica. In Duso G (ed) *Il potere. Per la storia della filosofia politica moderna*. Roma: Carocci, 372–383.

Merlo M (2023 [2020]) The Social Object. Marx, the Economists, the Mercantile Society. In Battistini M, Cappuccilli E and Ricciardi M (eds) *Global Marx. History and Critique of the Social Movement in the World Market*. Leiden: Brill, 28–43.

Mezzadra S (2018 [2014]) *In the Marxian Workshops. Producing Subjects*. London – New York: Rowman & Littlefield.

Mezzadra S and Neilson B (2013) *Border as Method, or, the Multiplication of Labor*. Durham – London: Duke University Press.

Mezzadra S and Ricciardi M (2002) Introduzione. In *Marx. Antologia degli scritti politici*. Roma: Carocci: 11–43.

Mies M (1998) *Patriarchy and Accumulation on a World Scale. Women in the International Division of Labour*. London: Zed books.

Miles R (1987) *Capitalism and Unfree Labour. Anomaly or Necessity*. London – New York: Tavistock.

Mohanty CT (2003) *Feminism without Borders. Decolonizing Theory, Practicing Solidarity*. Durham – London: Duke University Press.

Montesquieu C (1989 [1748]) *The Spirit of the Laws*. Cambridge: Cambridge University Press.

Morfino V (2013) Marx lettore di Spinoza. Democrazia, immaginazione, rivoluzione. *Consecutio rerum. Rivista critica della Postmodernità* vol 5: 141–167.

Moulier Boutang Y (1998) *De l'esclavage au salariat. Économie historique du salariat bride*. Paris: Puf.

Musto M (2018a) Marx militante: teoria e organizzazione politica ai tempi dell'Associazione internazionale dei lavoratori. In Petrucciani S (ed) *Il pensiero di Karl Marx. Filosofia, politica, economia*. Roma: Carocci, 209–241.

Musto M (2018b) *Karl Marx. Biografia intellettuale e politica. 1857–1883*. Torino: Einaudi.

Napoleon III (1953a) Proclamation du 2 décembre 1851. In *Discours et messages de Louis-Napoléon Bonaparte, Depuis son retour en France jusqu'au 2 décembre 1852*. Paris: Plon Frères, 191–194.

Napoleon III (1953b) Préambule de la Constitution. In *Discours et messages de Louis-Napoléon Bonaparte, Depuis son retour en France jusqu'au 2 décembre 1852*. Paris: Plon Frères, 203–211.

Negri A (1982) *Macchina tempo. Rompicapi, liberazione, costituzione*. Milano: Feltrinelli.

Negri A (1991 [1984]) *Marx Beyond Marx. Lessons on the* Grundrisse. New York: Autonomedia; London: Pluto Press.

Negri A (1992) *Il potere costituente. Saggio sulle alternative del moderno*. Milano: Sugarco.

Negri A (2016) *Marx and Foucault*. London – Malden: Polity Press.

Neocleous M (2005) *The Monstrous and the Dead: Burke, Marx, Fascism*. Cardiff: University of Wales Press.

Nipperdey T (1984) *Deutsche Geschichte 1800–1866. Bürgerwelt und starker Staat*. München: Beck.

Nobili Schiera G (2015) A proposito della traduzione recente di un'opera di Otto Brunner. *Scienza & Politica* vol 27(52): 221–237.

Pandolfi A (2016) La dialettica della repressione. Michel Foucault e la nascita delle istituzioni penali. *Science & Politica* vol 28(55): 131–149.

Patterson TC (2009) *Karl Marx Anthropologist*. Oxford – New York: Berg.

Petrucciani S (2018) Les multiples dimensions de la critique marxienne du droit. *Droit & Philosophie* vol 10. Available (consulted December 1, 2023) at: http://www.droitphilosophie.com/article/lecture/the-dimensioni-multiple-della-critica-marxiana-del-diritto-249.

Piccinini M (1989) Leo Strauss ed il problema teologico-politico alle soglie degli anni '30. Duso G (ed) *Filosofia politica e pratica del pensiero*. Milano: Franco Angeli, 193–233.

Piccinini M (2003) *Tra legge e contratto. Una lettura di Ancient law di Henry S. Maine*. Milano: Giuffrè.

Piccinini M (2004–2005) The forms of business. Immaginario costituzionale e governo delle dipendenze. *Quaderni fiorentini per la storia del pensiero giuridico moderno* vol 33/34: 73–114.

Piccinini M and Rametta G (1987) Introduzione a O. Brunner, *Osservazioni sui concetti di «dominio» e di «legittimità»*. *Filosofia politica* vol 1: 103–120.

Pradella L (2015) *Globalization and the Critique of Political Economy. New Insights from Marx's Writings*. London: Routledge.

Rancière J (1976 [1965]) The Concept of 'Critique' and the 'Critique of Political Economy' (from the *1844 Manuscript* to *Capital*). *Economy and Society* vol 5(3): 352–376.

Rancière J (1996) Le concept d'anachronisme et la vérité de l'historien. *L'inactuel* vol 6: 53–68.

Reichelt H (1973) *La struttura logica del concetto di capitale di Marx*. Bari: De Donato.

Renault E (2001) *Le vocabulaire de Marx*. Paris: Ellipses.

Renault E (2013) *Marx et la philosophie*. Paris: PUF.

Ricciardi J (2015) Marx on Financial Intermediation: Lessons from the French Crédit Mobilier in the New York Daily Tribune. *Science & Society* vol 79(4): 497–526.

Ricciardi M (1995) Lavoro, cittadinanza, costituzione. Dottrina della società e diritti fondamentali tra movimento sociale e rivoluzione. In Gherardi R and Gozzi G (eds) *Saperi della borghesia e storia dei concetti fra Otto e Novecento*. Bologna: Il Mulino, 119–159.

Ricciardi M (2001) *Rivoluzione*. Bologna: Il Mulino.

Ricciardi M (2010) *La società come ordine. Storia e teoria politica dei concetti sociali*. Macerata: EUM.

Ricciardi M (2012a) Ideologi prima dell'ideologia. Linguet e i paradossi sociali della politica. *Scienza & Politica* vol 24(47): 67–87.

Ricciardi M (2012b) La società di tutto il popolo. Linee storiche sui concetti politici del socialismo tedesco dopo il 1848. In Ruocco G and Scuccimarra S (eds) *Il governo del popolo 2. Dalla Restaurazione alla guerra franco-prussiana*. Rome: Viella, 289–309.

Ricciardi M (2015) L'ideologia come scienza politica del sociale. *Scienza & Politica* vol 27(52): 165–195.

Ricciardi M (2017) Tempo, ordine, potere. Su alcuni presupposti concettuali del programma neoliberale. *Scienza & Politica* vol 29(57): 11–30.

Ricciardi M (2023 [2020]) Germany as an Anachronism. Marx, Social Science and the State. In Battistini M, Cappuccilli E and Ricciardi M (eds) *Global Marx. History and Critique of the Social Movement in the World Market*. Leiden: Brill, 109–121.

Ripstein A (1987) Commodity Fetishism. *Canadian Journal of Philosophy* vol 17(4): 733–748.

Ritter J (1982) Person und Eigentum. Zu Hegels „Grundlinien der Philosophie des Rechts". In Riedel M (ed) *Zwischen Tradition und Revolution: Studien zu Hegels Rechtsphilosophie*. Volume 2. Stuttgart: Klett-Cotta, 152–175.

Roberts D (1960) *Victorian Origins of the British Welfare State*. New Haven: Yale University Press.

Roberts WC (2016) *Marx's Inferno. The Political Theory of Capital*. Princeton: Princeton University Press.

Rosdolsky R (1977 [1968]) *The Making of Marx's 'Capital'*. London: Pluto Press.

Rossi M (1974) *Da Hegel a Marx*. Vol. 3: *La Scuola hegeliana. Il giovane Marx*. Milano: Feltrinelli.

Rudan P (2013) *L'inventore della costituzione. Jeremy Bentham e il governo della società*. Bologna: Il Mulino.

Rudan P (2023 [2020]) The Artificial Nature and the Genetic History of Capital. Marx and the Modern Theory of Colonization. In Battistini M, Cappuccilli E and Ricciardi M (eds) *Global Marx. History and Critique of the Social Movement in the World Market*. Leiden: Brill, 44–57.

Ruge A (1975 [1844]) Der König von Preußen und die Sozialreform. *Vorwärts! Pariser deutsche Zeitschrift*, 27 July, Reprint: Leipzig, Zentralantiquariat der deutschen demokratischen Republik.

Sammadar R (2007) *The Materiality of Politics. The Technologies of Rule*. London: Anthem Press.

Saunders R (2008) Chartism from above: British Elites and the Interpretation of Chartism. *Historical Research* vol 81(213): 463–484.

Scattola M (2007) *Teologia Politica*. Bologna: Il Mulino.

Schieder W (1991) *Marx als Politiker*. München – Zürich: Piper.

Schiera P (1987) *Il laboratorio borghese. Scienza e Politica nella Germania dell'Ottocento*. Bologna: Il Mulino.

Schiera P (2004) *Lo Stato moderno. Origini e degenerazioni*. Bologna: Clueb.

Schiera P (2007) Stato. In Pomarici U (ed) *Filosofia del diritto. Concetti fondamentali*. Torino: Giappichelli, 563–568.

Schmidt VH (2020). Eight Theories of Societalization: Toward a Theoretically Sustainable Concept of Society. *European Journal of Social Theory* Vol. 23(3): 411–430.

Schmitt C (1995) *Briefwechsel mit einem seiner Schüler*. Berlin: Akademie.

Schmitt C (2003) *Der Begriff des Politischen. Ein kooperativer Kommentar*. Edited by Mehring R. Berlin: Akademie Verlag.

Schmitt C (2006 [1922]) *Political Theology. Four Chapters on the Concept of Sovereignty*. Chicago – London: University of Chicago Press.

Schmitt C (2013 [1921]) *Dictatorship*. Cambridge: Polity Press.

Screpanti E (2013) *Marx dalla totalità alla moltitudine (1841–1843)*. Pistoia: Petite Plaisance.

Scuccimarra L (2006) Il cuneo bonapartista: governo delle élites e sovranità popolare in Francia agli albori del Secondo Impero. *Giornale di storia costituzionale* vol 12(2): 129–148.

Sewell Jr. WH (1980) *Work and Revolution in France. The Language of Labor from the Old Regime to 1848*. Cambridge: Cambridge University Press.

Sgro' G (2017) *Friedrich Engels e il punto d'approdo della filosofia classica tedesca*. Napoli – Salerno: Orthonotes.

Small AW (1972 [1907]) *Adam Smith and Modern Sociology. A Study in the Methodology of the Social Science*. Clifton: Augustus M. Kelley Publishers.

Smith A (1981 [1776]) *An Inquiry into the Nature and Causes of the Wealth of Nations*. Volume 1. Indianapolis: Liberty Classics.

Smith DE (2004) Ideology, Science and Social Relations. A Reinterpretation of Marx's Epistemology. *European Journal of Social Theory* vol 7(4): 445–462.

Spivak GC (1996a) Feminism and Critical Theory. In *The Spivak Reader*. New York – London: Routledge, 53–74.

Spivak GC (1996b) Scattered Speculations on the Question of Value. In *The Spivak Reader*. New York – London: Routledge, 107–140.
Spivak GC (1999) *A Critique of Postcolonial Reason. Toward a History of the Vanishing Present*. Cambridge – London: Harvard University Press.
Stallybrass P (1990) Marx and Heterogeneity: Thinking the Lumpenproletariat. *Representations* vol 31: 69–95.
Stedman Jones G (1983) *Languages of Class. Studies in English Working Class History 1832–1982*. Cambridge: Cambridge University Press.
Stedman Jones G (2016) *Karl Marx. Greatness and Illusion*. Cambridge: Harvard University Press.
Steele ED (1991) *Palmerston and Liberalism 1855–1865*. Cambridge: Cambridge University Press.
Taubes J (1996) Theologie und politische Theorie. In Taubes J, *Vom Kult zur Kultur. Bausteine zu einer Kritik der historischen Vernunft*. München: Fink.
Taubes J (2009 [1947]) *Occidental Eschatology*. Standford: Standford University Press.
Taylor A (1994) Palmerston and Radicalism, 1847–1865. *The Journal of British Studies* vol 33(2): 157–179.
Theunissen M (1970) *Hegels Lehre vom absoluten Geist als theologisch-politischer Traktat*. Berlin: De Gruyter.
Thomas R (1997) Enigmatic Writings: Karl Marx's *The Civil War in France* and the Paris Commune of 1871. *History of Political Thought* vol 18(3), 483–511.
Thompson EP (1966) *The Making of the English Working Class*. New York: Vintage Books.
Thompson D (1971) *The Early Chartists*. London: Palgrave Macmillan.
Tocqueville A (1948 [1896]) *The Recollections of Alexis de Tocqueville*. London: The Harvill Press.
Tommasello F (2012) Dal popolo al proletariato. Marx e la costruzione del soggetto rivoluzionario. In Scuccimarra L and Ruocco G (eds) *Il governo del popolo*. Volume 2: *Dalla Restaurazione alla guerra franco-Prussiana*, Roma: Viella, 261–287.
Tommasello F (2018) *L'inizio del lavoro. Teoria politica e questione sociale nella Francia di prima metà Ottocento*. Roma: Carocci.
Tomba M (2013 [2010]) *Marx's Temporalities*. Leiden: Brill.
Tönnies F (1927), Demokratie. In *Verhandlungen des Fünften Deutschen Soziologentages vom 26. Bis 29 September 1926 in Wien*, Frankfurt am Main: Sauer & Auvermann: 12–36.
Touboul H (2004) *Marx, Engels et la question de l'individu*. Paris: PUF.
Tronti M (2019 [1966]) *Workers and Capital*. London: Verso.
Ure A (1967 [1835]) *The Philosophy of Manufactures: Or, An Exposition of the Scientific, Moral, and Commercial Economy of the Factory of Great Britain*. New York: Augustus M. Kelley.
Van Ree E (2013) Marxism as Permanent Revolution. *History of Political Thought* vol 34(3): 540–563.

Vincent A (1993) Marx and Law. *Journal of Law and Society* vol 20(4): 361–371.
Wacquant LJD (1985) Heuristic Models in Marxian Theory. *Social Forces* vol 64(1): 17–45.
Wainwright J (2008) Uneven Developments: From the *Grundrisse* to *Capital*. *Antipode* vol 40(5): 879–897.
Weber M (2005 [1921]) *Economia e società: Comunità*. Roma: Donzelli.
Wendling AE (2009) *Karl Marx on Technology and Alienation*. Houndmills: Palgrave Macmillan.
Wetherly P (2002) Making Sense of the 'Relative Autonomy' of the State. In Cowling M and Martin J (eds) *'Marx's Eighteenth Brumaire'. (Post)modern Interpretations*. London: Pluto Press, 195–208.
Winkler H A (2000) *Die lange Weg nach Westen. 1. Deutsche Geschichte vom Ende des Alten Reiches bis zum Untergang der Weimarer Republik*. München: Beck.
Wolff W (1952 [1844]) *Das Elend und der Aufruhr in Schlesien*. Berlin: Verlag Tribüne.
Wolin S (2016) On Reading Marx Politically. In *Fugitive Democracy and Other Essays*. Princeton – Oxford: Princeton University Press, 173–194.
Zamagni G (2002) Oriente ideologico e Asia reale. Apologie e critiche del dispotismo nel secondo Settecento francese. In Felice D (ed) *Dispotismo. Genesi e sviluppi di un concetto storico-politico*. Napoli: Liguori: 357–390.
Ziegler PR (2003) *Palmerston*. Houndmills: Palgrave Macmillan.

Index

Abensour M 7n
Aberdeen GH-G Earl of 77
Abramsky C 70n
Administration 16, 17, 39, 40, 60, 70, 74, 77, 80, 126, 136
Agamben G 45
Alquati R 118n
Althusser L 36, 135
Anachronism IX, 11, 12, 17, 18, 44, 47–49, 62, 65, 80, 86, 92–94, 97, 100, 115, 139
Anceau É 56
Anderson KB 80n
Anderson O 74
Annenkov PV 18
Antagonism VIII, XIV, 2, 17, 40, 42, 57, 69, 85–87, 89, 112, 117, 118, 120, 129, 135–137, 141
Anthropology 24, 107, 109, 121, 124, 126, 129
Appropriation 22, 93, 98, 102, 112, 118, 129, 130
Aristocracy 47, 58, 63, 65, 69, 70, 73, 75, 77, 80
Aristotle 5n, 27n, 118, 119
Arndt A 4n
Arthur CJ 116
Association démocratique 1
Association for Administrative Reform 74, 75
Austin J 131
Authority XI, XII, XIV, 3, 46, 48, 60, 62, 64, 76, 96, 113, 114, 120, 121, 130, 137

Bakunin MA 136, 141
Balibar E 6, 20, 35, 50, 98, 102n, 135
Barrow CW 62
Barthes R VII
Basso L 22, 102n, 138n
Basso M 31n, 46n
Bastiat F 84
Battistini M 34, 138
Bauer B 26
Bearer VIII, 8, 97, 117, 120
Bentham J 76, 77, 99, 100, 130
Bensaïd D 115
Berki RN 107n

Berta G 69
Bihr A 116
Blanqui LA 49
Blumenberg H 13, 37
Böchenförde EW 108n
Boesche R 123
Bologna S 66
Bolte F 106, 107
Bonaparte (Napoleon I) 46, 56, 61, 126
Bonaparte L (Napoleon III) XIV, 53, 55, 56, 58–61, 65, 66, 72, 73, 76, 79, 89, 118
Bongiovanni B 9n, 47
Borkenau F 108
Born S 29, 30
Bourdieu P 26, 65
Bourgeoisie 25, 26, 31, 32, 37–39, 41, 42n, 44, 45, 47, 51, 53, 55, 58, 61, 63, 65, 67, 69–71, 73–75, 79, 125
Bowring J 76, 77
Bravo GM 83n
Briggs A 68
Brocker M 30n
Brown D 78n
Brown H 130n
Brown ME 86
Brunkhorst H 84n
Buonarroti F 50
Bureaucracy XII, XIV, 9, 10, 40, 47, 51, 59–62, 80, 91, 136
Burkett JP 46

Campbell M 98
Camphausen L 51
Cappuccilli E 130n
Capital IX, XIII, XIV, 14, 21, 25, 38, 39, 45, 50, 57, 58, 64–66, 69, 71, 83–86, 89, 92, 93, 95, 97–106, 108–111, 113–119, 121, 125, 133, 134, 136, 138, 139, 141
Capitalism 18, 37, 50, 67, 81n, 102n, 107n, 113, 123, 132
Capitalist 14, 15, 38, 61, 81, 89, 92, 93, 97, 99, 100, 103, 104, 106, 111–114, 116–119, 126
Capital Relation VII, IX, X, XIV, 31, 66, 70, 85, 91, 93, 95, 97, 98, 101, 102, 105, 107, 109, 112, 114, 115, 119, 125

INDEX   165

Capital (cont.)
   Capitalist Development   16, 79, 92
   Capitalist Production   50, 64, 103, 105,
      111, 112, 119n, 129. *See also* Mode of
      Production
   Capitalists   IX, XIV, 93, 99, 103–105, 114,
      116–118, 120
   Overall Capitalist   102, 103, 127, 135
Carey HJ   8n
Carlyle Th   13
Carver T   19n, 35, 48n, 130n
Cavaignac LE   51
Centralization   59, 60, 61, 65, 81, 84, 110, 124,
   126, 136
Cervelli I   133n
Cesaroni P   6
Chakrabarty D   127n
Chartism   33, 34, 67, 68, 70n, 76
Chartists   XI, XIV, 34, 67–69, 71, 74, 75,
   78, 106
Chase M   68
Chauí M   8
Chignola S   134
China   76, 77, 81
Cioli M   109
Circulation   84, 88–90, 92, 98, 100, 132
Citizenship   38, 68, 71, 96
Civil War   VIII, 37, 38, 47, 52, 58, 71, 105, 114n,
   134, 138
Class(es)   2, 17, 20, 25–27, 30–33, 36n, 37–41,
   49, 50, 52–54, 57–59, 61, 63–65, 68, 70–
   72, 74, 83, 85, 89, 95, 99, 103, 105, 106,
   116, 118, 119, 130, 135
   Bourgeois Class/Ranks   31, 32, 37, 58
   Class Struggle   VIII, IX, X, XI, XIV, 33, 35,
      37–39, 50, 55, 57, 67, 69, 71, 74, 77, 79,
      86, 102, 104, 106, 134, 137, 138
   Ruling Class   X, 1, 24, 25, 33, 49, 50, 74, 76,
      89, 106, 107, 135
   Working Class   IX–XII, XIV, 13n, 28, 33, 34,
      36n, 39, 52, 63, 68, 69, 71, 73–75, 83, 101,
      103n, 104–106, 109, 110, 111, 118, 135, 138
Collins H   70n
Collision(s)   1, 2, 3, 8, 11, 15, 17, 18, 25, 33, 39,
   42, 47, 51, 52, 88, 89, 105, 131
Colonialism   XII, 78n, 80n
   Colonial Domination   80
   Colonial Politics   79, 81
   Colonial Power   55, 77, 128

Colonial Rule   76, 80, 81
Colonial System   132
Command   VIII, IX–XII, XIV, 14, 15, 59, 62,
   63, 69, 70, 87, 101, 108, 110–114, 116, 118n,
   119, 122, 123, 124–126, 133
   Command of Capital   IX, XI, 108, 111, 133
Commodity(ies)   88n, 91, 94–101, 117, 120, 136
   Commodity Fetishism   VIII, 98, 102
Commune   XI, XIV, 40, 50, 66, 133n, 134, 135,
   136n, 137, 138n, 139
Communism   17, 20, 24, 28, 29, 35, 36, 57,
   107n, 140
Community(ies)   13, 19–22, 24, 25, 27–29, 61,
   91, 120, 124, 127, 128, 137
Competition   27, 33, 34, 37, 77, 103, 112,
   117, 119n
Compulsion(s)   20, 30, 48, 73, 81, 107, 115, 141
Consolati I   47
Constitution   X, XIII, XIV, 5–9, 12, 16, 17, 21,
   24, 28–30, 35, 37, 40–43, 47, 51, 53, 56,
   57, 62–64, 66, 68–70, 73, 78, 85–87, 91,
   95, 105, 107, 122, 123, 125, 127n, 136
Contingency   3, 26n, 30, 90, 130
Contradiction(s)   12, 13n, 21, 25, 42, 43, 46, 53,
   77, 78, 86, 95, 103, 139
Cooperation   X, XI, XIV, 23, 47, 63, 85, 100,
   106–114
Cowling M   62, 130
Crisis   VII, 3, 56, 57, 65, 66, 71–74, 77, 78, 81,
   82, 105
Crusoe R   94
Curtis N   128n

Dardot P   23, 112n, 114n, 136n
De Boni C   56, 84
De Brunhoff S   87
Defoe D   94, 95
DeGolyer M   5
Demirović A   39n
Durkheim É   100
Democracy   X, XII, XIII, 1, 2, 5–7, 9, 11, 12, 13n,
   14–17, 20, 24, 25, 28, 30, 33–35, 36n, 38n,
   40–42, 50, 53, 57, 58, 70, 77, 78n, 90, 91,
   130, 139
   Political Democracy   12, 14, 34
   Pure Democracy   16, 34
   Social Democracy   11, 14, 51, 57
Dependence   4, 20, 22, 66, 83, 87, 89, 90, 115
Derrida J   43

INDEX

Despotism   VIII, IX, XI, XII, 11, 30, 39, 52, 65, 110, 114, 120–131, 135, 138
   Despotism of Capital   XI, XIV, 62, 125, 138, 141
   Asiatic/Oriental Despotism   121, 124, 126, 127
Deutsche-Brüsseler-Zeitung   1, 29
Deutscher Arbeiter Verein   1
Dictatorship   VIII, XII, XIII, 37, 41, 42, 47, 50, 51n, 78
   Dictatorship of the Proletariat   49, 50, 51n, 52, 53, 55, 137
Didry C   106
Direction   X, 3, 112, 137
Discipline   88, 111, 112, 116, 125
Domination/Pre-Dominance/Dominion   IX, X, XII, XIII, XIV, 1, 3, 12, 15, 17, 21, 24, 25, 31, 37–39, 46, 49–51, 55, 58–65, 67, 71, 77, 79–81, 85, 88, 89, 91–97, 99, 104, 106, 114–119, 125, 126, 129, 130, 136, 141
   Capitalistic Domination/Domination of Capital   VIII, IX, X, XII, XIV, 21, 25, 63, 65, 83–85, 88, 97, 104, 105, 107, 110, 113, 117–119, 126, 132, 136, 139
   Political Domination   31, 32, 71
   Social Domination   VIII, 32, 40, 52, 53, 58, 69, 70, 81, 82
Draper H   49, 62
Dummer I   101
Duso G   8

Elster J   27n
Emancipation   23, 53, 69, 78, 83, 128, 130, 134, 137, 138
Empire   XIV, 55, 58, 61–67, 77, 135
Engels F   XIII, 1, 13n, 19n, 20, 24–30, 33–41, 42n, 48–50, 62n, 73, 103n, 105, 116, 128, 134, 135, 137, 139
Equality   XIV, 1, 5, 10, 12, 24, 56, 75, 87, 88, 90, 91, 94, 96, 99, 121, 140, 141
Espinoza Pino M   90
Estate(s)   2, 8, 10, 11, 12, 41, 44, 46, 47, 55, 65, 84, 88
Europe   16, 43, 65, 67, 126, 128, 131–134
Evolution   VIII, 17, 18, 27, 36, 39, 41, 63, 85, 86, 93, 107, 115, 130, 133
Exploitation   17, 41, 64, 66, 80, 81, 104, 107, 109–113, 118, 119, 132, 133

Expropriation   76, 102, 108, 110, 121

Factory   XIV, 74, 76, 91, 101, 103–106, 108, 112, 124, 126, 128
Family   3, 4, 122, 128, 129, 130
Farr J   6
Federalist Papers   34
Fenton L   78
Fernbach D   41
Ferrari R   130n
Feuerbach LA   6, 121
Fine B   116
Finelli R   6, 84n
Forbes I   27n
Force   XII, 19, 20, 22–24, 26, 39, 43, 45, 51, 67, 68, 70, 81, 89n, 97, 99, 101, 102n, 103, 107, 113, 116, 123, 124, 132, 135, 141
Productive Forces   18, 23, 25, 94, 112
Foucault M   112n
Fourier C   108n
France   XI, XIII, XIV, 12, 32, 47, 51n, 55, 56, 58, 61, 64, 66, 67, 70–72, 75, 76, 78, 79, 82, 95n, 103, 104, 121, 124, 134, 135
Free trade   69, 70, 71, 79, 136
Freedom   4n, 22, 24, 58, 62, 78n, 88, 90–92, 96, 99, 105, 107, 110, 123, 124, 129, 137, 138, 141

Galli C   38
Gilbert L   27n
Girard L   56
Government/Governance   IX, 1, 7–10, 13n, 15, 35, 41–45, 55, 56, 59, 60, 64–74, 76, 80, 81, 83, 87, 90, 100, 103n, 115, 119, 120, 121, 123, 124, 126, 131, 136, 137, 138. *See also* Rule; Governmental Power
Granjonc J   20
Great Britain   XI, XIII, 67, 73, 76
   England   13n, 55, 67, 68, 70, 71, 73–77, 81, 82, 132
Guastini R   45
Gurney PJ   70
Guizot F   47, 57, 75

Hall S   41, 86, 141
Hampton M   92
Harney GJ   69
Harootunian HD   115n

INDEX

Hartog F 113
Haug WF 119n
Hawkings A 69
Hegel GWF IX, XIII, 1, 2, 3, 4n, 5, 6, 7, 8, 9, 10n, 11, 12, 13n, 14, 15, 18, 20, 24, 25, 35, 39, 43, 59, 63, 65, 122
Heinzen K XIII, 28, 29, 30, 31, 32, 33, 52, 97
Hierarchy 2, 10, 59, 60, 74, 101, 112, 120, 121, 137
Hindrichs G 35
History XI, XIII, 1, 8, 17, 18, 23–25, 27, 31, 36n, 38, 41, 43, 48, 49, 55, 59, 65, 70, 72, 75, 80, 84n, 85, 86, 90, 91, 102n, 110, 121, 126, 127, 129, 131–135, 138
   Constitutional History VII, 69, 112, 126
   World History 21, 24, 69, 133
Hobbes T VIII, 1, 5, 14, 15n, 77, 131
Hudelson R 6

Iacono AM 121
India 70, 80, 81n, 127, 128
Individual(s) *passim*
   Empirically Universal Individuals 24, 25, 38, 90, 107, 111, 141
   Individuality 10, 11, 23, 27n, 90, 91, 96, 107, 130, 140, 141
Industry 3, 33, 46, 65, 80, 103n, 109n, 110
Institution(s) 8, 33, 50, 54, 55, 57, 58, 69, 72, 81, 109, 126, 129, 135
   Institutionalization VIII, X, 7, 8, 38, 53, 137
   International Working Men's Association 70, 74, 83n, 84, 138
Iorio M 38n

Jung S 95

Kaiwar V 127n
Kant I 5, 34, 123
Kelley DR 46n
Kouvélakis S 9
Krader L 126
Krätke MR 24, 66
Kugelmann L 133, 134
Kuczynski T 101

Labour XI, XIV, 10, 14–17, 19, 25, 50, 63, 66, 68, 83, 89, 91, 93, 96, 97, 98, 100, 101, 103–105, 108–120, 128, 132, 134, 135, 137, 138, 140

Dead/Past Labour IX, 94, 97, 99, 100, 101, 115
Division of Labour 19, 26n, 112, 128
Labour Force/Labour Power IX, 15, 91, 94, 97–105, 112, 114–119, 132, 133
Labour Process XI, 100, 108, 111, 112, 114, 120, 125
Living Labour IX, 94, 97, 99–101, 115
Wage Labour VIII, XIV, 57, 85, 91–93, 100, 116, 119, 120
Landau P 141n
Lascoumes P 45
Laval C 112n, 114n, 136n
Law VIII, XII, 2, 3, 4n, 6–8, 12, 17, 18, 20, 23, 24, 28, 29, 39, 40, 43–45, 46n, 47, 50, 53, 63, 69, 72, 74, 83, 87, 91, 94–96, 99, 101–103, 105, 106, 116, 118, 119n, 120, 122–125, 131, 132, 133, 139–141
Lebowitz MA 110
Le Chapelier IRG 103
Legitimacy 2, 3, 12, 13, 43, 45, 53, 56, 76, 81, 103, 123, 139
Lemercier de la Rivière P-P 124
Lenin VI 43
Leonelli RM 112n
Leopold D 7n
Levine N 46n
Liberation XIII, 17, 46, 67, 90, 138
Lichtblau K 108
Liebich A 60
Liebknecht W 134
Liedman S-E 13n
Lieven M 103n
Limit(s) X, 9, 11, 16, 17, 22, 23, 37, 44, 50, 52, 73, 75, 90–92, 94, 98, 101, 103, 137–139
Lincoln A 137, 138
Linguet S-N-H 124, 131
Locke J 29
Lohmann G 113
Louis Philippe I 12
Lubasz H 8n
Luhmann N 83, 84, 114n
Luporini C 39
Luxemburg R 36n

Mably de G 33
Macherey P 95n, 112
Machiavelli N 131

Machine(s)   61, 65, 80, 93, 109n, 110, 111, 118, 123
Machinery   60, 109, 110, 117, 135, 136
Maine HS   128, 130, 131, 141
Management   23, 50, 53, 58, 114, 120, 133
Market   15, 33, 70, 98, 119n, 125, 137
   World Market   XI, XIII, 3, 21, 23–25, 33, 67, 77, 82, 90, 92, 93, 107, 110, 111, 127n
Marsden R   112n
Martin J   35
Mascat MHJ   46n
Marrast A   51
Mattingly G   132
Mayer H   41
Merlo M   98, 106
Mezzadra S   90, 92, 112, 120
Mies M   113
Might   XII, 5, 17, 18, 19, 20, 22, 23, 25, 28, 30, 31, 36, 47, 65, 68, 86, 87, 89, 99, 108, 110
   Alien Might   19, 22, 89, 113
   Societal Might   38, 58, 84, 86–89, 91, 92, 99, 101, 116, 117, 118, 134
   State Might   31, 32, 38, 132
Miles R   91
Mode of Production   VII, 46, 94, 108, 109, 112, 115, 120, 122, 123, 125, 129
   Capitalist Mode of Production   VII, IX, 92, 94, 106, 115–117, 120, 122, 124, 125n, 128, 131, 132
Mohanty CT   113
Monarchy   XII, 5–7, 11, 12, 30, 32, 33, 46, 47, 59, 61, 130
Money   IX, XIV, 21–23, 25, 28, 30, 32, 65, 66, 79, 84–87, 88n, 89–96, 98, 99, 100, 101, 117
   Power of Money   IX, XIV, 25, 50, 80, 86
   Societal Might of Money   84, 88, 92, 101, 116. *See also* Societal Might
Montesquieu C   11, 112, 123, 124
Morfino V   8
Moulier Boutang Y   91
Movement(s)   VII, VIII, X, 2–4, 6–8, 16, 17, 24, 25, 29, 41–43, 45, 47–49, 55, 57, 61, 62n, 68, 69, 72, 75, 81, 83, 85, 86, 89, 90, 94, 96–98, 102, 106, 107, 114–117, 119, 123, 127n, 128, 133, 135, 136
   Chartist Movement   34. *See also* Chartism; Chartists
   Democratic movement   5, 18, 28, 34, 41, 42n, 43, 58, 81. *See also* Democracy
   Labour/Workers' Movement   16, 36n, 41, 68, 75, 106
   Movements of Society   16, 55, 57, 70, 74, 102
   Political Movement   XIV, 35, 83, 106
   Revolutionary Movement   40–43. *See also* Revolution
   Social Movement(s)   XIV, 17, 40–42, 58, 60, 106, 128
Multitude   X, XIII, 4–6, 9, 10, 11, 31, 40, 52, 63, 100, 111, 138
Musto M   83n, 139

Napoleon I. *See* Bonaparte
Napoleon III. *See* Bonaparte L
Nation(s)   21, 27, 38, 63, 67, 77, 79, 132, 136
Negri A   89, 112n, 115n, 134n
Neocleous M   115
Neue Rheinische Zeitung   1, 41
New York Daily Tribune   VII, XIII, 71, 77, 81n
Nietzsche F   94
Nipperdey T   43
Nobili Schiera G   31n

O'Conor C   119
Order   IX, 2, 3, 8, 10, 13, 16, 17, 25, 30, 34, 36n, 37, 38, 39, 43–46, 52, 56, 65, 66, 68, 74, 84, 103n, 104, 131, 132, 138–141
Orders. *See* Estate(s)

Palmerston HG   XIV, 51, 72–77, 78n, 79, 81
Pandolfi A   112
Patriarchy   XIV, 113
Patterson TC   129
People   VIII, XIII, 1, 2, 5, 6, 7n, 8–10, 18, 24, 25, 35, 36n, 44, 45, 48, 53, 55–59, 65, 67, 68, 72, 73, 75–77, 78n, 79, 81, 85, 89, 95, 120, 122, 123, 137–139
Peasant(s)   1, 53, 51, 63, 64, 88
Petrucciani S   141n
Piccinini M   31n, 45, 81, 131
Political Economy   VII, 14, 83, 102n, 104, 106, 120, 132
Political Theology   VIII, 12, 13n, 44, 45, 139
Political Subject   XIII, 1, 6, 7, 57
Politics   VII, VIII, XIII, 2, 5, 6, 7n, 9n, 11, 13, 14, 18, 28, 34, 36n, 38, 39n, 45, 50, 70, 72–76, 79, 81, 84, 91, 107, 131, 134, 139, 141
Power *Passim*
   Becoming Power   X, XIV, 27, 53, 97

INDEX

Power *Passim* (cont.)
  Bureaucratic Power   40. *See also* Bureaucracy
  Capitalist Power/Power of Capital   XIV, 39, 109, 135
  Collective Power   23, 28, 63, 97, 100, 107
  Conquering Power   XI, 52, 53, 67, 83, 101
  Constituent Power   8
  Executive Power   XIII, XIV, 53, 57, 60, 62–64, 73
  Governmental Power/Power of Government/Governing Power   XIII, 8–10, 14, 15, 55, 64, 67, 72
  Legislative Power/Legislature   XIII, 8, 9, 11, 57, 79
  Personal Power   XIV, 26, 31, 72, 78, 122
  Productive Power(s)   15, 106
  Provisional Power   28, 32, 36
  Military Power   15, 80
  Political Power   VIII, X, 11, 18, 20, 23, 28–32, 34, 36n, 38, 40, 49, 50, 52, 53, 58, 59, 68, 69–72, 75, 81, 82, 101, 106, 107, 128, 130, 131, 134, 137, 138
  Power of Money   IX, XIV, 50, 80, 86
  Purchasing Power   14, 15, 87
  Societal Power   94, 98, 100, 130. *See also* Societal Might
  Social Power   XIII, XIV, 22, 39, 50, 53, 55, 58, 59, 70, 72, 92, 137
  Workers' Power   X, 36n
Pradella L   127n
Proletariat   X, XI, XIII, XIV, 1, 6, 13, 16, 24, 26, 28, 32, 33, 35, 36n, 37–41, 49, 50, 51n, 52, 53, 55, 58, 59, 67, 69, 71, 79, 83, 133, 134, 135, 137
  Industrial Proletariat   63, 64, 69
  Lumpenproletariat   62n, 63
Property   XIII, 1, 3, 17, 22, 29–33, 39, 49, 53, 66, 75, 92, 95, 99, 102, 108, 110, 124, 128–130
  Collective/Communal Property   1, 61, 132
  Private Property   XIII, 10, 19, 22, 23, 29, 102, 109, 118n, 124, 130, 132
Proudhon P-J   84n, 85
Prussia   2, 43, 121

Rametta G   31n
Rancière J   84, 139n
Ranke von L   12

Reform(s)   XI, 11, 16, 18, 29, 36n, 52, 55, 67, 74, 75, 124, 139
Regime   VII, 7, 17, 56, 60, 65, 113, 117, 122, 123, 128
Reichelt H   88n
Relation(s)/Relationship(s) *passim*. *See also* Capital Relations
  Economic Relation(s)/Relationship(s)   24, 81, 84, 101, 121
  Political Relation(s)/Relationship(s)   XIII, 32, 85, 124, 139
  Power Relation(s)/Relationship(s)   IX, 24, 31, 53, 67, 85, 93, 102, 109, 111, 112, 114, 118, 124, 131–133
  Property Relation(s)/Relationship(s)   23, 30, 31
  Relations of Domination   XIV, 93, 115
  Relation(s) of Lordship   88, 90, 92, 93, 119
  Relations of Production   25, 32, 94, 100, 120, 131
  Social Relation(s)/Relationship(s)   XIV, 17–20, 22, 25, 29, 40, 43, 53, 54, 60, 61, 63, 85, 88, 97, 98, 102, 117, 124, 129, 130, 139, 141
  Societal Relation(s)/Relationship(s)   VIII, XIII, 18, 32, 85, 86, 95n, 96, 97, 100, 103, 130, 131
Renault E   6n, 89
Representation   VIII, XIII, 6, 7, 9, 11, 13, 20, 40, 46, 50, 57, 60, 63, 64, 78, 81, 94, 122, 135
Reproduction   IX, X, XIII, 15, 19, 25, 27, 28, 33, 39, 47, 56, 63, 87, 92, 93, 96, 100, 101, 106, 112, 114, 116–118, 128, 133
Republic   6, 29, 30, 32, 33, 39, 42, 51, 52, 57, 58, 61, 70, 123, 135
  Democratic Republic   30, 33, 52, 55, 57
Revolution(s)   8, 9, 22, 23, 28, 32, 33, 36n, 40, 42n, 43–58, 60n, 61, 63, 66–68, 70, 72, 116, 121, 125, 127, 138–140
  French Revolution   XIII, 2, 6, 8, 9n, 24, 48, 56, 59, 60, 124, 135
  Bourgeois Revolution   32, 48
  Counter-Revolution   69
  Political Revolution   17, 32, 38, 49
  Proletarian Revolution   32, 41, 48, 49, 62n
  Revolution of 1848   1, 41, 43–45, 50, 51, 66, 83
  Social Revolution   41, 48, 67, 69–71
  Revolutionary Process   IX, 44, 48, 68

Ricciardi M   16, 17, 24, 26n, 49, 121, 124, 139
Ripstein A   98
Ritter J   3
Roberts D   83n
Roberts WC   84
Rosdolsky R   87
Rossi M   6
Roulet G   6
Rousseau JJ   9n, 23, 33
Rudan P   77n, 102
Ruge A   16, 121
Rule   31, 32, 40, 50, 52, 56, 58, 59, 61, 62, 76, 79, 80, 81n, 89, 119, 123, 124, 128, 141

Saad-Filho A   116
Sammadar R   81
Saunders R   75
Scattola M   13
Schieder W   43
Schiera P   108n, 131n, 134
Schmidt VH   108n
Schmitt C   13, 24, 38, 45, 51n
Screpanti E   9n
Scuccimarra L   56
Sociology   24, 85, 91, 108
Sewell Jr WH   59
Sgrò G   13n
Small AW   15n
Slave(s)   91, 92, 93, 104, 118, 119, 133, 138
Slavery   VIII, XII, XIV, 50, 91–93, 105, 114, 119, 120, 127–129, 133, 138
Smith A   14, 21, 15, 84, 86, 87, 113
Smith DE   86
Socialism   17, 29, 56
Society *Passim*
   Ancient Estate-based Society   44, 46, 47, 55, 84, 88
   Bourgeois/Civil Society   3, 4, 8, 10, 11, 12, 17, 22, 39, 42, 46, 47, 51, 57, 59, 61, 63, 73, 82, 85, 86, 88, 124
   Capitalist Society/Society of Capital   XII, XIV, 18, 45, 46, 64, 103n, 107, 118
   Democratic Society   33
   Modern Society   34
Societalization   XII, 108–110, 114
Sovereignty   IX, XI, 38, 45, 47, 62, 67, 82, 122, 125, 131
   People's Sovereignty   7, 56

Societal Sovereignty   98
   See also State Power
Spain   55, 126
Spinoza B   7
Spivak GC   54n, 97n, 113, 126
Stallybrass P   62
State *passim*
   Democratic State   20, 29
   Political State   7, 8, 16
   State Might   32, 38
   State of Siege   43, 44, 45
   State Power/Power of the State   VIII, XIII, XIV, 2, 7, 15, 31, 32, 36, 37n, 49–51, 60, 62, 64, 65, 78, 102, 105, 106, 124, 135–138
Stedman Jones G   41, 68
Steele ED   78n
Stein L von   17, 18, 39, 106, 134
Subjugation   XII, XIII, XIV, 17, 32, 113, 124
Submission   21, 31, 124, 129
Subordination   VIII, X, XIV, 4, 38, 58, 62, 66, 84, 87, 88, 89, 92, 93, 99, 107, 110, 112, 125, 126
Suffrage   51–53, 57, 58, 71, 75, 78, 81, 82, 106
Supremacy   X, XIV, 30, 31, 38, 39, 71n, 75, 81, 114

Taubes J   13
Taylor A   75
Technology   15n, 21, 109
Temporality(ies)   49, 54, 115, 121, 139
Theunissen M   13n
Thierry A   47
Thiers A   138
Thomas R   138n
Thompson EP   68
Thompson D   68
Tocqueville A de   59
Tomba M   115n
Tommasello F   6, 59
Tönnies F   91
Touboul H   5n
Trendelenburg FA   6
Tradition   VIII, IX, 5, 13, 27, 28, 39, 48, 53, 54n, 70, 73, 75, 79, 110
Traffic   14, 16, 18, 19, 23–25, 27, 28, 30, 42, 46, 67, 89, 140
Trincia FS   6

Tronti M   103*n*

United States of America   28, 30, 33, 92, 128, 131, 138
Universal/Universality   XIII, 3, 4, 6, 9*n*, 10–12, 16, 17, 19, 20, 21, 23, 24, 25, 40, 50, 60, 62, 87, 90, 91, 94, 122, 128, 140
   Universalism   5, 23, 24
   Universal Subject   VIII, XIII, 15, 25, 35, 36, 53
Ure A   83, 103*n*, 119

Valorization   VII, 11, 93, 100, 101, 104, 110, 112, 115, 116, 125
Value   IX, 14, 15, 22, 29, 64, 66, 87, 88*n*, 90, 92, 94–101, 111, 113, 115–117
Van Ree E   49
Vincent A   141*n*
Violence   VIII, XII, 20, 29–31, 80, 81*n*, 98, 101, 102*n*, 116, 132, 133. *See also* State; Law

Wacquant LJD   86
Wainwright J   131

Weber M   31*n*, 108*n*
Weitling W   41
Wendling AE   109*n*
Wetherly P   65
Weydemeyer J   50
Winkler HA   43
Wolff W   16
Wolin S   125*n*
Worker(s)/Wage-Labourer(s)   XIII, X, IX, 15, 16, 31, 33–35, 36*n*, 37, 41, 42, 44, 52, 66–69, 81, 83, 89, 91–93, 97, 99, 101, 102, 104–109, 111, 113, 114, 119, 125, 129, 132, 133, 137, 138
   Overall Worker   63, 88, 93, 102–104, 108, 110, 111
Working Day   43, 83, 101, 103–106, 110, 111, 116, 134, 138
World Market   XI, XIII, 3, 21, 23–25, 33, 67, 77, 82, 90, 92, 93, 107, 110, 111, 127*n*

Zamagni G   124
Ziegler PR   78*n*

npliance